W9-CEJ-701

How Armstrong Floored America
The People Who Made It Happen, 1945–1995

C. Eugene Moore

Lancaster County Historical Society

Lancaster, Pennsylvania

For Jan Moore
and
Dawn Johnston

Front cover: Armstrong's Colonial Classic Designer Solarian (no-wax) flooring found a home in many American kitchens. Its design was based on a linoleum pattern known as 5352, which represented the best-selling pattern in the entire flooring industry. Photo courtesy Armstrong World Industries.

Photo credits: All photographs courtesy Armstrong World Industries, Inc.

Editor: James T. Alton
Design: Michael L. Abel, FLCHS
Printed by Cadmus Communications, Lancaster, Pennsylvania

ISBN 978-0-9740162-4-5
Library of Congress Control Number 2007932523

Published by Lancaster County Historical Society
230 North President Avenue, Lancaster, Pennsylvania, 17603
www.lancasterhistory.org

Contents

The printing and distribution of this book

were made possible by the generous support of the

RICHARD C. VON HESS FOUNDATION

Foreword

In November 2005, a group of former executives of Armstrong World Industries gathered at the Lancaster County Historical Society in Lancaster, Pennsylvania. The group numbered more than forty, all of them retired for at least five years, many after working for the company their entire adult lives. The scene resembled a spirited college reunion, as men who spent years together creating, manufacturing, and promoting coverings for America's floors caught up on each others' lives and reminisced about the past. That meeting served as the launching pad for the interviews that became this book.

When George F. Johnston first approached me a few years ago about recording the post–World War II history of Armstrong's U.S. Floor Products Operations, I already knew it was a story with deep local roots. For most of the twentieth century Armstrong dominated the Lancaster skyline both literally and figuratively. During the years covered by this book the company consistently ranked as one of Lancaster County's largest employers. Armstrong's actions, whether moving part of its operations into the middle of downtown Lancaster or bringing hundreds of wholesalers to town for its annual convention, had a significant impact on the community, and the company's employees participated in and sat on the boards of numerous nonprofit organizations and religious and civic groups. Employee or not, in the second half of the twentieth century, an awareness of Armstrong's presence embedded itself in the consciousness of most residents.

This book was never intended to be the definitive treatise on Armstrong's flooring operations. It's really a story about the people—and how they created a new business model that blended manufacturing with fashion. By listening carefully to consumers, Armstrong's people succeeded in designing, producing, marketing, and delivering consumer and commercial goods that were widely acclaimed and enormously popular, and their success translated into a period of remarkable growth and profitability for the company. Fortunately, the majority of the people who ushered in that transformation are still around to tell the stories. Their recollections enable us to witness the creative transformation of an industry and that industry's power to reshape the appearance of the American home. From the historian's perspective, this book serves as a model for involving the people in preserving and interpreting the history of their community. The finished product illustrates the tremendous value of collecting twentieth-century history before it slips away.

George Johnston and author Gene Moore are to be commended for their dedication to making this book a reality, as are all those who agreed to share their memories and their financial resources in support of this publication. We can all learn from their example of setting important events to paper and passing along stories for future generations.

The Lancaster County Historical Society is particularly grateful to the Richard C. von Hess Foundation for underwriting the printing and distribution of this book. The foundation's support is fitting given the role that Armstrong played in the life of its namesake. Richard von Hess was an award-winning art director for Armstrong for more than a decade. I express my personal appreciation to the foundation's current chairman, Thomas Hills Cook—who spent much of his career as part of Armstrong's Interior Design department and retired as its Corporate Creative Director—for his support of this project and this institution.

Ironically, this book goes to press just as crews complete the demolition of most of the Lancaster Floor Plant, where Armstrong employees crafted many of the flooring products mentioned in the following pages. On this site a new chapter in Lancaster County's history is beginning exactly one hundred years after the Armstrong Cork Company built a new linoleum factory in a cornfield. For those future generations that will know the huge manufacturing plant only from photographs, this book preserves the remarkable occurrences of the intervening century. It's a piece of American history that happened in Lancaster County, Pennsylvania.

I invite you now to discover *How Armstrong Floored America*.

Thomas R. Ryan, Ph.D.
President and CEO
Lancaster County Historical Society

Acknowledgments

So many fine men and women played a part in putting together this story that I should be embarrassed to have my name alone appearing as author.

George F. Johnston certainly deserves equal billing. The project would not have been completed, or even begun, without his vision and his determination. But it goes beyond that. Throughout, his powers of persuasion, his organizing skills, and his polished sense of historical balance kept the wheels turning. As advisor, director, and producer behind the entire effort, he was its propellant force. He is the *sine qua non* of the project. (And I wonder whether he ever has been called a *sine qua non* before.)

Thanks to his tireless oversight, more than half a hundred people contributed memories or money, often both, to assure that the story would be told. They believe that what occurred not only was important to their careers but also to the growth of Armstrong as a corporation and to Lancaster as a community. They are right. As we gathered information from them, my admiration grew for their collective genius. What they accomplished in working together at Armstrong was a mountainous economic miracle, one that has seldom been matched. Their names are listed in Appendix C.

Dr. Thomas R. Ryan, president and CEO of the Lancaster County Historical Society, acting on the society's *carpe diem* dictum—"seize the day" to capture first-person recollections while you still can—offered numerous suggestions. Every suggestion was a good one. Members of the society's staff and volunteers, especially James T. Alton, Donna Hermany-Pflum, Michael L. Abel, and John W. W. Loose, made valuable contributions, usually unheralded.

My deep gratitude goes to William A. Mehler, whose books *H. W. Prentis, Jr.*, and *Let the Buyer Have Faith* were rich, reliable sources of Armstrong history. These, along with another, unattributed book, *History of the Floor Plant, 1908–1980*, were especially valuable in helping us record highlights of the early years of Armstrong's existence.

Sacrifices made by spouses are often ignored in such accounts as this. I don't want to ignore those of my own wife, Jan. As the work progressed, she never wavered in her loyal support of this research and writing project. Along the way she provided many helpful suggestions for its improvement.

In telling this story, whom did we miss? So many. Thousands of Armstrong employees were involved in making the company's flooring business such a success. Some made the products in the manufacturing plants or sold them in the marketplace. Others, at the highest levels of executive management, did their part by directing the overall effort, encouraging innovation, and financing the business. Still others were involved peripherally, generally in staff departments. All played important parts in the glory years of Armstrong flooring. Relatively few are recognized here by name. To those who are not, my apologies. It simply was not possible to interview everyone who was involved and still complete this in a timely manner. As they read this I hope that all of them can recognize how valuable their contributions were.

All of those who offered comments were as interested as I in providing historical accuracy in this account. If factual errors or misquotes are included, and that is a possibility, let it be understood that I take sole responsibility for them.

This is a story of multiple triumphs. Occasionally mistakes were made, and they're part of the story, too. The lesson here is simply that Armstrong people learned from their mistakes. They bestrode the rubble of failure, then stepped onto a higher rung on the ladder of success.

They were good at that. They were good at so many things. It's a pleasure to tell their story.

Introduction

In the years following World War II an economic miracle began to take shape in Lancaster County, Pennsylvania.

At the time, few people except those directly involved recognized what was happening. But its effects would spread through the county—and eventually throughout the entire world.

At the end of the war, the U.S. resilient flooring business of Lancaster's Armstrong World Industries, Inc., took one deep breath. Then, belly to the ground and breathing fire, it roared into life. Drawing on the talents and energy of a remarkable team of people, it began a period of exceptional activity that would last for half a century. Its history is marked by dynamic, profitable growth that few other American manufacturing companies could match during this period, or any period.

What accounts for this remarkable record? Was it:

- The research and development program, which led the effort to move the company away from commodity products, especially linoleum and asphalt tile, and into those that offered proprietary advantages?

- Armstrong's product styling and design organization, which allowed consumers to add to their homes and businesses decorative effects never before possible?

- Engineering and manufacturing teams, which pioneered in finding new ways to produce the flooring effects dreamed up by research and design staffs—and then worked up the production capacity to meet demand?

- A distribution system that was the lodestar of the flooring industry, one that directed the finished product from Armstrong factories through wholesalers and retail dealers into the hands of waiting consumers?

- Advertising and promotion programs that, year after year, were sizable enough to place Armstrong among the top 100 advertisers in the United States?

Truly it was all of these. But it was something more. What brought all these elements together, allowing them to work toward a common end, was a marketing effort in the United States that proved sublimely effective.

Undergirding the marketing program was the company's general management, and its support, too, was vital to the effort. Armstrong's top management team deserves credit, first, for maintaining the base of ethical principles, sound decision-making, and business strengths that had been established by the company's founder and early managers and, second, for turning loose the creative minds that contributed to its flooring operations. Time after time, someone came up with an idea for a better product, or an improved way to make that product, or a more effective means of delivering it into the hands of consumers. When that occurred the corporate leadership could be counted on to evaluate the new approach and usually, if it fit Armstrong's plans, to fund it and give it unalloyed support.

This support enabled the flooring organization to fill unmet consumer needs by understanding market forces and manufacturing products to satisfy those needs. The result was marketing success that was classic enough to serve as a model for a college course.

Along the way, it would lead Armstrong into innovations that its founders and early managers could scarcely have imagined.

PART I

The Early Years

An Ethical Base to Build On

The enterprise that evolved into Armstrong World Industries, a multibillion-dollar corporation, didn't start as a flooring company. Its origins were much more modest and less promising. It all traces back to cork—an unusual raw material that is harvested from the bark of the cork oak, grown commercially only in several countries bordering the Mediterranean Sea.

John D. Glass wanted to buy the small cork-stopper business that employed him in Pittsburgh. The company was for sale, but the price was a staggering $300, and in 1860, with threats of a civil war rumbling through the economy, bankers weren't eager to lend money for uncertain ventures. Glass turned to a friend, Thomas Morton Armstrong, who had a bit of money to invest and was known to have an entrepreneurial turn of mind. They reached agreement: Glass would continue as the cork-cutter, and Armstrong would provide initial funding for the company in return for half the profits.

Armstrong was 24 years old and engaged to be married. Understandably, he was reluctant to commit all of his resources to the cork business. So he retained his job as shipping clerk for a local glass bottle manufacturer, though on some evenings he would stop by to help out at the cork shop on his way home from work.

The two partners worked hard. More important, they tried to work smart. The cylindrical corks they produced were used in home preserving and sealing beverage bottles. Each cork, cut by hand, differed in slight detail from every other cork. Glass and Armstrong sought ways to improve uniformity, to meet their customers' demands for perfection. The answer came in the form of a device known as the Improved Cork Cutting Machine. It was designed to produce tapered, not just cylindrical, corks. When the device became available, Tom Armstrong swallowed hard and invested in one, with exclusive rights to use it in Allegheny County. The machine cost a thousand dollars, more than three times his opening investment in the company.

The machine proved successful, and it enabled the two men to begin offering improvements in the products they made and sold—a marketing advantage that would characterize the company in later years. The enterprise grew and began slowly to establish itself among Pittsburgh companies, but not without difficulty. The cork business was not an easy one to manage even in boom times. With the Civil War raging, the partners found it increasingly difficult to purchase their cork raw material, every pound of which was imported.

Armstrong made another tough decision. He decided to leave his job at the glass bottle company to devote full time to the growing cork business.

In 1864, four years after they had established their company, John Glass died. Thomas Armstrong's brother, Robert D. Armstrong, left his employment at a Pittsburgh bank and joined the effort, which became known as Armstrong, Brother & Co.

By now the enterprise had gained a reputation for integrity. During the Civil War citizens of Pittsburgh donated money to be used for buying medical supplies for the war effort. The price of raw materials soared, and some suppliers attempted to circumvent this problem by shipping inferior finished products to the army hospitals. Not Thomas Armstrong. He insisted that any products made by his company be of the promised quality. In time authorities investigated medical suppliers. Their report singled out Armstrong, Brother & Co. as a manufacturer that demonstrated integrity and forthrightness in its business dealings.

Such an experience typified the young company. *Caveat emptor*—"Let the buyer beware"—was a guiding principle of business transactions. Tom Armstrong replaced it with a principle of his own: "Let the buyer have faith." Customers heard this and began to listen. A buyer could have confidence when dealing with Armstrong. (Revealingly, William A. Mehler chose as the title of his excellent history of Armstrong, *Let the Buyer Have Faith*.)

After several moves, each into larger quarters, the company bought a site in Pittsburgh, at 24th Street and the Allegheny River, where it built a factory in 1878. From this new nest there developed a company that would soon make its mark on American enterprise.

In the same year, Armstrong launched its first venture abroad. Up 'til now, it had acquired its primary raw material, corkwood, from importers. In 1878 it made arrangements with a direct representative in Spain to purchase, prepare, and ship corkwood and corks made in Spain to the parent company in Pittsburgh.

The business was going well. But markets change, and sometimes the results are unforeseen and devastating. In years to come, calculators would virtually eliminate the need for slide rules. For Thomas Armstrong's company, the invention of the Mason jar took away its biggest market: home preserving. The Mason jar's cap proved much more convenient than sealing with paraffin, and the Mason jar didn't need cork at all. In a similar manner, the development of the spring stopper replaced cork in the bottling of soda water.

Armstrong, Brother & Co., staggering from the loss of two of its major markets, intensified its efforts in other markets. The pasteurization process had by now made it possible to preserve beer in bottles. Beer bottlers became the largest customers of cork companies. They offered other opportunities as well. Every keg of beer had a bung cork, and Armstrong vigorously went after this business.

Soon the company was rolling again. In the years following the Civil War, family-run businesses found it difficult to generate the capital needed to expand their operations. The need for capital led to the formation of many corporate bodies. Armstrong, Brother & Co. was one of these, and it incorporated in 1891. Four years later, in a merger with several other companies, it incorporated under a new name: Armstrong Cork Company. Three of the combining companies were situated in Lancaster, Pennsylvania, and these melded into one, the Lancaster Cork Works (later known as the Lancaster Closure Plant). Although little noted at the time, this geographical coincidence would have significant meaning in the years to come.

Back in Pittsburgh, adversity and necessity led the company in a new direction. Picture the scene in the cork-cutting room. A cork factory turned out a lot of scrap, as round corks were cut from rectangular chunks of cork bark. In Armstrong's plant, something like 65 percent of the raw cork that came through the door was wasted as cork dust or chips. The waste amounted to a carload a day, and getting rid of it was more than an annoyance. It was wasteful. It was costly. Clearly, some solution was needed for this problem.

From corks to cork products

A solution was found. It came through the production of corkboard, even today considered an efficient insulation material. The waste particles of cork were pressed into sheets or blocks that could be used to insulate breweries and other cold-storage facilities. Armstrong pounced on the process, and soon it was producing corkboard insulation in two plants, at Beaver Falls, Pennsylvania, and Camden, New Jersey.

In Pittsburgh, meanwhile, the company had decided in 1900 to construct a seven-story brick, fireproof building to be used for manufacturing. The old buildings on the property were restricted to storage and shipping. By February of the following year the new building was about three stories in height when disaster smashed into the plan. In a frame portion of the plant facing the Allegheny River, the sprinkler system sprang a leak. It was shut off so repairs could be made. In an ugly instant, fire broke out in bags containing cork shavings. It took almost no time for the fire to spread through the frame building. The flames grew so hot that workmen found it impossible to get to the valve controlling the sprinklers, and within minutes it was clear that the entire rear section of the plant was doomed.

Time and time again in its history, the people of Armstrong have shown that they can rebound from catastrophic events. This fire was the first. The loss amounted to more than half a million dollars. Fortunately it was covered by insurance. Charles D. Armstrong, the president of the company and the son of its founder, wasted no time. He leased temporary quarters at two other Pittsburgh locations and put through rush orders for production machinery. In a fortnight operations were underway on a small scale, and within weeks the two temporary factories in Pittsburgh, along with the Cork Works in Lancaster, operated day and night to fill customers' orders in a timely manner. Out of the fire grew a spirit of mutual determination and cooperation that would underlie Armstrong employees' efforts for years to come.

The success of the business no longer depended on the cork stopper alone. Corkboard began to exercise its dominance in Armstrong's corporate attention. Some prospective customers at first showed resistance to the idea of insulating their facilities with cork. So Armstrong installed equipment at Pittsburgh to measure the thermal conductivity of materials being used for insulation, to demonstrate cork's effectiveness. This action is considered to be the first time the company drew on product research to aid in its marketing efforts. It was a long way from the extensive research and development programs that would come in the future, but it was a sensible start. In time Armstrong became the nation's principal producer of corkboard, a position it held for many years.

If cork could be formed into corkboard, then what other uses might be found for it? This question must have occurred to the company's management more than once as it saw its insulation business expand.

Cork is an unusual natural material, with characteristics unmatched by other materials. Its cellular structure entraps air, making it an efficient heat insulator. Cork can be compressed with little lateral flow; that is, when squeezed between two flat surfaces it doesn't squash outward the way rubber or some other material might do, and that too provides for interesting consideration. Cork is resilient, tending to rebound to its original size when a weight is placed on it, then removed. It can be carved and cut into various configurations, and cork particles can be molded to fit around just about any shape. What additional product applications might these promising characteristics suggest?

Answers came in 1904, when Armstrong Cork Company entered two new businesses. One was a natural outgrowth of the corkboard insulation business, with the company offering sectional cork insulation for pipes and fittings that carried brine, ammonia, and cold water. The second business, though, was a real departure. Armstrong began making cork flooring tile. This 1904 venture represented the narrow gateway that would lead to an astounding record in resilient flooring for years.

Other products followed. Corkboard, when painted white, could serve as an acoustical material for lining the walls and ceilings of natatoria (indoor swimming pools) and radio broadcasting studios. The small start of this business would later blossom into Armstrong's full range of acoustical ceiling materials. Products to add comfort and bulk to shoes could be made of cork composition materials. Its compressibility and no-lateral-flow characteristics lent cork a special advantage when used as a gasket material. Textile cots and aprons, used by the tens of thousands in a cotton spinning mill, could be made of cork compositions. The company's product line diversified, and sales grew.

Two points are worth noting about this parade of products that began to march forth from the active minds in the company's Pittsburgh headquarters. First, they permitted Armstrong to venture far beyond its original business, packaging materials (more specifically, cork stoppers), and into a panoply of new industries. Second, every one of the new products used cork, in some form or another, as a raw material.

Rolling into a new market

Then came linoleum.

Several considerations must have influenced the decision to manufacture linoleum. One was the successful experience with the geographical location and the industrious employees of the Lancaster Cork Works. Another was the concern of Charles D. Armstrong. The oldest son of Thomas Morton Armstrong, Charles was by now serving as directing head of the company. He worried that the national prohibition movement might make alcoholic beverages illegal and thus threaten the cork-stopper business. Probably the greatest impetus came from the fact that one of the raw materials of linoleum was cork flour. The piles of cork dust that accumulated in the Pittsburgh factory remained a concern. The company needed to find uses for it, if possible.

The decision was made in 1907. Armstrong's Board of Directors voted to buy land in Manheim Township, Pennsylvania, just north of the border of the City of Lancaster, and to build a linoleum factory there.

Linoleum had been invented in England by Frederick Walton in 1863 — coincidentally, about the same time that Armstrong and Glass founded their cork-cutting business in Pittsburgh. Walton was an experimenter with an innovative mind. One evening as he closed up his laboratory, he forgot to replace the lid on a can of oil-based paint. When he entered the lab the next morning, he found that the linseed oil in the paint had oxidized because of its exposure to air. Now a skin of linseed oil covered the surface of the paint. Annoyed, he lifted it off with a spatula, then wiped the spatula on a piece of canvas lying on his workbench. He became interested when he saw that the oxidized linseed oil adhered to the canvas to provide a tough, flexible coating. In a brilliant burst of serendipity, Walton recognized that he had stumbled upon something that could possibly be used as flooring.

At that time, floors of British residences ranged from stone slabs in baronial manors through rough wooden floors in middle-income homes to tamped earth covered with straw in homes occupied by those less fortunate economically. For years a better type of flooring had been sought. About the best anyone could come up with was a grainy, rough-surfaced material called kamptulicon. It offered resilience underfoot, but kamptulicon had little durability and was difficult to keep clean. Walton thought his oxidized-linseed oil discovery might be the answer, if the process of making it uniformly could be perfected. He went to work, and he succeeded. Drawing on his knowledge of Latin, he named his new product "linoleum" for *linum*, flax (the source of linseed oil), and *oleum*, oil.

By the time Armstrong entered the business, half a dozen manufacturers were already making linoleum in the United States, with total sales of perhaps $10 to $15 million a year. In Europe the industry was quite a bit larger and concentrated in Great Britain. Armstrong supplied cork flour to some of these manufacturers, so the company's Board of Directors knew that competition was firmly in place. The board members were undeterred, though, and by the summer of 1907 construction was underway in a former cornfield just north of the City of Lancaster.

Armstrong had purchased about 31 acres of land for $25,663.10. The company paid in cash, down to the last dime. The initial contracts called for buildings to be constructed for $425,700, and for the machinery to cost $375,000. As often occurs, costs mounted somewhat during construction. Some of the people involved in the project later estimated that the actual costs climbed to about $1,500,000. This was a lot of money for that era. But now, not quite half a century since its founding, Armstrong was moving into the big time, and the focus was on flooring.

Launching linoleum from Lancaster

Building and equipping a new factory was one thing. Getting it to run was something else. The process proved more difficult than the board had at first imagined. Armstrong managers went to Europe to recruit help—a superintendent, a designer, and a block-cutter foreman from Dundee, Scotland, and an assistant superintendent from Delmonhurst, Germany.

On July 5, 1908, Armstrong fired the first boiler in the new plant, and that November came trial runs of plain linoleum. Regrettably, Thomas Morton Armstrong, founder of the company, was not around to witness these events. He had died on May 9, at the age of 72.

The following year Armstrong offered to the trade the first runs of plain linoleum. But success in getting the production line to run well came slowly, and the company took on a new superintendent in September. The first major decision made after he came in was to discontinue "flat-rack" stoving, used by most U.S. manufacturers, and to begin "festoon stoving," which involved hanging great loops of linoleum in ovens several stories high while the flooring cured. In the late fall Armstrong began selling the first runs of the more advanced printed linoleum and molded inlaid linoleum. During 1909 the plant in Lancaster had average employment of 246, paying a minimum wage of 14 cents an hour.

For some years the company's Pittsburgh operations had run small, modest advertisements for its line of cork stoppers and corkboard insulation, primarily in trade magazines aimed at brewers. Beginning on March 1, 1907, a young man began his employment as assistant to the manager of the newly formed Insulation Department. He was to have a monumental effect on the direction that Armstrong's advertising would take, and indeed on the future course of the company. His name was Henning W. Prentis, Jr.

At the time he joined the organization, a number of letters were pouring in from schoolchildren, teachers, even businessmen, asking, "What is cork?" As one of his early assignments, Prentis was asked to produce a pamphlet that would answer the question and tell the story of cork's unusual characteristics as a raw material. He went to work on it, and "Cork—Its Origin and Uses" was issued in 1909. It was the first piece of product literature produced by Armstrong.

By the end of 1911 Prentis had been named manager of the first advertising department for the company, which had never thought it would need one. In 1913 the company began advertising linoleum in trade magazines. The potential offered through advertising increasingly occupied Prentis's attention. He had convinced himself that advertising could play a significant role in the company's future. Convincing Armstrong's general management would prove more difficult. Prentis produced a series of articles under the heading "Told in the Store," aimed at helping wholesalers and retailers sell more flooring. The articles then were combined in a booklet that related successful selling techniques, with a section on interior decoration for the home. There must have been nothing else like it in the flooring industry. Requests came flooding in, and the company had to reprint the booklet to meet the demand. As Prentis would later recall, this event was the watershed in his attempts to demonstrate the positive power that advertising could provide to Armstrong.

America's entry into World War I meant changes at Armstrong. In addition to the move of sizable numbers of its employees into the armed forces, the company faced shortages of raw materials such as burlap. A dramatic new venture began in 1918, when the flooring plant at Lancaster began production of high-explosive shells for the army. It marked the company's first experience in making munitions. But even the changes mandated by the war did not get in the way of Armstrong's view to the horizon and its determination to continue its growth when conditions once again made this possible.

Sensing that he needed to bolster his views with ideas from professional advertising people, Prentis sought the help of the George Batten Company. Then, equipped with the facts and figures he had sought, Prentis asked Armstrong's Board of Directors for a sizable commitment: $50,000 to be invested over a three-year period in consumer magazine advertising. "This young man will break the company," one director reportedly said. Prentis held firm, contending that it would take the span of three years to make the investment pay off and that trying to accomplish its goals in less time would only be a wasted effort. Finally the board assented. A determined Prentis had won his case.

The first national consumer advertisement for Armstrong linoleum ran in the September 1, 1917, issue of *Saturday Evening Post*. The black-and-white ad occupied a full page.

Other magazines, including *Ladies' Home Journal* and *Good Housekeeping*, were added to the schedule, and the ads began running in color. The theme was "Armstrong's Linoleum: For Every Room in the House." The idea was to gain Armstrong an increased share of the linoleum market. But it was more than this. Prentis believed that, with the proper message to consumers, the ads could expand the breadth of the total market. If so, linoleum would no longer be merely the lure that brought people into a retail store, where they could be sold the retailer's line of rugs and carpet. He wanted linoleum, through effective advertising, merchandising, and sales training, to be the focus of attention as the customer entered the store.

In 1918 Armstrong took another unprecedented step when it established its Bureau of Interior Decoration. This innovation marked the first time in the flooring industry that a company purposefully set out to make people think of their floors as contributing significantly to the overall attractiveness of their homes.

*O*ne story has it that Prentis had wanted to talk with another ad agency in the same New York City office building as Batten. He arrived early one morning and, walking up several flights of stairs, found that no one had yet arrived at the chosen agency. Disappointed, he headed down the stairs. When he had gone down one flight, he noticed that the door to the Batten agency was open. On impulse he stopped in, and a long-term relationship began with that visit. (Later, through a merger, the George Batten Company became Batten, Barton, Durstine and Osborn, which evolved into BBDO. For nearly a hundred years it has served as Armstrong's advertising agency.)

Homing in on the wholesale distributor

Before 1920, Armstrong had virtually no internal floor covering sales organization. The company sold linoleum through an agent, George B. Swayne & Co. But Swayne also sold other products, such as rugs and carpeting, which diluted his attention to selling linoleum. Prentis recognized this weakness and wanted to develop a closer tie to the firms that sold Armstrong linoleum to retail dealers. In 1917 he held the first "jobbers' convention"; it would evolve into an annual event that for many years was an important part of Armstrong's relationship with wholesale distributors.

By the beginning of 1920 George Swayne's health was failing. The management at Armstrong sensed that it needed to develop a new arrangement for distributing linoleum. It purchased Swayne's business. Prentis became general sales manager of the Floor Division and moved to Lancaster, where the linoleum was being made.

With the support of John J. Evans, general manager of the division, Prentis decided that the time had come for Armstrong to develop its own sales force. He began visiting college campuses, interviewing young men who were about to be graduated—and thus pioneering one of the nation's first college recruiting programs. Some people in the flooring industry made fun of the effort, referring to "Prentis's rah-rah college boys." As usual, he persevered. And, as usual, his innovative ideas proved to be successful. His system of developing a sales staff through recruitment and training would in time be widely emulated by other companies.

Building Armstrong's own sales force for linoleum was just one click in the busy whirring going on in Prentis's mind. During the first half of the 1920s he envisioned a new method of marketing, one radically different from anything the flooring industry had ever experienced.

At that time the retail dealer bought his linoleum inventory from wherever he could clench the best deal, whether this meant negotiating with a wholesale distributor or directly with a manufacturer. The price paid depended on the buyer's ability to bargain with the seller. Linoleum was, after all, just a basic commodity, and the practice was accepted by everyone. Everyone but Prentis. He believed that the addition of more inviting color and design to this product would be embraced by the public and would stimulate sales. But better styling wouldn't be enough in itself. There had to be an efficient way to deliver the product to the ultimate customer, the consumer. Every link in the chain from manufacturer to wholesaler to retailer to consumer would benefit from a more orderly approach to distribution.

Prentis concentrated on the wholesaler system, which he felt was the best way of distributing a bulky product offered in a variety of patterns and sizes. A relatively small number of wholesale distributors handled Armstrong flooring, with a limited number of stocking points in the United States. Prentis wanted to increase the number of wholesalers, so they could provide better coverage coast to coast, and he was determined to develop them into a team with more merchandising muscle and more selling savvy.

Armstrong and the wholesalers with which it did business were strong in rural areas. By contrast, their competitors, with smaller product lines to offer, specialized in selected urban areas. Armstrong generally sought out wholesalers that had had success in the dry-goods business, selling such items as housewares, furniture, baby carriages, even hardware. These wholesalers in turn set up exclusive retail distribution rights within certain areas. The system worked satisfactorily for its day. Prentis recognized that Armstrong would have a much bigger impact in its markets, especially in urban areas, if it could develop proprietary products, those that the competition could not offer. He led the company's research and production people and the Floor Division's marketing group toward the development of such exclusive products.

To help develop trust between wholesale distributors and their manufacturing supplier, he outlined the rights and responsibilities of each party in a series of actions. One of the most important was based on his belief that the function one carries out should determine compensation. Even the smallest wholesaler, he reasoned, was entitled to a price proportionately lower than that paid by the largest retailer. Doing so recognized the service provided by the wholesaler. He startled the industry by publishing price lists for Armstrong linoleum. Now lower prices could be earned by purchasing larger quantities, rather than through secret negotiations between buyer and seller. He knew that this "open book" approach would be ridiculed, and initially it was. Retail dealers, however, accepted it when they saw that now they could compete more evenly in the marketplace. They knew what other retailers were paying for their goods. Prentis saw it as "equality of competitive opportunity," a fairer, more equitable way of doing business with all of the company's customers.

He asked the wholesale distributors for detailed reports on their shipments to retail dealers, believing that this information would help him understand how well the distribution system worked in each area of the country. He also invited wholesalers to send elected representatives to regular meetings of a Wholesalers' Policy Committee. Its members met with Armstrong management to go over marketing plans and policies before they were put into effect.

These and other innovations, such as training in sales, financial management, and flooring installation, generated a mutual trust and spirit of cooperation that pervaded every level of Armstrong's flooring business. Its sales rose steadily.

In 1921 Armstrong began making and offering patterns in Straight Line Inlaid Linoleum. By the end of 1922, the Floor Division's district office network was in place. Most of the field marketing representatives worked out of district offices. To cover sparsely populated areas of the United States, some, known as resident sales-men, worked out of their homes. Now any Armstrong wholesaler in the nation was no more than 12 hours' distance from an Armstrong sales representative. In 1923 the company completed a six-story building in the flooring plant at Lancaster to house a new rotary inlaid machine, which could make Straight Line Inlaid Linoleum more efficiently. The company also established in Lancaster the Armstrong Laying School (later known as the Installation School), which trained the linoleum mechanics of retail dealers in proper installation techniques. It concentrated on the Armstrong-recommended "felt-layer method" of installation. This called for a layer of dry felt to be installed over the floorboards before the application of the linoleum, so the felt could take up any movement in the floorboards.

Several notable events occurred in 1925. Construction began on the first unit of the company's general office building on Lancaster's West Liberty Street. In the summer Armstrong received a license to produce felt-base rugs with borders, under patents held by Congoleum-Nairn, Inc. Of particular significance, the com-pany applied for patents for making Embossed Molded Inlaid Linoleum. For several years, Armstrong molded inlaid products had suffered in comparison to inlaid products made by the straight-line process. The molded product line would probably have died had it not been for the novel idea of embossing its surface to achieve more realistic simulations of tile and stone effects. Indeed, some people later credited embossed flooring with the company's survival.

In 1926, Armstrong validated Prentis's influence, electing him to the Board of Directors and appointing him a vice-president of the company. The following year the company tapped Alfred Jones, who had headed operations at the linoleum plant since 1909, to become manager of a new Research Division.

Three years later, with the company's annual sales having grown to more than $25 million and with linoleum now the flagship product, Armstrong moved its cor-porate headquarters to Lancaster. John J. Evans, who had been leading the linoleum operations in Lancaster, moved up to president, succeeding Charles D. Armstrong, who became chairman of the board. Prentis became first vice-president.

Almost before they had warmed their new office chairs, members of this man-agement team faced a critical problem. The years of the Great Depression saw sales slide off. In three of those years—1930, 1931, and 1932—the company oper-ated at a loss. Even during those grim times, though, Evans and Prentis planned for the future. The company bought the Arrowhead Mills felt products plant at Fulton, New York, in 1929. The purchase gave Armstrong full control of the man-ufacture of felt-base floor coverings. They were gaining in importance within the company's sales, possibly because such enamel-decorated products sold at retail for only about a third as much as the more durable true linoleum goods. In 1930 Armstrong undertook a joint venture with Newport Industries, Inc., opening a plant in Pensacola, Florida. The fiberboard products, sold under the name Temlok, laid the foundation for the diverse line of ceiling materials the company markets today. Over a period of several years Armstrong entered the asphalt tile business and then, through the purchase of Stedman Rubber Company's plant at South Braintree, Massachusetts, introduced rubber tile to broaden its line of resilient tile flooring.

The introduction of asphalt tile to the Armstrong line in 1931 was especially noteworthy. Linoleum, with all its attractive features, suffered from one great liability. Because alkaline moisture could make it brittle, linoleum could not be safely installed on concrete that was in contact with the ground. Asphalt tile could be. It found ready acceptance for basement recreation rooms in the nation's homes and also for commercial and institutional structures, such as schools, hospitals, stores, and office buildings.

Asphalt tile was not a perfect flooring. It offered poor resistance to grease. After extensive research, the company introduced a "greaseproof" type of asphalt tile. It was especially suited for use in areas subject to the spillage of oils, fats, and greases. Conductive asphalt tile, another variant of this flooring material, was made for areas in which static electricity presented a hazard, such as powder plants and hospital operating rooms. Then—improvement upon improvement—there was greaseproof conductive asphalt tile, which combined several advantages for special-purpose installations.

In 1934, as sales and earnings slowly rebounded from their Depression lows, Evans was named chairman of the board. Prentis was in line to succeed him as president, and he did so on March 28.

For about 20 years Armstrong had been making a heavy-duty product called Linotile flooring. It was made of the same basic ingredients as linoleum but was specially matured to a greater hardness and durability. By the mid-1930s Linotile, together with asphalt tile, cork tile, and a relatively thick sheet material known as battleship linoleum, constituted a strong package that could be sold through flooring contractors, especially for commercial and institutional buildings. The contract department of the Floor Division handled their marketing.

In 1935, though, this picture changed. The company assigned the three tile products to the newly formed Building Materials Division, which brought them together with the Insulation Division and the Temlok Division. Some in the Floor Division protested because the sale of battleship linoleum was an important part of the contract business. They did not want to see this business divided, with one Armstrong division selling tile while another division handled battleship linoleum, both to the same contractors. Despite their opposition, the move took place. The general management likely recognized that the insulation and Temlok parts of the new division were struggling. Adding flooring tile to the mix would bolster the line of products sold through contractors.

Sales of insulation products and acoustical materials remained sluggish. But asphalt tile? It took flight. Sales were so strong that in 1937 Armstrong built a new asphalt tile plant at South Gate, California. The facility provided faster service to West Coast markets and lessened freight costs for shipping this heavy product. In that same year the company announced an important development for felt-base products: full 12-foot-wide floor coverings and rugs in sizes 12' x 12' and 12' x 15'. Now only Armstrong offered such products in widths greater than 9 feet.

Competitive pressures amid the rigors of the Depression led Armstrong into an additional change affecting felt-base rugs and floor coverings. The felt-base products were made eligible for freight equalization. (Prior to this, the equalization had been made available only to linoleum.) With freight equalization, Armstrong applied the same freight charges to customers located near competitors' plants as customers near its own plants, so Armstrong products would not be at a competitive disadvantage. The company also provided 180-day protection against any decline in prices for its goods in transit or in wholesalers' inventories.

In 1937 nonsupervisory employees of the flooring plant at Lancaster formed the Linoleum Workers' Protective Union. It represented hourly paid production employees until 1944, when it was supplanted by Local 285, United Rubber Workers.

Also in 1937, Prentis initiated the company's first five-year planning meetings. Some of his managers were unaccustomed to thinking so far ahead, but Prentis's persuasiveness won out. The company had at least a better start on what the future would require of it.

Wartime—more than a mild interruption

By the late 1930s the clouds were gathering. When war became a reality in Europe, Henning Prentis believed that entry of the United States into the conflict was all but inevitable. He wanted Armstrong to prepare itself, to take steps that would help the survival of both the nation and the company. In 1940 a War Activities Committee undertook a study to determine whether it was advisable for Armstrong to bid on government contracts for munitions. Experience in making shells during World War I proved valuable in this regard, and by the end of the year the War Department had awarded the flooring plant a contract to make five thousand 75-millimeter shells.

It may seem strange that Armstrong Cork Company, with its concentration on linoleum, would be selected to make shells for the armed forces, but there's a simple explanation. Only a few U.S. companies made linoleum. Because the production equipment used in the process was not generally available from machinery manufacturers, Armstrong's engineers and production specialists had to devise and perfect much of it at the plant in Lancaster. This capability especially applied to innovative, proprietary processes. As a result, over the years the people at this plant had honed their skills in metalworking as they learned to make the machinery they needed. Moving from developing linoleum-making machinery to precision turning of shells for the war effort was a demanding but not impossible transition.

After Pearl Harbor, as America's need for war matériel intensified, Armstrong entered more contracts for producing shells for the army and navy. The company also found ways to convert some of its linoleum production lines into specialized goods. For example, it had a lot of experience in moving lengthy sheets of linoleum down inspection tables. That experience could be turned to making other types of flexible materials that moved across these tables, such as camouflage netting and rubberized duck to use in tents and water-resistant clothing. The work in metals continued as well. The know-how of the company's artisans aided in the production of component parts of military aircraft—wingtips, rudders, and even the entire fuselages of some planes, such as the Navy Corsair fighter.

During World War II Armstrong made nearly three million bomb racks, more than 60 million navy projectiles, and 27,000 plastic canopies for airplanes. Its early work garnered national recognition. In 1942 the Lancaster plant received the Army-Navy "E" award for excellence in war production.

By the time the war ended in 1945, more than 5,000 Armstrong men and women had entered the armed services. Naturally, this drawdown of the company's employee force, as important as it was to the war effort, presented a compelling manpower problem: How was Armstrong to keep its plants and offices going with a greatly diminished number of employees? Meeting the demands of government contracts, many of which were quite labor-intensive, presented the most arduous challenge.

At the time the government strictly controlled companies' recruiting practices. But because of its fine record in producing war matériel, Armstrong was granted an exception and was allowed to recruit employees from outside its own locations. The company sent a mobile office into the Pennsylvania coal regions to recruit new employees. Armstrong then began busing a number of women to Lancaster on Monday mornings, returning them to their homes elsewhere in the Commonwealth on Friday evenings. To house them during the week, the company leased an entire dormitory at nearby Millersville State Teachers' College (now known as Millersville University). The war years marked the first time that Armstrong's linoleum plant in Lancaster employed women in production activities.

If the demands of the war necessitated burdensome adjustments on the part of Armstrong's U.S. operations, the company's subsidiaries overseas encountered even more severe problems. During the war in North Africa, Allied troops took over buildings of Armstrong's French subsidiary in several areas of Algeria. Enemy air raids destroyed a plant at Djidjelli. In Great Britain, Armstrong managed to maintain manufacturing activities despite the ravages of bombings, wartime shortages, and severe reductions in manpower. During 1941 through 1943, sales volume in nations other than the United States remained about steady, though profits earned in these nations evaporated in 1943 and 1944. Sales rose sharply in 1945, though, and 1946, the first full year after the war's cessation, saw sales and profits of Armstrong's Foreign Operations increase to nearly five times their 1940 totals.

Management attempted to devote at least some attention during the war-torn years to preparing for the postwar period. This planning, however, had to be done without any letup on the war effort. It was. The company showed such devotion to its home-front responsibilities that, according to one contemporary report, Prentis had to be talked out of offering to build ships.

Advertising helped prepare for the future. While many companies saved money by curtailing their advertising, Armstrong continued to feature linoleum "for every room in the house." Other ads informed consumers that Armstrong, maker of by-now familiar products for their homes, also turned out products for the soldiers in the foxholes. The slogan read, "Armstrong Cork Company— makers of hundreds of products for Home, Industry, and Victory." The inquiries pouring in reached record numbers. Clearly, Americans sensed that the Allied effort was turning the war around, that peace would eventually be achieved, that better times lay ahead. Unsatisfied demand was building up. Armstrong wanted to be ready to meet that demand, and it wanted to make sure that its name was one Mr. and Mrs. Consumer would think of when they began choosing products for their peacetime home.

Another important step in the preparations for postwar operations came with the completion in 1943 of a massive five-year plan. It was much more compre- hensive than the one Prentis had inaugurated in the mid-1930s. Under the new plan, every division would be equipped with the right products, manufacturing plants, distribution systems, sales organizations, and support personnel. Each divi- sion in the company had two days to go over its part of the plan with representatives of top management. Out of these planning meetings grew a more clearly defined future for the company, one that was to be ready for implementa- tion once the war came to a close.

Then 1945 arrived. The war in Europe ended with the collapse of Italy and, shortly afterward, Germany. A few months later, the war in Asia ended with the defeat of Japan. It was time for Armstrong to get going, with products to meet the pent-up needs of the civilian population.

Within the company, ideas were pent-up, too. They came boiling forth, more than ever before in Armstrong's history. The Floor Division, for example, had its eye on a new kind of linoleum, one made with different kinds of raw materials. It wanted to enlarge its advertising program and enhance its merchandising activities.

By this time, some of the major markets in the country had grown too large to be handled by just one wholesaler. The Floor Division wanted at least two active wholesalers in every important metropolitan area in the United States. With two distributors covering one metro area, it would be possible for each, if appropriate, to specialize within ethnic neighborhoods.

Every one of such plans depended on Armstrong's being able to rebuild its employee force, because well-qualified people could turn the postwar dreams into success. Even before the war ended, the company sent letters to its men and women employees in the armed forces, letting them know that they were welcome to return. As of the end of 1945, more than 1,200 had come back to Armstrong. By the close of 1946, that number had grown to 2,740. Others went to college under the GI Bill, then rejoined the company after earning their degrees.

The organization was being replenished with good men and women. The plans were waiting. It was time to unleash the thunder.

Pouring new power into peacetime

At the beginning of 1946, the first full year of peace following World War II, Armstrong Cork Company was pulsating with potential. It was ready to pour its energies into serving a nation at peace, one resolved to rebuild.

The company had made significant contributions to the war effort and had weathered that tortured four years of world conflict better than many American corporations. Annual net sales for Armstrong Cork Company and its subsidiaries in the United States had held fairly steady during the war years and were hovering around the $100 million mark, climbing to $108.8 million in 1945. After-tax earnings also were on a plateau, a low plateau, and had dipped somewhat from their 1944 level, to $3.1 million in 1945. Armstrong's total assets amounted to $77.1 million. If you were to plot the almost-level 1941-to-1945 results on a bar graph, you might conclude that the company had been sluggish during the war years—a wounded patient still breathing but with no vigor and little hope for buoyant health.

Such a conclusion would be wrong.

Remember that Henning W. Prentis, Jr., was at the helm throughout the war. As president, this remarkably prescient and perspicacious man led the company through the struggle while always looking for ways to meet its obligations toward the national defense effort. Armstrong's team of upper and middle management, salaried employees, and hourly paid employees made innovation after innovation as they learned to make new kinds of products in new ways. They found out how to work around shortages of raw materials, and they solved multiple distribution problems. They conquered each new obstacle they encountered, then moved on to the next.

Prentis didn't let them stop with that wartime success. He kept one eye cocked on the postwar period. Even during the rigors of wartime, he was pondering, predicting, planning. Halfway through World War II, in 1943, Prentis led his management people through the completion of a massive five-year plan, more extensive than anything Armstrong had ever before undertaken. The company purchased land at Jackson, Mississippi, and Kankakee, Illinois, with the recognition that additional flooring tile plants would be needed to meet postwar demands for housing and home furnishings. Projects were also put into force to increase capacity for the flooring-related plants at Fulton, New York; South Braintree, Massachusetts; South Gate, California; and Lancaster. Armstrong managers began searching for answers to pertinent personnel questions: Where will our employees come from? How will we train them? How can we deploy them for greatest effectiveness in serving our customers? Such measures, companywide, helped Armstrong people enter peacetime with a sense of preparedness, a readiness to move forward with seamless progress.

Though confident in its success, Armstrong Cork Company must have been regarded as only modest in size. In mid-1946 it employed 11,667 men and women in the United States and 2,333 in other countries, a total of 14,000. According to the 1946 edition of *Partners in Business*, a publication issued for Armstrong shareholders, "On the basis of a recent survey which showed an average of 3.2 persons per employee family, the economic lives of approximately 45,000 men, women and children are directly dependent on the Company. This is approximately equivalent to the entire population of a city the size of Elmira, N. Y.; Green Bay, Wis.; or Ogden, Utah."

At this time there were 9,524 registered holders of the company's common stock and 1,272 holders of the preferred stock. They lived in all of the 48 states and in numerous foreign countries. No shareholder was known to own as much as five percent of the outstanding common stock. Not counting brokerage and business houses and trusteeships, *Partners in Business* noted, "Women stockholders of the Company on December 31, 1945, represented 56.4 percent of such individuals… owning Preferred Stock and 49.4 percent of those persons holding Common Stock." Since the corporation had begun to operate under the name Armstrong Cork Company in 1895, it had rewarded its shareholders with cash dividends in every single year except for the two Great Depression years of 1932 and 1933.

The opening of 1946 found the company the largest producer of linoleum and asphalt tile flooring in the United States. It also was the largest producer of corks, corkboard insulation, cork pipe covering, cork composition, and textile cots. (Clearly, the "cork" in the name Armstrong Cork Company still had lots of weight.) It was the second largest manufacturer of felt-base rugs and floor covering, one of the largest producers of insulating fire brick, and a significant supplier of glass containers, crown caps, molded plastic closures, and several other specialty products.

*B*raintreee occupies its own special place in American history. It had been the home of John and Abigail Adams, the first First Family to occupy the White House in Washington, D.C. Armstrong people who staffed the company's plant at Braintree were fond of informing visitors, "You are standing on the very spot where Paul Revere used to stable his horses."

In 1946 the company operated 17 plants in the United States. Of these, six made products related to the flooring business: the flooring plant in Lancaster (linoleum, felt-base rugs and floor coverings, Linotile, asphalt tile, and sundries); the Arrowhead plant at Fulton, New York (flooring felt); Gloucester City, New Jersey (asphalt emulsions); Pittsburgh (cork tile); South Braintree, Massachusetts (rubber tile); and South Gate, California (asphalt tile and linoleum paste). Three more U.S. plants were being built. Two of these—at Jackson, Mississippi, and Kankakee, Illinois—were designed to produce asphalt tile. Asphalt tile plants were also under construction in Canada and England.

Armstrong manufactured three different types of flooring or floor covering products: first, sheet flooring (6-foot widths); second, felt-base floor coverings (6-, 9-, and 12-foot widths) and felt-base rugs (various sizes); and third, tiles (9 x 9 inch and 9 x 12 inch). It also offered a collection of products, called sundries, that were used to install and maintain its flooring products.

Let's look more closely at the first of the major product categories, sheet flooring. In its manufacturing operations, Armstrong drew on three different processes or capabilities to make its sheet flooring materials.

The oldest and simplest of these was calendering, which fed granules of linoleum mix through heated rolls under great pressure. The resulting product could be a plain linoleum or a directional, striated design effect known as jaspe linoleum.

A second method, known as the molded process, also dated back to the early days of the Lancaster plant. It made linoleum on a stencil machine that was fascinating to watch. As a felt blanket, or "carrier," moved through the several stations on this machine, it would slide a few feet, then stop. At each station, the sweep of a brush would transfer linoleum granules of a specific color mix through the openings of a stencil onto the blanket. Then the blanket would slide forward the precise distance needed and stop. The brushes would go to work again, depositing the linoleum mix onto the carrier. Each station used a different color and a different stencil design. By the time a given section of the blanket had moved through every station, the design was complete. Heavy presses then heated and compressed the mix into place against the blanket and, after aging in the linoleum stoves, the product was complete. This step-and-repeat process was a slow, painstaking procedure, but the results it achieved, including embossing across the surface of the linoleum design, could not be matched by Armstrong's competitors.

A third process involved the seven-story-high rotary machine, which somewhat resembled a ferris wheel and had cost about $2 million to build in the early 1920s. It represented the company's third attempt at a rotary machine at the plant in Lancaster. After the first two attempts had not adequately succeeded, the Board of Directors made the decision to invest fully in the process, acknowledging that Armstrong could not afford to lag behind the competition. The rotary machine produced overall marbleized design effects, such as the extremely successful Marbelle Linoleum. It also was capable of making Straight Line Linoleum, a new type of increasingly popular flooring. This linoleum featured geometric design effects with true, straight lines, as contrasted with the irregular lines and graduated colors that the molded process turned out. Armstrong's rotary machine processes, an English expert said, "incorporated all the good points of existing machines, left out the bad ones, and added some novel ones of their own." Once again Armstrong demonstrated its willingness to make an investment that resulted in the best product for the consumer.

At the close of World War II Armstrong was the only manufacturer in the United States that offered its customers a full line of flooring products. They included linoleum, felt-base floor covering, cork tile, Linotile, asphalt tile, and rubber tile. The Floor Division also provided to flooring installers and consumers a variety of sundries used in the installation and maintenance of its flooring products, such as lining felt, cove base, adhesives, linoleum knives and other tools, furniture rests, cleaners, and waxes. Armstrong had established a brawny base on which to build, and in years to come the company's team of cooperating specialists would do just that.

In 1946 the Floor Division maintained district sales offices in 19 U.S. cities. These were Atlanta, Boston, Buffalo, Chicago, Cincinnati, Cleveland, Dallas, Denver, Detroit, Kansas City, Los Angeles, Minneapolis, New Orleans, New York, Philadelphia, Pittsburgh, San Francisco, Seattle, and St. Louis. In the next decade it would raise the total to 21, adding offices in High Point, North Carolina, and Baltimore.

By now the list of products being offered by the company's various divisions numbered about 360. A product was defined as an item that was produced through its own process of manufacture, excluding simple differences in size, color, or design.

Being marketed by the Floor Division, in addition to its flooring and floor covering materials used in homes and commercial and institutional buildings, was a bewildering assortment of items used by manufacturers of airplanes, buses, desks, display fixtures, motor boats, kitchen cabinets, railroad cars, and trolley cars. If you made a product that incorporated linoleum or something like it, Armstrong could probably make it available to you—and would. But such a willingness to supply a classified-telephone-directory mix of customers took up too much time and attention for the total sales it generated, and in years to come the division began to concentrate its efforts on those broader markets that offered the greatest potential.

The move toward defining discrete market segments

As the national economy shifted to more peacetime operations, Armstrong's Floor Division gradually entered a process of looking in a new way at the markets it served.

The essence of "marketing," as contrasted with mere "selling," is to let customers, not producers, dictate the products and services they want. "You can't push a rope," as the old saying goes. Armstrong, like almost every other successful marketing company, had followed this pattern. It could have produced flooring materials of various types, with the hope that consumers would want to buy those products. That would have been operating by guesswork. Instead, the company and its Floor Division had been quick to test products in the marketplace, discontinuing those that had outlived their usefulness and adding new products to meet customers' needs and desires.

What were those needs and desires? What did people want in their flooring materials? Specific preferences changed from time to time, especially as technology made new choices available. But in general, what the consumer sought was a product that was fashionable in design and color, one that provided durability, easy maintenance, and underfoot comfort, one that for a reasonable price would add value to the home, and one that offered a reassuring sense of satisfaction as you entered the room in which it was installed.

With a new team of eager young men entering the Floor Division's ranks came, step by step, a move toward a more advanced approach to serving various market segments. The result was a sophisticated delineation of discrete markets for the division's products. The differences may have been subtle, but they were there.

Consider hospitals as an example of how this delineation was carried out in practice. Back in the 1930s the company had offered a conductive asphalt tile to reduce the risk of sparks in locations where static electricity was a potential hazard. Hospital operating rooms, with the highly combustible oxygen they contained, had a need for this type of flooring. Armstrong responded. That response was marketing—finding a product to match a specific requirement—but of an obvious, rather elementary sort.

Half a century later, in 1983, the company introduced Medintech sheet flooring for medical facilities and clean rooms. This innovation arose from a careful study of hospitals' needs. Medintech was created for clinical environments in which productivity and precision depended on cleanliness. This product, an unbacked vinyl sheet flooring, was quiet underfoot and comfortable to walk on. It offered outstanding resistance to staining, acids, and other chemicals, and it was designed for especially easy maintenance. Its seams could be sealed with either a chemical process or heat, so it offered no crevices in which germs or dirt could take residence. In short, it was made to meet the special requirements of hospitals. This more thorough type of marketing, with products designed through and through to meet the specific needs of discrete marketing segments, represented a much more comprehensive approach to serving consumers of various kinds.

A similar story could be told about the development of products that served much broader market areas than did the specialized Medintech flooring. Natural raw materials were gradually replaced by manmade materials, which offered significant advantages to the consumer. With this change, Armstrong greatly improved its ability to respond to customers' desires. Asphalt tile in time would be superseded by the vinyl-based Excelon Tile. From linoleum would spring such advanced products as Cushioned Vinyl Corlon sheet material.

Out of these evolutions grew better methods for serving the company's various consumer targets. Not every effort was successful, and the changes didn't take place all at once. But each successive generation of management examined what it was handed and then buffed it to a new patina of effectiveness.

In the early years of the twentieth century, sales of Armstrong products were handled by the appropriate sales divisions. For example, the Linoleum Division marketed resilient flooring and related products. The company's production operations were centralized within one organization that served all of the divisions. In 1952, though, Floor Products Operations was established. The operations comprised, first, the Floor Division, which had responsibility for sales and marketing, and, second, production, which had responsibility for all floor products manufacturing plants in the United States. This and other operations established within Armstrong were now known as "profit centers" for the company because they had dual accountability. They were responsible both for bringing in sales income and for the expenditures encountered in doing business, such as manufacturing the product. Floor Products Operations eventually adopted this statement as its mission and guide: "Manufacturing and marketing resilient floors, tiles, floor coverings, and sundries through wholesalers, retailers, contractors, and mass merchandisers to residential, commercial, and institutional users in the domestic United States."

Let's look more closely at Armstrong's discrete markets for flooring, as these markets matured and were identified from 1945 into the early 1990s. It may be

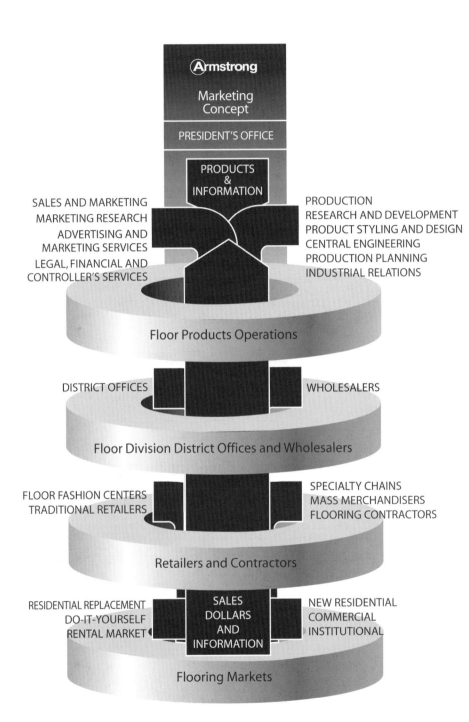

ILLUSTRATION BY C. RICHARD WHITSON

helpful to visualize four toroids, or doughnut shapes, lying atop one another, with their center holes aligned, as shown on page 24.

The first toroid, the uppermost one, represents the Lancaster-based management of Armstrong's Floor Products Operations. Clustered near the center are activities vital to its success: sales and marketing, research and development, product styling, central engineering, manufacturing at all U.S. flooring plants, and advertising and marketing services. Around the edges are the strong, centralized support organizations that permit the operations to carry out its work effectively, such as production planning, industrial relations, controller's, finance, marketing research, and legal services.

The second toroid encompasses the Floor Division field organization, including district offices nationwide and the field marketing representatives assigned to them. Also at this level are the wholesale distributors.

The third doughnut contains retail dealers, mass merchandisers, flooring contractors, and architect and interior design specifiers.

The fourth toroid represents all the discrete end-use segments to which Armstrong flooring products could be marketed.

Down through the center of this stack—through the aligned doughnut holes—flowed Armstrong products of various kinds. As sales took place, flowing up through the holes was money, with each level being compensated for what it provided to the success of the whole. Flowing both up and down through the stack was information, which was necessary for the smooth functioning of each level. The company's marketing organization, in the topmost toroid, had responsibility for starting the flow of information. It reached all the way down through the stack to pull up details of what consumers wanted and needed, and that's what allowed it to develop appropriate products for the various market segments found in the fourth-level doughnut.

Within this fourth doughnut, we can identify five major segments: the residential remodeling and replacement market, the do-it-yourself market, the new residential construction market, the rental market, and the commercial and institutional market. Each of these grew in size and significance between 1945 and 1995, and each deserves a closer look.

(1) The residential remodeling and replacement market. Largest of all the market segments, this one is called to mind by the wife who said, "Harvey, I think it's time we do something about our basement. We could put a floor down there, and a ceiling, and we could have some cabinets put in and maybe a television set, and the kids could play down there after school, and it would be like adding another room to our house, and I don't think it would cost that much to do, and you know the Wilsons just did that at their house and it's beautiful." Once he heard those words, Harvey had to stir himself. When he looked over his basement he decided that, yes, something could be done to add living space to the home and increase its value. Chances are, he found that the way to begin was to have a new resilient floor installed. Once he had done this, he showed it to his neighbor, Braxton, who was reminded that he and his wife had been thinking about replacing their kitchen and bathroom floors. Nationwide, of course, kitchens and baths represented much bigger market opportunities than Harvey's basement. And so the links were added to the chain.

The increase in home ownership following World War II reflected the "American dream" of purchasing one's own home. Fulfillment of the dream was of course aided by the GI Bill, which offered low-interest mortgage loans to veterans. It meant something significant to Armstrong, too. Consumers in the remodeling and replacement market, who were buying professionally installed floors for their homes, tended to choose better, higher-margin products than their counterparts in the do-it-yourself, new residential construction, and rental market segments.

Harvey had a number of places to which he could turn for help. The retail outlets serving the residential remodeling and replacement market included flooring specialty stores; Armstrong Floor Fashion Centers (beginning in the mid-1960s); furniture, hardware, and building supply stores; department stores; and chain stores such as Montgomery Ward and Sears, Roebuck. These outlets provided professional flooring installation or arranged for it to be provided by others.

Through the years, several Armstrong products were major factors within the residential remodeling and replacement market. They included Standard Marbelle, Straight Line Inlaid, Spatter, and Embossed Inlaid Linoleum and, in more recent years, Futuresq, Tessera, Montina, and Coronelle Corlon; Castilian Vinyl; Designer Solarian, Sundial Solarian, and other Solarian sheet flooring and tile; and Glazecraft Tile.

For clarification, it may be helpful to note that "Corlon" was Armstrong's trademark for vinyl sheet flooring. The name "Castilian" was given to rotogravure-printed vinyl flooring. A product using the trademark "Solarian" had a no-wax surface—a surface known as "Mirabond" in sheet goods and as "Duracote" in tile. "Excelon" referred to the company's vinyl-content tile flooring, whether for residential or commercial use.

(2) The do-it-yourself market. Maybe Harvey wanted to save some money and, in a burst of creative pride, decided to install his new floor all by himself. (All right, he might call on his brother-in-law for a little help along the way, but it's mostly all by himself.) Now he became a part of this market segment.

Here, too, he could draw on the services of a number of different types of retail outlets. They included Montgomery Ward and Sears, Roebuck catalog and retail stores; specialty flooring tile chains; furniture stores; and such mass merchandisers as Home Depot, Lowe's, and Hechinger's. Though Harvey was determined to take on his basement flooring installation on his own, he may still have needed advice and calm counsel to do the job right. Most of the outlets catering to this segment were able to offer such help to their customers.

Armstrong products that proved popular within the do-it-yourself segment included Asphalt Tile (9 x 9 inch), Jaspe Linoleum Tile (6 x 12), Excelon Tile (service gauge, 12 x 12—an especially big seller through the years), self-adhering Place 'n Press Excelon Tile (service gauge, 12 x 12); Vernay and Stylistik rotogravure-printed tile; Solarian Tile with the no-wax Duracote finish; At Ease rotogravure-printed sheet vinyl flooring; Quaker Rugs (various sizes) and Quaker Floor Covering (12-foot widths); rotogravure-printed Vinyl Accolon Rugs (various sizes), and Vinyl Accolon Floor Covering (6-, 9- and 12-foot widths).

(3) The new residential construction market. This is the market segment represented by the home builder, whether he was a large tract developer, a builder who erected a single house on speculation, or a builder who contracted with a potential homeowner to construct a house for him. Such builders typically purchased their flooring through builder contractors (that is, flooring contractors who specialized in selling to new home builders), building materials stores, or, starting in the mid-1960s, Armstrong Floor Fashion Centers. The flooring materials placed into new houses were professionally installed, almost always.

Which Armstrong products went into new houses? The favorites included such "builder basic" materials as standard-gauge Marbelle Linoleum, Terrazzo Vinyl Corlon, and service-gauge Excelon Tile. But that's not quite the whole picture. Many a tract builder, at the entrance to his housing development, outfitted a demonstration home with choices "beyond basic" in such areas as kitchen appliances, plumbing fixtures, built-in cupboards, and, yes, resilient flooring. The home buyer, by agreeing to pay something extra, could elect any number of options to customize his new house beyond the standard, basic model. Armstrong flooring materials that fit the definition of "builder upgrades" included Straight Line Inlaid, Spatter, and Embossed Inlaid Linoleum; Futuresq, Patrician, Tessera, Montina, and Coronelle Vinyl Corlon; rotogravure-printed Castilian Vinyl; and no-wax Solarian sheet flooring and tile.

(4) The rental market. Across the nation, from Brooklyn to Watts by way of Chicago's Maxwell Street, American families occupied apartments. They rented. Many such people didn't consider their living arrangements permanent. They knew they'd be moving to other apartments after a year or so, or perhaps they intended to occupy homes they would purchase. They were not interested in investing in permanently installed flooring materials if instead they could buy something that could be loose-laid in their apartments, then replaced every few years if and when it wore out. What they wanted were floor coverings, not floors. Those who lived in farm homes, with a number of large rooms to cover, often fit into this market segment, also.

They bought their Armstrong products through furniture, hardware, and building supply stores and mass merchandisers, as well as floor covering retailers. These were loose-laid products, which the purchaser generally unrolled onto his own floor when he got them home. They were considered floor coverings, not true flooring materials, and they were not intended to be professionally, permanently installed. They included Quaker Rugs of all sizes, Quaker Floor Coverings (in 6-, 9-, and 12-foot widths), Vinyl Accolon Rugs (9 x 12, 12 x 12, and 12 x 15 feet in size), and Vinyl Accolon Floor Coverings (6-, 9-, and 12-foot widths).

At one time, peaking in the mid-1950s, this market segment was immensely important in the flooring business. Sales of such loose-lay floor coverings at that time amounted to perhaps 50 million square yards a year.

(5) The commercial and institutional market. Here lodge the nonresidental structures, an enormous variety of them, that people encountered in their day-to-day lives: stores, shopping centers, restaurants, banks, office buildings, hotels and motels, museums, libraries, hospitals and medical centers, churches and temples, schools, colleges and universities, government buildings. The list goes on.

The flooring materials for such buildings were professionally installed by flooring contractors, through whom they were usually sold. The materials were selected by architect specifiers or sometimes by interior design specifiers or even by specifiers for the building owners themselves.

As you would expect, the flooring used in this market segment differed from that used in residential buildings. It tended to be heavier-gauge and longer-wearing even under heavy foot traffic. The Armstrong materials designed for commercial-institutional use included Plain and Marbelle Linoleum (1/8-inch gauge); Linotile, Rubber Tile, Cork Tile, Custom Corlon Tile (1/8-inch gauge, 9 x 9 inch), and Asphalt Tile (9 x 9); Excelon Tile (1/8-inch, 12 x 12) and Imperial Excelon Tile (3/32- and 1/8-inch gauge, 12 x 12); Brigantine, Montina, Palestra, Sandoval, and Seagate Vinyl Corlon sheet flooring in the .090 gauge; and such specialty products as Medintech and Crosswalk flooring. In the mid-1920s, Armstrong even made linoleum in what was known as "heavy battleship" gauge—a full quarter-inch thick. What a job it must have been to transport that to the job site and install it!

It should be noted that Rubber Tile and Custom Vinyl Tile were not sold in great quantities for this market segment, but they helped to round out the line that could be offered to building owners and specifiers. Armstrong took pride in being a full-line company, one with certain exclusive products (such as Linotile) that competitors didn't offer, one with self-contained manufacturing services capable of serving each segment of the market.

As can be inferred from this discussion, each of the five discrete market segments had its own requirements, its own retail distribution outlets, its own product needs. As the years following World War II rolled by, Armstrong marketing teams became expert at identifying the special characteristics of each.

That skill enabled them to serve each market segment and subsegment in ways that satisfied customers. And that resulted in an extended period of profitable growth for Floor Products Operations and for Armstrong.

A *quick chronology of flooring at Armstrong, 1904–1945*

For more than a century, virtually every year brought significant events affecting Armstrong's Floor Products Operations. Some years these came in a trickle. Other years, as a result of deliberate effort, in a steady stream. All played their part in the success that would roll out during the period following World War II.

It's worth retracing this trail to see how the picture developed.

In 1904 the company began making cork tile. This was Armstrong's first venture into flooring. Back then was anyone farsighted enough to see where it would lead? Possibly, possibly not. But it's clear that, over the next couple of years, the company's management in Pittsburgh recognized that something new, something exciting was occurring. They liked what was going on at the Cork Works, over in southeastern Pennsylvania. Lancaster was nicely situated from a geographical standpoint. It was on the main line of the Pennsylvania Railroad. It lay within easy reach of some of the most important metropolitan centers in the United States — New York, Philadelphia, Baltimore. The steady industriousness of the work force at Lancaster had exceeded expectations. And oh, yes, the pile of waste cork dust in the corner of the plant at Pittsburgh was still there, still growing, reminding management that it would be helpful to find other cork-containing products that Armstrong might make to reduce the scrap.

Linoleum! The answer must have come like a thunderclap. A new business, of course. But by now Armstrong had had at least a bit of experience in making flooring tile. Linoleum seemed a logical extension.

In 1907 came the decision to build a linoleum plant at Lancaster. Armstrong wasted no time. Ground was broken that same summer.

During the next year or so, while construction was going on, lots of planning, preparation, and staffing needed to be done. Even in those days, the company was intent on maintaining the highest standards. C. F. Humphreys, who was hired from Scotland to head the design department for the new plant (and would remain there for a career lasting 35 years), later recalled a telling incident. It was time to begin cutting the blocks that would be used for printing on linoleum. Humphreys went to Charles D. Armstrong, the directing head of the company, with a question: "Do you want to use brassed blocks or typed blocks?"

Armstrong had no idea. "What's the difference?"

"Typed blocks are used in America, brassed blocks in England," Humphreys informed him. "The brass blocks will cost several times more but will give much better printing."

Armstrong didn't hesitate. "Then we want brassed blocks, for we want the best product it's possible to make, even it if does cost more."

A year of celebration was 1909. The first run of Plain Linoleum rolled off the calender line and was offered to the trade. Then came Molded Inlaid Linoleum. The plant was turning out salable goods!

So successful were the early runs of the new product that just a year later the Board of Directors appropriated $240,000 for additions to the calender machine. If you're going to create consumer demand, you'd better be ready to keep up with it.

The expansion-minded management of the company continued its willingness to invest. In 1911 they had a rotary print machine installed. This method was speedy, but the results proved to be disappointing overall because the finished product had a thin, poor-lasting wear surface. The first rotary print machine was dismantled within a few years.

Just before the end of 1912, the Lancaster plant's employees came together to organize the Employees' Beneficial Association. It provided sickness and death benefits to the plant's personnel. Average employment for the year was 480, and the minimum wage was 16 cents an hour. Both represented sizable jumps from 1908, when the plant had been under construction. In that earlier year average employment had been 169, with the minimum wage 9 cents an hour. For a bench-mark, consider that Armstrong and other manufacturing companies trailed Ford Motor Company. Within five years, by 1914, Ford introduced a precedent-setting "$5-a-day" wage at its new plant in Highland Park, Michigan. At Armstrong's floor-ing plant in 1914, average wages were 17 cents an hour, or $2.04 for a 12-hour workday.

The first advertisements for Armstrong linoleum appeared in 1913 in trade magazines. Though advertising to the consumer was still several years in the future, it's clear that Henning Prentis and his belief in the power of advertising were already beginning to shape a new look for Armstrong.

Though the flooring plant at Lancaster had been producing salable goods for only five years, by 1914 it was into innovation. In that year the company installed a machine to make Straight Line Inlaid Linoleum to meet the growing demand for this type of material. The plant also developed an important new product. Known as Linotile flooring, it was made of linoleum mix but was stoved and matured to a greater hardness and durability than ordinary linoleum. At first Linotile was not distributed through the usual wholesaler-retailer channels. Instead, it was sold by the company's Insulation Department, which also installed it on the job.

The innovation continued over the next several years with the introduction of new products, some successful, some not.

In 1917 war raged in Europe, and America's entry into the conflict appeared to be growing more certain. That led to a problem for Armstrong, when its usual sources of burlap (used as backing for linoleum) dried up because burlap cloth was needed to make sandbags for trench warfare. Special looms were installed at the Lancaster Cork Works, and they soon turned out a satisfactory substitute.

But 1917, the year the United States directly entered the war, was notable at Armstrong for several other reasons, too. In March the company set up an emergency hospital and medical dispensary in the flooring plant, and the services of a visiting nurse were made available to employees and their families. That same month, Armstrong purchased a plot of ground at the west end of Liberty Street and deeded it to the city. Management's hope was that a roadway could be constructed, with a bridge over the Pennsylvania and Reading Railroad tracks just south of the plant, that would connect Liberty Street with Harrisburg Pike. Fifty years later, though a footbridge for pedestrians was in place there, that roadway still had not been built!

In 1917 Armstrong introduced the felt-layer method of installing linoleum. It involved placing a layer of dry felt over the floorboards of a room to absorb the movement that took place in the floorboards, then cementing the linoleum into place over the felt. This process was considered a true departure in the flooring business, and it took years for it to be generally accepted. Competitors resisted the idea, insisting that no felt underlayment was necessary with their products. But Armstrong's method worked, and eventually it became the industry standard.

Additionally, in this mountaintop year of 1917, the company held its first "jobbers' convention." In later years this would become known as the annual convention of Armstrong flooring wholesalers and would attract to Lancaster distributors from all over the United States and Canada.

Finally, 1917 was the year in which Armstrong began a program of national consumer advertising. The first ad, in black and white, appeared in the *Saturday Evening Post*. It promoted "Armstrong's Linoleum: For Every Room in the House." The campaign soon broadened to include ads in other magazines: *Ladies' Home Journal, Good Housekeeping,* and *The Delineator.* These pioneering efforts grew into one of the most-acclaimed, longest-sustained programs in American advertising history.

The following year Armstrong, continuing to make pioneering footsteps through the deep snow of innovation, established its Bureau of Interior Decoration. (Later the name would be changed to the Bureau of Interior Design.) Its purpose was to show consumers through example and advice how linoleum could make any room in the home more inviting. The Lancaster plant began to produce a striated effect in linoleum, the first to be made in the United States. The plant also began to turn out high-explosive shells for the army fighting World War I. This venture marked Armstrong's entry into the munitions business.

Some manufacturers of felt-base floor coverings at this time advertised their products as "linoleum." This tactic upset manufacturers of true linoleum, which was a far superior product. In 1919 Armstrong joined with several other manufacturers of linoleum to formally protest the practice. The protest was successful, and in June the Federal Trade Commission ordered Ringwalt Linoleum Works, Inc., to discontinue using the word "linoleum" to describe its products.

When George B. Swayne, selling agent for Armstrong flooring, retired in early 1920, Armstrong took over the responsibility for selling its Linoleum Division products. It began training its own sales force and, to house the new salesmen while they were undergoing their training in Lancaster, the company purchased an old farmhouse on the Lititz Pike. After reconditioning, this house became known as the Armstrong Manor. It served as the Lancaster home for generation after generation of sales trainees, some of whom went on to manage Floor Products Operations and even to head the company. During this same year management decided to invest $2 million to build a new rotary machine for the manufacture of Straight Line Inlaid Linoleum.

Something else occurred in 1920, something that was more important than anyone involved would have imagined at the time. The plant began making the earliest "5352-type" inlaid design in linoleum sheet goods. It resembled a layout of tiles in various sizes and coordinated colors, with grout lines between the tiles. Its sales eventually shot heavenward like a howitzer, and this design effect, in its various permutations, became the most popular ever to be offered in linoleum—Armstrong's linoleum, or anybody else's.

The company strove to make and market exclusive products, those that competitors did not or could not match. In 1921 it introduced to the trade patterns in Straight Line Inlaid Linoleum that featured marbleized graining. In a burst of manufacturing creativity, the production people had found a way to make it on a flat-bed machine. Design plans for the rotary machine were still being worked out.

Asphalt tile debuted on the market the following year—but not Armstrong's. The company didn't make and sell this product for almost another decade. The asphalt tile business quickly became quite important within the flooring industry. Why did Armstrong delay entering it? Probably nobody remembers for sure. Most likely Armstrong saw itself as a linoleum manufacturer, a sheet flooring manufacturer, and wanted to concentrate its attention on that.

For distribution 1922 was a landmark year. During the annual flooring whole-salers' convention in the spring, Armstrong detailed plans for a new selling arrangement and fixed price policy to replace the customary barter-and-trade prac-tice. The purpose was to support the wholesaler method of distribution, and it was a revolutionary move within the flooring industry. It proved to be of immense importance in developing solid, sustainable wholesaler outlets. Perhaps it wasn't just coincidence that by the end of the year Armstrong had realized its dream of having enough wholesale distributor locations in the United States that each was no more than 12 hours' travel away from an Armstrong sales representative.

A molded inlaid press installed during 1923 could make molded linoleum a full 12 feet wide. It ultimately led to the introduction of embossed linoleum. The plant in Lancaster completed the six-story building that was to house the new $2 million rotary machine and began to construct the machine itself. Another high-light of 1923 was the establishment of the Armstrong Laying School (later to be known as the Installation School), which trained the linoleum installers employed by retail dealers and helped to promote the felt-layer method of installation.

The dawn of 1924 brought exciting news for Lancastrians: Hourly employees of the flooring plant would now receive paid vacations. The announcement came at a time when few major industries offered such an employee benefit. The new rotary machine issued its first product runs as well. The first year's production sold out almost at once.

Meanwhile, sales of felt-base floor coverings, of lower cost and of lower quality compared with true linoleum, had begun to grow significantly. Armstrong intro-duced Fiberlin Rugs into the low-price floor covering market in 1916, meticulously noting that this product was a printed felt paper material, not linoleum. It began offering printed linoleum rugs the following year. They proved so popular that it discontinued the Fiberlin Rugs in 1920. But now, four years later, trouble hovered on the horizon. Two competitors, Congoleum Company, which made felt-base floor coverings, and Nairn Linoleum Company, which made linoleum, merged in 1924 to form Congoleum-Nairn, Inc. The newly formed company could include both linoleum and felt-base materials in carload shipments to wholesalers. To com-pete effectively, Armstrong needed to match this ability. The quickest answer was to buy an existing manufacturer of felt-base floor coverings. Armstrong did so, pur-chasing Waltona Works, Inc., of New Brunswick, New Jersey.

The products made at New Brunswick, which came on the market the follow-ing year, were given the name Quaker Rugs and Floor Coverings. The products marketed by Congoleum-Nairn dominated the felt-base floor covering market for more than a decade, but in time the Quaker name became established as one that America's homemakers recognized and trusted.

The company headquarters remained in Pittsburgh, but Lancaster was the starlet now taking the bows. In 1925 construction began on the first unit of a general office building along West Liberty Street in Lancaster. The people of Lancaster nodded their approval, recognizing that this could only be regarded as promising for their city. Toward the end of the year another big stride was taken when Armstrong applied for patents on a process of making Embossed Molded Inlaid Linoleum. For several years sales of the molded product had suffered in comparison with those of Straight Line Inlaid Linoleum. The novel idea of adding embossing to the molded product revitalized it and probably saved it from extinction. Certainly it contributed a great deal toward the exuberant survival of the company.

Consumers began to show their favoritism for large blocks and marbleization in Straight Line Inlaid Linoleum, with preferences shifting away from the small-block effects the company had been making. Responding to the change in demand, Armstrong in 1926 began producing marbleized patterns on the rotary machine. Even more significant, it began making molded inlaid effects with embossing added. It went after additional patents to protect the new embossing process.

During the next year the Linoleum Division introduced a number of new design effects, including the first marbleized printed patterns. Alfred Jones, who had served as superintendent of the Lancaster flooring plant since its beginnings in 1909, was named manager of the company's new Research Division.

In 1928 the validity of Armstrong's patents on the embossing process, which had been challenged by a competitor, were upheld by the U.S. Circuit Court of Appeals. In December the company approved a $200,000 expenditure for a "horseshoe" (U-shaped) coating and saturating unit to be added to the manufacturing facilities for felt-base floor coverings. Clearly, Armstrong's top management was willing to invest in new processes to keep the Lancaster plant at the forefront of technology.

For Armstrong, 1929 started on a hopeful note. John J. Evans was elected president, succeeding Charles D. Armstrong, who became chairman of the board. In January the company purchased the Arrowhead Plant at Fulton, New York, which made gray felt. Armstrong previously had obtained its felt from various sources. With the purchase of this plant, it had control of the full manufacturing process for felt-base floor coverings, which were growing in importance. April 1 of 1929 marked the official transfer of the company's headquarters from Pittsburgh to Lancaster.

It was a heady time, a time of excitement and optimism. Then, in October, came Black Friday. At the time, few people—whether hourly employees, business managers, government figures, or renowned economists—sensed how deeply the Great Depression, as it would become known, would affect the United States and other nations around the globe—and Armstrong.

Swept along by momentum from the past, Armstrong entered 1930 on a strong note. Construction started on the west wing of the general office building on West Liberty Street. The first unit of the building, the east wing along North Charlotte Street, had been pretty well filled when the company's headquarters moved to Lancaster. In the flooring plant, the south wing of the factory administration building was completed. The flow of new products continued. Most notable was the introduction of the first felt-base material in the industry to be offered in widths greater than 9 feet.

Armstrong, long a leader in benefits programs for its employees, had announced a broad program that included life insurance, accident and sickness insurance, retirement annuities, and disability income plans. The program was to go into effect on December 31, 1930. By that date, though, the strangling effects of the Depression made themselves felt across the United States. Armstrong's sales slid off materially from those of 1929, and profits evaporated. Contemplating a loss of some $3 million in 1930, and possibly even worse times ahead, the company's management ruefully postponed the pension part of the plan.

Certainly the company's benefits programs helped to offset the hardship that the Depression brought to many an individual employee. The economic suffering was widespread, nonetheless. Prentis outlined what he called "the four specters that loom behind every man and woman who works for a living—the specters of sickness, death, old age, and unemployment." To help ease the last of these, Armstrong plants cut the standard workday from 12 hours to 8, to spread out the work available among a greater number of those employed. Employees still encountered reductions in their wages and salaries over several years, and these would remain in effect until economic conditions improved in 1933. Stockholders paid a price, too. Armstrong declared no dividends during 1932 and 1933.

Even during the Depression doldrums, though, Prentis and the company's top management looked toward a future that they believed would bring "fair skies and a following wind." The year 1931 saw Armstrong's entry into the asphalt tile business to help fill out the line of commercial flooring sold through flooring contractors (as were cork tile, Linotile, and heavy-gauge "battleship linoleum"). The initial entry was asphalt tile in 3/16- and 1/8-inch gauges and in nine dark, plain colors. In jest, the pattern line was sometimes referred to as "shades of black," because the primary raw material, asphalt, made it difficult to achieve lighter colorations. By the end of that year, Marbelle had become one of the most popular design effects in linoleum. It was made in standard gauge for residential markets and in heavy gauge for use in commercial and institutional buildings.

"Hey!" some manager at Armstrong must have cried more than once. "We're doing well in flooring. But the walls of a room represent four times as many surfaces as the floor. Why don't we get into the wall covering business, too?" The song of the wall covering siren proved irresistible, and in 1932 came the introduction of Linowall, which was made by calendering a thin layer of linoleum mix onto a cotton backing. Linowall remained in the product line for several years. While it added some volume to sales, it never lived up to the rosiest expectations.

But 1932 was the year of another introduction, also, and this one would have a profound effect on the company's sales. To the line of embossed inlaid linoleum was added, without particular fanfare, the pattern that was to became famous throughout the flooring industry. It was known simply by its pattern number, 5352. In various colorations, primarily reds, this 6-foot-wide product resembled a geometrically diverse arrangement of bricks or tiles in various sizes, with grout lines separating each tile from its neighbors. A design effect similar to this had been introduced in 1920, with fair success. What made this one different, evidently, was that the grout lines were embossed. Whatever it was, many of America's homemakers found that they had to have it in their kitchens. Pattern 5352's success became a legend. This pattern rose to the top of the best-seller list and remained there, standing as the all-time most popular pattern in the flooring industry. In time, enough of this single pattern was sold that it could have formed a 6-foot golden pathway halfway around the world.

The Depression dragged on. Armstrong continued struggling to introduce successful new designs in flooring. In 1933 arose "shaded" effects in embossed linoleum, which featured gradations in colors within a single block of the design. The company patented the new process that permitted this shading, which became a significant selling point. This also was the year in which the Linoleum Division established the Bureau of Retail Merchandising, to help retail dealers serve consumers more effectively.

Important news about management people marked the next couple of years. In 1934 John J. Evans was elected chairman of the Board of Directors. He was succeeded as president by Henning W. Prentis, Jr. Both men had been instrumental in leading the company's flooring business to its solid position in the industry. The following year Charles D. Armstrong, who had served as chief executive officer from 1908 to 1929 and was the son of founder Thomas M. Armstrong, died in his 73rd year.

Though remnants of the Depression were still sucking at its work shoes as it struggled to emerge from the quicksand, the nation was rallying. Armstrong, too, began to show slow progress. By the end of 1933 it again operated with a before-tax profit instead of a loss. Over the next few years the company introduced several new products—Accoflor, Mastic Armoflor, Monobelle—that today are remembered only as minor blips in an overall pattern of success.

In 1938 the plant at Fulton, New York, placed in operation a new felt machine. It could make higher quality felt in 12-foot widths to help meet the growing demand for wide-goods linoleum and felt-base floor covering. The new plant at

*I*t's high noon on Broadway." *Even today, well over half a century
after they were first heard on the radio, these words fan the fond
memories of many an American. They opened each weekly broadcast
of "Armstrong Theatre of Today," which began airing in 1941. The
company had had earlier experience with radio. In 1928 it launched
"The Armstrong Quakers," a vocal octette whose programs advertised
Quaker Rugs and Floor Coverings. The program was heard on 17
stations east of the Rocky Mountains until the Great Depression ended
it at the close of 1931. By 1938 the number of American families
owning receivers had almost doubled over the 1931 figure, so Armstrong
tried again, this time with a serialized romantic drama, "The Heart of
Julia Blake," aimed at homemakers. Each week the program
highlighted one pattern in Quaker Rugs, attempting through the magic
of words to let listeners visualize the details of the design so they would
want it in their own homes.*

*With "Theatre of Today" Armstrong broke new ground in radio.
Each week, the 30-minute program opened with a five-minute summary
of the latest news. Some item in that day's news then became the focus
of the drama that filled out the remainder of the half hour. Before long
more listeners were tuning in to "Theatre of Today" than to any other
half-hour daytime radio show in the country. As their sales rose, Quaker
Rugs were feeling the electricity in the air.*

South Gate, California, began production of asphalt tile. At this time it and other
tile products were still being sold not by the company's flooring people but by the
Building Products Division.

At the flooring plant in Lancaster, mid-1939 saw construction work begin on
an addition to the 10-story warehouse. The "horseshoe" coating and saturating unit
for felt-base floor covering production finally came into operation. Financing for
this unit had been approved more than 10 years earlier, but Depression strictures
held up its completion. Once on-line, it was considered the most advanced operation of its kind in the entire floor covering industry.

By 1940 the waves of war engulfed Europe and lapped at the shores of the
United States. Armstrong formed a War Activities Committee to consider the
advisability of bidding on munitions projects, and soon the Lancaster Floor Plant
was at work making five thousand 75-millimeter shells for the War Department. In
that year the Bureau of Retail Merchandising went on the road. Its representatives

visited 34 cities coast to coast to present seminars aimed at helping retailers to merchandise Armstrong products more effectively on the sales floor.

Then came 1941. Long before the Japanese attacked Pearl Harbor on December 7, the war in Europe was an increasing center of attention here at home. Armstrong formed a Munitions Division and began to go after contracts for products that would aid the armed forces. While production moved apace on 75-millimeter shells, another contract came in. This time it was for 3-inch antiaircraft shells. Then another, for 105-millimeter shells. Soon the plant in Lancaster was making wing tips for Martin PBM-3 flying boats and filling an order for 50,000 square yards of camouflage material. By the end of the year it had begun making bomb racks for U.S. planes.

Meanwhile, the plant personnel labored to maintain production on their more traditional products, but with increasing difficulty. The demand for flooring rose steadily in anticipation of shortages caused by wartime activities. The plant pro-rated its production output so that products could be meted out fairly to all wholesale distributors.

The conflict between Allied and Axis powers was by now being called World War II. The United States became more fully involved as 1942 limped its way through a calendar pockmarked by savage struggles in the European and Pacific theaters. On the homefront, Armstrong's Lancaster Floor Plant hastened to fulfill its contracts for products to aid the military effort, the main ones being for aircraft structural parts and various kinds of shells.

James H. Binns, a former Floor Division sales representative, served during the wartime period as assistant general manager of the Munitions Division and later became president of the company. Years afterward he recalled the contributions Armstrong made to the war effort. In 1942 German tanks were much better armored than U.S. tanks. When American forces landed in North Africa, Erwin Rommel, the German field marshal in charge of the Panzer divisions there, almost ran the Americans back into the sea. Binns said, "Armstrong was one of several companies given the contract to produce a new design for a 20-millimeter armor-piercing shot that could be fired from an aircraft. The specification required that it had to pierce 3/4-inch face-hardened armor at a 45-degree angle. Armstrong was the first contractor to manufacture shot that passed." Allegedly, he added, it was this shot that made the difference at the Battle of the Kasserine Pass, the first time Rommel's forces were held.

Government restrictions on the use of burlap, and later on linseed oil, hampered flooring production. Manufacturing shifted to concentrate on products that did not incorporate these raw materials or that used substitutes. Employable males were scarce, of course, so the company hired and trained sizable numbers of women to make war matériel. In November 1942 the plant received the Army-

Navy "E" Award for excellence in aiding the war effort, the first of four such awards Armstrong's Lancaster facilities would earn.

During the next two years, Armstrong continued to produce matériel to help the Allied cause. By the end of 1943 such products included fins and rudders for the naval scout planes made by Curtis-Wright and fuselages for the Corsair naval fighter plane made by Chance Vought. The company continued its tradition of innovation. For example, it developed a technique for spot-welding aircraft structural members so good that the navy sent in representatives from other companies to observe. Armstrong also improved paints for duck camouflage that an infrared camera would photograph as natural vegetation.

In late summer 1944 the United Rubber Workers won bargaining rights for hourly paid production employees at the Lancaster Floor Plant. In December of the following year the first agreement was signed with Local 285 of the union, ending negotiations that had been going on for more than a year.

During 1945, with the defeat of the Axis powers in sight, munitions activities waned. The government lifted restrictions on the use of burlap. Restrictions on the use of linseed oil were lessened, though supplies were still limited. In the Lancaster plant, a department to make flooring adhesives and sundries was formally established about mid-year. Along with their partners in the manufacturing plants, the people of the Floor Division, as it was now being called, looked forward to a restoration of peacetime activities.

One of the greatest challenges faced by the Floor Division during the war years was to maintain its network of wholesale distributors. Field sales representatives had relatively little to sell because of product allocations. Wartime travel restrictions, which had already led to the cancellation of the annual wholesaler conventions in Lancaster, necessitated care in planning the week's sales activities. Despite such problems, Armstrong district office personnel still made regular visits to their customers as best they could, helping to strengthen their relationships for the days that lay ahead.

At this time the Floor Division handled sheet flooring and floor covering products, including both linoleum and felt-base materials. The Building Products Division, which had been organized about 10 years earlier, handled tile flooring products, including asphalt tile. This tile was bulky and heavy, expensive to ship. That factor led the company in 1938 to augment its tile production at Lancaster by opening an asphalt tile plant at South Gate, California. Now it planned to open new tile plants in the Midwest and the South, so as to serve customers better in those regions without encountering huge freight costs.

With wartime activities drawing to an end, a question arose with increasing urgency within the executive offices at Armstrong: Where is the best place within the company to position flooring tile?

The people of the Building Products Division could argue that they had nurtured the tile business into rosy respectability. Asphalt tile, in fact, was now the most profitable part of their line. Moreover, they had carefully developed relationships with contractors, who were accustomed to buying direct. They feared that such relationships would be badly dented if the tile products were shifted to the Floor Division, with its highly structured pricing policies and wholesaler method of distribution. The current system worked. Why change it?

The Floor Division had some arrows in its quiver, also. With its nation-spanning distribution system, it could argue, taking the tile products under its broad wings provided much greater opportunity for growth. This was especially true if tiles were to be promoted for residential as well as commercial and institutional use. The Floor Division had a well-established consumer advertising program, and tile products could benefit from that.

In the end, maybe the strongest argument proved to be the simplest. Flooring tiles were floors. Clearly, some said, they belonged in the Floor Division.

That's how it turned out. The Floor Division won the intramural battle for control of tile flooring. To help offset the loss of its profitable asphalt tile business, Building Products was promised a new plant for ceiling materials, to be built without delay at Macon, Georgia.

Now, as 1945 made way for a peacetime, promising 1946, the war was over. Now, suddenly, soaringly, as a nation people were eager to get back to normal, whatever that was, and draw up even with their dreams. GIs were coming home, forming their families, resuming their educational pursuits, learning unaccustomed skills and trades, needing homes to live in, kick-starting their lives into new beginnings.

PART II

The Postwar Period

The Hive Starts to Hum

Floor Products Operations was not yet the giant it would become within a few years, but it was waking, stretching, flexing. It had not forsaken its dreams. Instead, within the limits imposed by the war, it had worked to prepare itself for peace. Peace had arrived, and the organization was ready to move ahead on several fronts. Now was the time for a lusty lunge forward.

The candle burns brighter, 1945–1953

In terms of flooring production, Armstrong had the capabilities for making linoleum through several different processes, including calendering, the giant rotary machine, and the molded inlaid tables. The company also produced Quaker rugs and floor coverings and asphalt tile. Construction was underway on the two new tile plants at Jackson, Mississippi, and Kankakee, Illinois. By 1946 being planned in Lancaster was a technically advanced calender on which plain and jaspe linoleum could be made, along with a new mixing line for linoleum raw materials. Also, the plant received approval to go ahead with construction of a 12-foot printing machine. Expansions were taking place at other flooring-related plants, especially those at Fulton, New York, and South Gate, California.

The Floor Division, still dealing with allocations of products in short supply, was eager to get back to business with its full line: plain, jaspe, Marbelle, embossed, and Straight Line Inlaid Linoleum; Linowall wall covering; flooring sundries, including felt underlayment, cove base, and adhesives; Quaker Rugs and Floor Coverings; asphalt tile, Linotile, rubber tile, and cork tile.

Bulking up with the strongest possible manpower was one of the first priorities. In 1946 Floor Products Operations welcomed to Lancaster its first post–World War II training class. Its members included not only marketing trainees but also those headed for manufacturing and staff assignments.

Activity was everywhere, almost feverish at times. Clifford J. Backstrand, first vice-president of the company (he would become president in 1950), put it into perspective in mid-1946 with this prescient statement to employees: "Right now, while industry is recovering from the effects of the war, there is a seller's market for many products—a greater demand than can be met with the goods on hand. But with industries all over the country prepared to step up production, this condition cannot last. Sooner or later—and probably sooner—customers will not have to sign up on waiting lists. Suppliers will be able to deliver the goods on demand and, what's more, they will be able to offer a choice between the products of different manufacturers. Armstrong products must be made available in sufficient quantities as soon as possible or the customers may not wait for them. Improvements must be made in manufacturing methods and equipment so that we can offer the customer the best possible buy for his money. Otherwise he may pass up our products even if there are plenty of them on the market."

Backstrand's comments seem to have been directed primarily to the company's production organization. They applied also to the marketing team, which reacted to the postwar economy with renewed concentration.

During this first full year following the war, Armstrong bought its first airplane. It was a war-surplus Lockheed 12 seating four passengers. Intended primarily for executive travel, it was christened *Orion*. Two years later came *Orion II*, a Douglas DC-3 and another veteran of the war. It held 15 passengers and was used for employee travel, then eventually for transporting customer groups, such as retailers, wholesalers, architects, and builders, to Lancaster and other company locations. By 1964, such customer travel accounted for four-fifths of its use.

In 1947 the company put into effect a group hospitalization and surgical benefits program for employees. Employees were always a top concern at Armstrong, which continued to believe that the success of the business depended on hiring and training the best available people and treating them properly. Recruiting on college campuses, which Prentis had originated in the 1920s, picked up its pace. By now staff departments, not just the sales divisions, asked to be supplied with new employees just off the campus. For the first time the company's recruiters visited colleges on the West Coast. From 1946 through 1948, about a hundred college trainees were hired each year.

Some said that Lancaster, since 1929 the site of Armstrong's headquarters, was the oldest inland city in the United States. Whether this was true or not (several other cities made the same claim), it certainly had been the largest inland city in the Colonies and an important jumping-off place for people moving westward to the Kentucky frontier. Lancaster's planner, James Hamilton, laid out the city as a perfect rectangle, occupying four square miles and extending one mile north, south, east, and west from the town center, today known as Penn Square. In 1947 this changed. Back in the 1920s, Charles Dickey Armstrong, second president of the company, had established a strong tradition for corporate community-mindedness as he led a group of businessmen to develop the Pittsburgh City Plan, from which grew that city's Golden Triangle district. Now, as fourth president of the company, Henning W. Prentis followed a similar path when he recognized that the City of Lancaster needed tax revenues if it was to adequately serve the needs of its citizens—many Armstrong employees among them. At the midpoint of 1947, the company signed an annexation agreement that made its property in Manheim Township, including the property on which stood the general offices and the adjoining Lancaster Floor Plant, a part of the City of Lancaster. The town lost its attractive symmetry, but it richly gained from the added property taxes it now received.

By the end of 1948 plans were underway for a new research and development center to be built on the Lincoln Highway west of Lancaster, about five miles from the company's Liberty Street headquarters. Also in 1948, the new printing machine, authorized two years earlier, went on line at the manufacturing plant in Lancaster. It provided additional capacity for making Quaker Floor Coverings in the 12-foot width, an Armstrong exclusive. This feature, together with the company's capability of controlling its own backing systems for such products, represented a significant advantage. Such product improvements, added to the strong Armstrong distribution system and the record of advertising that had continued even during the war years, had by now made the Quaker brand the leader in the market for felt-base products. True, some people still came into retail stores asking for "Armstrong's Congoleum," but they were an anomaly. The Lancaster Floor Plant churned out Quaker goods like never before.

Felt-base goods featured painted surfaces. That is, various bright colors of enamel paint came together to create the design of each pattern. Armstrong's success with felt-base floor covering and certain other products, such as acoustical ceiling tile, made the company one of the world's largest industrial users of paint. One of the early challenges with felt-base materials was to find paints that would dry properly as the materials were festooned vertically in ovens. Another challenge was to develop paints that would last consistently in the finished product, no matter what the color, so some parts of the pattern wouldn't wear out faster than others. A real breakthrough occurred in the late 1940s when the research and development organization, after seven years' work, perfected what the company called the K-99 finish for felt-base products. Heavily promoted in advertising and merchandising programs, it became known as the finest surfacing substance in the felt-base floor covering field.

The buzz was hardly limited to felt-base materials. Other parts of the plant were humming as well. It was already necessary to expand the adhesives and sundries operations, new since 1945, and a million-dollar addition to warehouse facilities was approved. The latter part of the year saw the completion of the large auditorium, with its technically advanced staging possibilities, being added to the general offices on West Liberty Street, in time for the 1948 Floor Division wholesalers' convention.

Also making its appearance was *The Floor Plant Journal,* a newspaper for plant employees.

Every workday, the employees demonstrated why the company's management had been attracted to Lancaster when it decided to locate its linoleum manufacturing activities here in the early part of the twentieth century. These were industrious people, local people who had demonstrated a willingness to learn new trades and had shown an understanding of how making the best product in the industry would help secure their employment in the future. More than that, they were proud to regard themselves as Armstrong employees. In general, they tended to have the most enviable jobs in the community. They were paid better than most, with better benefits packages. Armstrong was sometimes accused of being paternalistic, but it wasn't that. The top management of the company truly saw its employees as its major asset, and it tried to treat them that way. Most of these employees responded with loyalty to their employer that may have been unsurpassed anywhere in America's industrial heartland.

In the Floor Division's all-star team, nothing obscured linoleum. And in 1949 came two new products whose significance would grow in the coming years. The first of these was jaspe linoleum tile. It came in a 6 x 12-inch size, so it could be installed in an attractive herringbone effect. More important, it was the company's first flooring product specifically designed to be installed by the do-it-yourselfer. Jaspe was packaged with an adhesive appropriate for its use, along with printed instructions and other items to make the home handyman feel comfortable with the flooring job he had decided to undertake. Jaspe marked the beginning of a major marketing push to the do-it-yourselfer. In time it would lead to developments in product design, simpler installation techniques, and merchandising efforts that would continue to the present day.

The second 1949 offering was one that would have supernal sales success. This product was made through the molded process and was designed to resemble the splatterdash floors of colonial days, when a pioneer homeowner would take an almost-dry paintbrush and shake it vigorously across wooden floorboards. The result left small dots of color highlighting the neutral tones of the floor surface. Armstrong called its new product Spatter Linoleum, and it almost immediately showed that it was the most popular design effect since the introduction of embossing in linoleum about two decades earlier. Spatter at first came in only two patterns: a white with spatter dots in various colors, and a black with similar multicolored dots. Retailers could hardly stock enough of it. Recognizing that it had produced a hit, Armstrong's flooring team promptly began churning out effective displays and other point-of-sale merchandising aids, advertising campaigns, and even Spatter-design neckties for its salesmen. Spatter Linoleum remained such a hit that during the next decade Armstrong offered it in nearly 40 pattern colors.

One of the major events of 1950 occurred when Henning W. Prentis, Jr., retired as president and became chairman of the board. Clifford J. Backstrand, a Californian well-schooled in Armstrong flooring matters, succeeded him as president.

In this year Armstrong began its experience with the computer, or at least an early version of the computer. The company installed an IBM electronic calculator in the Tabulating Department at Lancaster. It could handle the calculations for 6,000 paychecks an hour, six times as fast as the mechanical equipment it replaced. And it had 1,400 electronic tubes.

Now, more than half a century later, it's easy to forget that for most parts of the United States television was still a novelty during this period. By 1950 the networks tied together perhaps 25 or 30 large cities. Other cities saw network television shows on delayed broadcasts, made possible through the delivery of film cans containing grainy kinescopes to local broadcasting studios. Audiences were small. Nonetheless, people across the country saw that television had enormous potential as an entertainment, education, and advertising medium.

Led by Cameron Hawley, director of advertising, Armstrong's team reacted quickly. On June 5, 1950, television viewers witnessed the debut of "Armstrong Circle Theatre." The half-hour dramatic program aired once a week. Undoubtedly it gained by occupying the time slot right after comedian Milton Berle's show, the most-watched television program of the day.

At first the "Circle Theatre" dramas were similar in format to those radio audiences had enjoyed on "Armstrong Theatre of Today" when it began airing in 1941. In time, though, the television show moved into a new kind of programming that was variously called "actuals" or "docudramas." Each presentation was an original drama based on recent actual events. Through the years "Armstrong Circle Theatre" informed audiences about the discovery of the Dead Sea scrolls, for example, or the modus operandi of a society jewel thief. Studies indicated that the show tended to attract the sort of viewers the company sought—thoughtful, upper-income people who wanted more than just to sit vacuously in front of a television set for entertainment. Of course the sound-and-picture capabilities of television provided an expanded opportunity to show these audiences how Armstrong products, especially flooring, could make their homes more attractive and more livable. Although "Circle Theatre" left the air in 1963, to be replaced with a chain of Armstrong-sponsored programs of other kinds, it was notable as the groundbreaker for the company's long experience with television.

Many a firecracker, occasionally a fizzle. Not every new product was a success, no matter how innovative. Limping out of the misty memories of 1951 come two examples. In the spring Strypelle Linoleum made its appearance. This was a straight line product made on the rotary machine. It must have seemed a natural successor to Spatter, which had debuted two years earlier, and it was introduced with an even bigger splash. Even the promotional necktie idea was repeated. The public, however, was not as excited as the Floor Division marketing staff about a linoleum design that incorporated built-in stripes against a marbleized background. Dealers, wholesalers, and Armstrong warehouses all found themselves overstocked with Strypelle, and the product soon died a merciful death.

Looking back on this chapter of Armstrong's flooring story, you might conclude that the flooring plant must have had excess capacity on its rotary machine, and that this seemed reason enough to get into Strypelle production. In other words, Armstrong made the product because it could make the product. This was not the pattern followed in classical marketing, and it was not typical of Armstrong's usual marketing practice. Whatever you wish to call it, the Strypelle experiment didn't work.

The other 1951 egg-layer also was a disappointment to Armstrong's marketing team, but at least out of this one came a brighter hope for the future. Marbelle Corlon sheet flooring was the company's long-awaited answer to plastic floors being introduced by some competitors. Marbelle was the first vinyl floor sold by Armstrong. It had several advantages over linoleum, especially in design and color. The company could finally escape the limitations imposed by linoleum's primary raw material, oxidized linseed oil, whose amber hue made it almost impossible to achieve bright, light colorations in linoleum patterns. Unfortunately, Marbelle had a problem of another kind. "It would snap at you!" recalls a long-time marketing man who attempted to place the product in dealer showrooms. "Plastic has a memory. When you unrolled Marbelle, it would try to go back to where it came from, right back on the roll. You'd have to jump out of the way to keep from being wrapped up in it!"

The introductory formulation for Marbelle Corlon didn't last long. Armstrong people learned from their mistakes, and the research scientists went to work on the problem. It wasn't long before the company's line of vinyl flooring products was so successful that the experiment with Marbelle was almost forgotten.

Another 1951 introduction had a quicker payoff. The Spatter design, still popular in linoleum, was added to Quaker Rugs and Floor Coverings, and it proved a success there also.

The new research and development center opened in 1952 with appropriate fanfare. No other company in the flooring industry had anything like it. At the ribbon-cutting ceremony, noted scientist Dr. Vannevar Bush, director of the federal Office of Scientific Research and Development, was the main speaker. At last Armstrong scientists had a modern laboratory building in which they could unfold their innovative wings and soar toward new horizons.

Years earlier, Prentis had recognized that as long as Armstrong made only commodity products, every buying decision would be based on price alone. But if the company could, through research, develop proprietary products that provided demonstrable benefit to the consumer, the company could make real gains and so could its customers. He and succeeding generations of top management, together with the company's Board of Directors, believed in research and development. They showed their willingness to invest in it. The new facility was an extension of this faith, and the men and women of R and D paid it off with a parade of new products and product improvements.

Something else notable occurred in 1952. The International Association of Machinists, in an election conducted by the National Labor Relations Board, won bargaining rights for machinists, electricians, pipefitters, welders, millwrights, and carpenters in the floor plant.

Having been president for two years, Clifford Backstrand and the company controllers initiated a new tool for valuing profitability and establishing accountability. Its essence was return on capital employed. This ROCE concept, as it quickly became known, was designed to help measure how well each business within the company was being managed. Up to now, the usual measurements were gross dollars of profit or sales margins (that is, the percentage of the selling price remaining after the deduction of manufacturing costs). These yardsticks had their usefulness, but they were of limited value in helping management decide where future investments could be made most effectively. ROCE added a new dimension to such decision-making. Each of the company's operations worked out its profit margin, as before, but then this number was multiplied by how many times the capital invested in that operating unit turned over in a year. Included in the "capital employed" part of the equation were not only the manufacturing plants and their machinery but also all the money invested in the business, such as capital employed in inventories and accounts receivable.

The ROCE concept, by combining responsibility, authority, and accountability within each of the company's various operations, turned them into profit centers. The five-year plans, which were updated each year, were now being examined in what became known as ROCE meetings. Managers came together to compare how Armstrong's corporate ROCE record fared against those of selected top-flight companies in other industries as well as its competitors.

In 1952 came Granette Vinyl Corlon material, a granitelike design effect introduced in several attractive patterns. It offered the consumer light colorations not possible with linoleum. And, unlike its predecessor vinyl product, Marbelle Corlon, Granette didn't insist on snapping back onto the roll when it was unfurled. Armstrong had found a solution to the earlier problem of unintended roll-ups.

With the sharply focused lens of hindsight, it isn't surprising to find that a few mistakes were made during this period of intense activity. Not all of the mistakes flowed out of the introduction of new products not ready for the market.

Consider asphalt tile, which was selling well in 1953. Armstrong had an exclusive here. Its asphalt tile featured a swirl-grain effect, whereas competitors' tile came only with directional streaks in an effect known as straight-graining. For years Armstrong had sold its 1/8-inch asphalt tiles with few complaints. That was when the tiles were handled by the Building Products Division. Now they were sold through the Floor Division, and suddenly problems were developing. Once the tiles were installed in a commercial or institutional building, the reports from the field said, they began curling like potato chips. That was an exaggeration, certainly, but nonetheless one could see the corners of the tiles rising above the surface of the floor. The company promptly started an investigation. It showed that the accent streaks forming the swirl-grain effect were pulling against one another, in time leading to a problem with dimensional stability. When the tile had been sold direct to contractors, then cemented into place shortly afterward, the instability did not have time to develop. With the tile now sold through wholesale distributors, that meant a delay in getting the product to the job. The longer it lingered in the wholesaler's warehouse, the more the problem grew. The solution proved to be simple: Forget about swirl-grain effects and, as competitors did, sell nothing but straight-grain asphalt tile. The fix produced happy results. Customers preferred it to the swirl-grain design, and it brought production advantages to Armstrong because it was less expensive to produce. "Going to straight-grain asphalt tile was a real breakthrough," remembers John H. "Jack" Young, a research scientist who was deeply involved in the changeover. "It meant less handling, less waste, better temperature control. Besides, Armstrong's straight-grain tile was better than the competitors'. We were able to add value through styling."

Lesson learned from the swirl-grain asphalt tile experience? An exclusive product doesn't mean much unless it's one that customers want to buy.

The following year witnessed two other strategic mistakes, though they must have seemed promising ideas at the time. First, the Floor Division introduced a high-pressure laminate, Corlex countertop material, made by General Electric. It was a good enough product, but the breadth of the pattern line was inadequate, deliveries were unreliable, and Armstrong was not able to devote enough time and money to the business to compete effectively against the big name in high-pressure laminates, Formica. Corlex lasted less than five years.

Second, Armstrong entered the carpet business, sort of. It purchased the family-owned Deltox Rug Company. At its plant in Wisconsin, Deltox produced a line of fiber rugs and carpets, sold mainly in the mid-Atlantic states to people who used them as summer floor coverings, often stowing them away during the colder months. The Floor Division leveled its biggest marketing guns on the Deltox opportunity. Another, more cynical way of putting that is that Armstrong tried to "linoleumize" Deltox, with a new basis of sale, published price lists, wholesaler distribution, and other characteristics borrowed from its successful resilient flooring business. These changes were not popular. Sears and some other large Deltox retailers decided to drop the line rather than play by the new rules.

Armstrong's experiment with Deltox was probably doomed anyhow. The company faced a couple of irresistible forces. About the time it began its efforts to promote Deltox products, tufted carpeting began to spread across the United States like daisies on a springtime hillside. Also, people nationwide were taking advantage of residential air-conditioning systems, which meant that changing a home's interior furnishings for the summer months no longer made sense. The timing of this acquisition could hardly have been worse. Armstrong's involvement with Deltox lasted about six years. Then it was farewell, fiber rugs.

The candle turns into a Roman candle, 1954–1969

Forget those two forgettable products, Corlex and Deltox. They were obscured by other developments. And these other developments make 1954 a standout year in the history of Armstrong flooring.

Armstrong took on a brighter look with a new corporate trademark. Even before the turn of the century the company had been using a capital "A" with a circle around it as a sign of quality. The new trademark retained this "Circle A" symbol, but now with the "A" included as the first letter of the word "Armstrong" in a clean, up-to-date typeface. Making such a transition was no simple snap of the fingers. It affected all the places in which the company name was officially used — stationery, business cards, more than a thousand different product labels, signs on manufacturing plants, product literature, retail signage, advertising, and many others. The change took three years to complete.

One interesting sidebar to the corporate trademark story involves identification right on the sheet flooring products the company sold. For years the word "Armstrong" had been printed on the back of sheet goods in a repeating pattern, but this didn't solve a problem that sometimes arose at retail. A customer might lift a corner of the goods off the roll and say something like, "This one looks pretty good. But I want Armstrong. Is this Armstrong?" The showroom salesman, eager to please and not careful with the truth, might say, "Oh yes, that's Armstrong, all right." To prevent such deception, the company began in the early 1950s to print its name right on the face of the goods, so the maker's name gleamed out from every square yard. Now it started face-printing sheet flooring with the new "Circle A Armstrong" trademark. No longer did the consumer have to wonder. Once the floor was installed, she could readily clean off the trademark with a damp sponge.

The face-printing was done on perfect goods. Following the admonition of its founder to "Let the buyer have faith," the company printed the word "Armstrong" only on the back sides of any seconds or remnants, which were considered off-goods and were to be priced as such at retail.

The Floor Division continued its innovative merchandising programs, using the strengths offered by its status as the industry's only full-line manufacturer. In 1954 it sent on the road two mammoth tractor trailers that could together form an auditorium seating more than a hundred people. This Merchandising Motorcade hummed its way out to 150 cities in 46 states. By the time its travels ended, it had taken the Armstrong story to 22,000 retail dealers and retail salespeople, offering them proven techniques on how to sell more effectively.

Plastics were beginning to poke their nose up in the flooring industry, saying, "Hey! Look at me! I'm the future!" Smaller manufacturers took the lead in their development, promising that their products would be longer wearing and easier to maintain than linoleum. Armstrong management looked on such claims with skepticism. Experiments with plastic flooring on the market, its own and others', suggested that such products sometimes shrank when they were installed, opening seams. In addition, their surfaces tended to show scratches and dents more readily than linoleum did. Still, the threat could not be ignored. Armstrong gingerly stepped onto the plastics playing field while its research people continued to seek product improvements to correct the inherent flaws in early plastic floors.

In 1954 Decoresq Corlon flooring debuted. It was notable as the first vinyl sheet flooring with a built-in design, in this instance an attractive arrangement of soft-edged stripes. Decoresq would not be the last design to feature built-in styling.

A plastic flooring with longer staying power in the marketplace was by now establishing its place within the highly competitive tile business. Armstrong first brought out Excelon Tile in a 1/8-inch thickness. It was an attractive product, durable and made with the kind of right-angle precision that tile requires if it is to fit properly when it's installed. Later, when many Excelon installations in commercial and institutional buildings had demonstrated its success, the company began making it in service gauge. This thinner gauge was intended for residential use, even for do-it-yourself installations. In time Excelon Tile had a stunning impact on Armstrong's flooring business.

When Terrazzo Corlon sheet flooring came on the market in 1955, the Floor Division discovered another reason to be cautious about vinyl materials. Terrazzo was a well-styled product, and it proved to be popular among customers. Then a problem popped up: In certain of its lighter colors, surface staining began showing up once Terrazzo Corlon was installed. Reports from Floor Division district offices affirmed that the problems were intensifying. Something had to be done before Armstrong's reputation for quality was eroded.

The research scientists went to work. The rampart they had to surmount was intimidating. What substances caused the stains, and how could their effects be counteracted? These were difficult questions. Eventually the researchers isolated several different types of staining that contributed to the problem. The staining of Terrazzo proved to be a more complicated problem than at first thought. Finding the solution took time and many a test of new raw materials and different processing methods. Eventually the problem was solved.

Dealing with such matters tended to reinforce the reluctance of some Armstrong managers to enter the plastic flooring field. By now, however, the plastics side of the business was growing too muscular to ignore any longer. Characteristically, the company took on the new challenge and beat it down. Once Armstrong people found the way to work with vinyls, they soon offered more opportunities than problems. The Product Styling staff especially found new excitement every day in the sharper, brighter colors possible with vinyl materials—colors that could not be achieved with linoleum because of its linseed oil base. Soon it was apparent to everyone in the industry that Armstrong had parted the waters in vinyls and was now clearly the dominant force in inlaid flooring of all kinds.

Ever since the experience with Linowall material in 1932, Armstrong had periodically renewed its search for a product that would be as accepted for the four walls of a room as those that found their way onto the floor. The walls offered much more square-footage potential, after all. Through the years, the parade of could-this-be-the-one attempts would include such products as Quakertex, cork wall covering, and Wall Corlon. Nothing succeeded as well as the marketing people hoped, and they all took time and attention away from the profitable, principal portion of the line, resilient flooring. The 1956 entry was vinyl wall tile. It didn't last long, either. Some began to reason that possibly the wall covering business was different from the flooring business, and that it needed the attention of people who could specialize in it, not just give it cursory attention.

Then came one of those watershed years, 1957. The new Styling Center opened in the floor plant, on the site of the old unromantic-sounding "crate shop." The men and women who worked in Product Styling and Design were accommodated in better quarters now than they had been. Although they were still a long way from the beautiful building that would house them within a few years, what they gave birth to in this interim setting was almost beyond anyone's dreams. It would be a product line unlike any that the flooring industry had ever seen, one that would open rich new pastures for the company.

Surprisingly, when one considers Armstrong's devotion to innovation, this one started elsewhere. Out at the new Disneyland theme park in California, Monsanto was to build the House of Tomorrow. It featured all-new ideas in residential living, with the emphasis on plastics. The chemical company invited Armstrong to create the Floor of Tomorrow, stipulating that this product couldn't be simply an adaptation of something already on the market.

Was Armstrong interested? Oh, yes. An opportunity like this couldn't be ignored. A team of people from Product Styling and Design, Research and Development, and the Lancaster Floor Plant eagerly went to work. What they eventually produced, everyone agreed, was simply magnificent—a sheet flooring that blended clear vinyl chips, colored chips, and glittering metallic chips. For the first time you could actually look down into the pattern, through a transparent layer of vinyl, so the flooring gave you an intriguing three-dimensional look past its surface. Nobody had ever seen a flooring material anything like it. Not ever.

In keeping with the Floor of Tomorrow theme, Armstrong named its new product Futuresq Corlon flooring. It would prove easier to name than to make. To meet the dizzying schedule of readying Monsanto's house at Disneyland, the first runs of Futuresq were rushed through, almost on a handmade basis. "Whew! We made it!" Not quite. The central portion of the House of Tomorrow boasted an impressive dome as its roof. Unfortunately, the Futuresq sheet material was installed before the dome was in place, just in time for an overnight Southern California soaking that drowned the whole project under several inches of rain. The flooring was sodden and deemed unfit for the heavy traffic the house was sure to attract. Back in Lancaster, the research, engineering, and production people had to start over again, making replacement flooring for the approaching kick-off. Some doubted it could be done in time. But determination and dogged persistence paid off, and the new shipment of Futuresq went out to Disneyland.

The new flooring design was a knockout. Of the thousands who trooped through the House of Tomorrow during the coming months, virtually everyone liked it. Many of the visitors went back to their hometown dealers, wanting to see more of the sparkling new flooring effects they had been introduced to at Disneyland.

This pull from the marketplace represented a great opportunity for the Floor Division. It also created a problem. The instant-hit demand for Futuresq meant that the new material would be in short supply for several months, until Armstrong could gear up to make sufficient quantities of it. What was to be done? Place it on allocation, as was done for products during World War II?

James H. Binns, who was then general sales manager of the Floor Division, made a brilliant marketing decision. Futuresq Corlon, he said, would be available to the retail dealer only as a package sale. Armstrong would sell it in initial quantities no smaller than six rolls and would offer a six-roll showroom rack on which to display it.

Some dealers threatened to rebel. In the first place, Futuresq was intended to sell at retail for about $7.95 a square yard. No sheet flooring had ever been priced so high. (The prevailing price for linoleum was only about $5.95 a square yard.) On top of that, Armstrong was saying that a retailer couldn't even stock the product unless he was willing to buy six rolls. Outrageous! For the retailer this required an investment of $1,200 to $1,500, and that was beyond anything most dealers would consider reasonable.

An Armstrong retiree who served as a field marketing representative at the time chuckled as he reminisced about the dealer reaction. "It seemed a tough sell at first," he acknowledged. "Then, as the retailers began to think it through, it suddenly became much easier. They all knew they had to have this product. Their customers were insisting on Futuresq. As salesmen in the field, all we'd have to say was, 'Okay, if you don't want to buy the package, that's fine. I understand. But I should mention that your competitor down the street has already signed on.' That would be the clincher. And do you know what? I doubt that there was any retail dealer in America who ever was sorry that he had bought that six-roll rack of material, even at $1,500. Futuresq made a lot of money for Armstrong dealers."

In addition to its styling, Futuresq offered another advantage. It was the first flooring offered with Hydrocord backing. Armstrong's flooring researchers had come up with Hydrocord, but, as they themselves pointed out, much of the credit properly went to Armstrong's gasket researchers. They had developed a highly effective gasket material through a process called "beater saturation." Then, in a splendid example of cross-fertilization, the flooring people recognized that beater saturation held great possibilities in their field also. From this came Hydrocord, and here is why it was so important, then and later, to Armstrong's flooring fortunes: A vinyl sheet flooring backed with Hydrocord could be installed over concrete in direct contact with the ground. For the first time, vinyl sheet flooring could be used in concrete-slab construction or even in a basement. Such installations were impossible with linoleum, as the alkaline moisture from the concrete tended to damage the linoleum. Even vinyl flooring could not be satisfactorily installed over ground-level or below-grade concrete. In a flash, the introduction of Hydrocord opened an entire new market area to vinyl sheet flooring. From this time on, virtually all of Armstrong's major vinyl sheet introductions included the Hydrocord backing. Its significance within the flooring industry could hardly be overestimated.

Concentric circles of success rippled out from Floor Products Operations. The following year, 1958, while still enjoying the success of the Futuresq Corlon introduction, Armstrong stood in the batter's box while three other new products were pitched. One resulted in a strikeout, but the other two proved to be home runs that soared over the upper deck.

The flop was called Vinyl Accolon floor covering. It represented Armstrong's answer to rotogravure-printed materials offered by competitors. These products were flooding the market, and their manufacturers promoted them heavily. In television ads, one competitor even showed elephants walking on its floor coverings to demonstrate durability. It was true that the rotogravure materials, printed by fast-turning rollers, offered processing advantages over felt-base floor coverings, which were block-printed in a slow process on flat tables. Felt-base couldn't possibly match up to the realistic designs available in roto goods.

Finally, Armstrong acquiesced by test-marketing its own product. It was a defensive move and, as one looks back on it now, it clearly seems a mistake. Vinyl Accolon was not a true rotogravure-printed vinyl floor covering worthy of the Armstrong trademark. It was not as durable or as well-styled or as salable as later introductions bearing the Vinyl Accolon name. This initial offering was made only in 6-foot widths, intended for the New York City market. It was a premature birth, uncharacteristic of Armstrong, and it was not much of a success even in New York. The test-market Vinyl Accolon was dropped a year later to allow the company to study the rotogravure possibilities more thoroughly and to prepare a better product.

Of 1958's two home runs, one was a tile, the other a sheet flooring product. The tile product Armstrong named Imperial Excelon Tile. The vinyl-content Excelon Tile had been on the market for several years and enjoyed at least modest success. Harry A. Jensen, who at that time was marketing manager for tile products and later would become president of the company, knew that much greater market potential lay ahead if only Armstrong could develop a proprietary form of Excelon, one that competitors didn't have. He worked with R and D, product styling specialists, and the production people at the tile plant in Kankakee, Illinois. Together they came up with a grand solution.

What put the "Imperial" in Imperial Excelon Tile was its through-graining. This feature allowed it to climb swiftly above its competition, even its Armstrong competition. Regular Excelon had its design applied basically to the surface of the material. Heavy traffic would eventually wear it off, down to the plain-colored vinyl mix below. With Imperial Excelon, the grains of contrasting colors that made up the design effect went right through the thickness of the tile, all the way to the very bottom. Armstrong had found a way to revolutionize something as ordinary-appearing as flooring tile. To demonstrate Imperial's competitive advantage, the company made up sample tiles with concentric circles carved into their surface, each one at a deeper level. Look! You can't wear off the design, because it goes right through! Imperial Excelon Tile was first made only at the Kankakee plant in the 1/8-inch and 3/32-inch gauges. Armstrong came up with a special pricing strategy for Imperial. It priced the 1/8-inch tile well above the similar thickness of regular, straight-grained Excelon Tile, but the 3/32-inch gauge Imperial was offered at a price slightly below the 3/32-inch straight-grain tile. Then it showed through demonstrations that the 3/32-inch Imperial flooring would maintain its handsome appearance longer than the thicker-gauge regular Excelon Tile. That was convincing.

When the commercial-institutional market made it a must-have product, the production of Imperial Excelon Tile expanded into the company's other three U.S. tile plants. At first the product was offered in a few standard pattern colors. When it became so popular, though, Armstrong turned its styling people loose. They created a dazzling palette of colors, including some that were unusual for flooring, aimed to please interior designers. Eventually the Floor Division offered it in an unusually broad selection of pattern colors, more than 30 in all. Imperial Excelon Tile sold in huge volume for many a year. It became a standard in the flooring industry, and it still is, half a century later.

The sheet flooring home run—named Tessera Vinyl Corlon because it some-what resembled the tesserae of classic mosaic floors in Ancient Rome—came about through a happy accident. Dr. David T. Zentmyer, an Armstrong research chemist, was seeking a new approach to making tile flooring. As he dribbled small cubes of vinyl onto a backing, he was surprised to find that they all lay flat on the surface, in an arrangement that seemed unusual and attractive without further manipulation. Additional experiments showed that the application of a molten clear vinyl would lock them into place on Hydrocord backing. Boom! Like that, a new sheet flooring was born. And what a flooring it was!

From the start, Tessera, made in a heavy .090-inch gauge, was intended for the commercial market. Everybody understood that. Everybody but the consumer. Once it hit retail showrooms, dealers were overwhelmed by people who thought Tessera was beautiful and wanted it installed in their homes. Armstrong marketing people shrugged and said, Okay, we'll promote it for residential use also.

Oddly, one of the characteristics that attracted consumers had at first seemed a flaw in the product. Contract floors were almost always made with a smooth, mir-rorlike surface. It's the way people expected them to be. Tessera, because of its embedded three-dimensional cubes, couldn't be made in a glasslike effect. Instead, it had slight surface irregularities that could be seen when the light hit them. What could be done about this problem? L. E. "Pop" Foster, an Auburn alumnus who was the marketing manager for linoleum and vinyl sheet flooring, said, "What problem?" He saw past the conventional thinking and wanted to make the pebbling a selling point. He emphasized that this made Tessera more closely resemble the mosaics of Ancient Rome, so that Tessera took its place among the truly classic floors of history. As a clincher, he showed how the slight irregularities in the surface of Tessera broke up reflected light, helping to hide any scratches or smudges.

In its advertising, the company began pointing out how that feature made Tessera more appealing for use in the home, but the sales pitch went further than that. Magazine ads often featured Tessera in close-ups, so readers could see its unusual appearance. The ads urged consumers to write in for free Tessera coast-ers, offered six to a set, die-cut right from actual swatches of the flooring. Was it this sampling program that led to a firestorm of demand, or was it simply the product's distinctive, never-seen-before appearance? It really doesn't matter. For many customers, once they had been exposed to Tessera, nothing else would do. They wanted it in their homes. Right now.

The big demand caused a problem for the company's production people. Not for the first time with a popular product, they found that their manufacturing process couldn't produce enough salable goods to keep up with the orders. The early runs of Tessera Vinyl Corlon were made on the Lancaster Floor Plant's molded line. It was a slow process, and at times difficult. "For the first three months of production, we lost a lot of money," recalls Joseph L. Jones, then production manager for the Tessera line and later Armstrong's chairman and president. "Then came a breakthrough. [Production manager] Ross McCray ran across a mention of a lower-density plastic resin that seemed to hold promise. We tried it, and it worked. It turned out that this resin was made by only one manufacturer, down in Pensacola. We phoned him and shocked him by saying, 'Send it to us by the carload.'"

The new resin solved one problem, but others remained. The molded production line just couldn't turn out enough Tessera to keep the material flowing through the pipelines. Clearly, some faster method was needed. A new approach was being tried out in the pilot plant at Research and Development, a continuous production method that became known as a "rolling press." If Armstrong's production teams could successfully use this process, through which the flooring could flow without interruption, in contrast to the start-and-stop molded line, it might be possible to substantially increase output.

Joe Jones approached Curtis N. Painter, vice-president and general manager of Floor Products Operations. "We can jury-rig a rolling press line in the plant, but we'll need $25,000 to set it up."

Painter said no: "You can't make this product on a continuous basis."

Jones insisted, "I'm convinced that we can. I've seen it work in the pilot plant, and we can make it work in the floor plant. But we need your okay to spend $25,000 on the project."

"All right," Painter grudgingly replied. "But I want you to call me as soon as you have it working. I want to see it for myself." It did work, and Painter was pleased to see it work. "By the end of the second year of production on that line," Jones remembers, "we were making Tessera at a third of its initial estimated cost."

Such cost effectiveness on the manufacturing line was important. Even more important was that the rolling press enabled the plant to make Tessera in volume, so the orders could be filled as they arrived. The rolling press line played a vital role in several key products that came along later, also.

Having had their tailfeathers scorched in the earlier failed attempt with an improvised product that was wrong for all time, some at Armstrong were reluctant to again enter the competitive conflict involving rotogravure-printed materials. They continued to ridicule such products with their thin wearing surface. "Nobody wants to walk on the funny papers," they said. The problem was that the competition from these floor coverings just didn't go away. With the rotogravure printing method, you could reproduce virtually any image on the backing, with photographic fidelity, before the clear vinyl wear layer was applied. The management of the company finally recognized that roto products were here to stay and that they had ignored competitors' efforts for too long.

In 1959 Armstrong disclosed its plans for re-entering the roto market. It would offer several designs in the 6-, 9-, and 12-foot widths. The company had no equipment capable of printing such products, so, unbeknownst to most, Armstrong arranged to ship its coated underlayment to Mannington Mills, a competitor. Mannington, for a specified amount per square yard, printed Armstrong's patterns on the felt, then shipped it back to Lancaster so Armstrong could apply the wear layer.

While this unorthodox procedure took place, Armstrong rushed to complete the installation of its own rotogravure printing presses in the flooring plant at Lancaster. During 1960 these presses began producing two designs, Treasure Trove and Pebblestone, in Vinyl Accolon rotogravure-printed floor covering.

Armstrong was late in plunging into the roto market, and when it did so it went in only up to its ankles at first. But finally it was there, and it was there to stay. Once the company had access to its own printing presses, it unleashed its styling people on the design of new patterns in rotogravure. What they produced was magnificent. Over the next decades, each year Armstrong sold millions of square yards of rotogravure-printed materials, and the company became the major player for such products.

For several years, the Floor Division had assumed the responsibility for marketing not only sheet flooring but also tile flooring. The latter had earlier been under the wing of the Building Products Division, which had sold direct to contractors. The Floor Division sold its products through a network of wholesale distributors. Tiles to be used in commercial and public buildings were purchased generally at the recommendation of professional specifiers, and such specifiers were usually not widely known by the wholesalers. To help ensure better relationships with the specifiers, the Floor Division in 1960 assigned some of its longer-service field representatives to a new function. They were now to be known as architect-builder-consultant specialists, working full-time with the specifier segment of the commercial-institutional market.

About the same time the company, in conjunction with the New York World's Fair, opened the Armstrong Product Center in Manhattan's Rockefeller Center. Specifiers could come to one central location to see the company's full line of flooring products. They also could obtain technical and decorating help while they were there.

"Beginning Our Second Century of Progress" was the theme for Armstrong's centennial observance, marked in 1960. The company had come a long way during its 100-year history, and it had a plenitude of plans for the future. The centennial celebration, in keeping with Armstrong's corporate demeanor, was observed with quiet dignity and was celebrated primarily among its employees and the people of its plant communities.

The great legacy of the company's centennial observance was the codification of Armstrong's Operating Principles. These principles, or at least the ideas behind them, were not new. They had begun with Thomas M. Armstrong, founder of the company, and had been rubbed to a new patina by each generation of management through which they were handed down. In 1960 Armstrong preserved them in written form for every employee, every shareholder, every customer:

1. To respect the dignity and inherent rights of the individual human being in all dealings with people.
2. To maintain high moral and ethical standards and to reflect honesty, integrity, reliability, and forthrightness in all relationships.
3. To reflect the tenets of good taste and common courtesy in all attitudes, words, and deeds.
4. To serve fairly and in proper balance the interests of all groups associated with the business—customers, stockholders, employees, suppliers, community neighbors, government, and the general public.

Armstrong expected its employees to live by these principles. They did, almost always, almost without fail.

Years later, during a time when newspapers seemed full of stories about corporate misdeeds, many a company worked out elaborate ethics manuals for their employees, carefully listing what sorts of conduct were and were not acceptable. Joseph Livingston, a business columnist for a Philadelphia newspaper, interviewed Jim Binns, Armstrong's president. "Will Armstrong adopt such a guide for its employees?"

"No," Binns answered. He handed the newspaperman a copy of Armstrong's Operating Principles. "We don't need a thick manual to tell our people what they should and shouldn't do. It's all summed up in these Operating Principles. As long as we follow these perfectly, we won't have ethical problems."

As tested over time, Binns was correct. Did Armstrong employees live by the principles perfectly? No, there was an occasional lapse. People are human beings, and they make mistakes. But it could be argued that, in every instance of a misstep, had the employee in question followed the Operating Principles, the misstep would not have occurred. They stood for years as the guiding beacon in the conduct of Armstrong employees, and the employees took great pride in that. The Operating Principles became the company's DNA.

As Armstrong began its second century of progress, in many respects Floor Products Operations showed the way. In 1961 Deltox Rug Company, which had operated as an Armstrong subsidiary, was sold back to its original owners. For many years the Floor Division's line of installation and maintenance products (or sundries, as the salesmen called them) had included Linogloss Floor Wax. Research into such floor maintenance substances had led to the development of a liquid product that could clean and wax resilient flooring simultaneously. Named Armstrong One-Step Floor Care, it became the initial product in the company's new Consumer Products Division. Test-marketing of the new One-Step product, sold primarily through supermarkets rather than flooring retailers, began in 1961.

Among the Floor Division's new products that year was Custom Vinyl Cork Tile. It featured the warm glow of actual cork but offered easier maintenance and more durability than the original cork tile; a wear layer of clear vinyl coated the cork.

Another new product in 1961 proved to be an all-star. The overwhelming success of Tessera Vinyl Corlon three years earlier and the development of the rolling press method of producing it had led farsighted Armstrong people to ask themselves, What's next? Richard Flanders Smith, vice-president and director of Product Styling and Design, had an answer. "The obvious next step with a Tessera-like floor design is to make the chips bigger and to marbleize them." He asked the styling people to make up a prototype to show what he had in mind.

Robert W. Snyder, then a member of the process development organization at R and D, picks up the story: "Rich Smith believed in starting at the top. He showed us his prototype and told us, 'This is it. It's been approved. This is what we'll be making. You can figure out how to do it.'" It wasn't easy. The new product, with its larger, variegated chips, was more difficult to make than Tessera. But working first in the pilot plant at research and development and then with the manufacturing equipment at the Lancaster Floor Plant, Armstrong's research scientists and production people figured out how to make it. The result was Montina Vinyl Corlon sheet flooring.

Montina was something special, and it called for unique approaches, even a new pricing strategy. George F. Johnston, at that time the marketing manager for linoleum and Corlon sheet flooring (he later would become general sales manager of the Floor Division) recalls the yeasty enthusiasm of those days: "So many people were involved, and it was a magnificent team effort." J. Ross McCray was general production manager of Floor Products Operations, and he and his manufacturing people had to learn to make the product. Harry A. Jensen was general sales manager of the Floor Division. He scrambled to bring Product Styling and Design on board and to develop a marketing plan. Both McCray and Jensen were deeply involved in christening Montina Vinyl Corlon in a way that could not be ignored. "But so many others also took part. It would be impossible to name them all, but their efforts can't be ignored," Johnston says. "People from research and development, product styling, engineering, production, marketing, advertising. It was like nothing Armstrong had ever seen before. Everyone recognized that Montina was an extraordinary product and that it deserved an extraordinary effort."

Adding energy to the mix was Armstrong's financial commitment. Curtis N. Painter, vice-president in charge of Floor Products Operations, authorized a multimillion-dollar production line for the plant in Lancaster specifically to make the new Montina product. "Everybody on the team was under great pressure to fill in what was needed," Johnston remembers. "We couldn't allow ourselves to fail."

The team included William W. Adams, who handled the product from an advertising standpoint (he would later serve as president, then chairman, of the company). Working together, the group rolled out Montina with a merchandising and advertising campaign previously unequaled at Armstrong. At the heart of the program was a motion picture that introduced the new product and its potential to wholesale distributors and retailers of Armstrong flooring.

Montina Vinyl Corlon flooring proved to be worth all the effort. Used in both commercial and residential interiors, it became as big a smash as Tessera. No, even bigger. Over the next quarter century the Floor Division sold more than 30 million square yards of Montina.

During 1962 Clifford J. Backstrand retired as president and became chairman of the board. Maurice J. Warnock succeeded him as president. He was a slim, quiet Oregonian, and somehow his appearance wasn't as imposing as the nickname he had been given during his college football days: "Moose." Yet a smoldering fire lay beneath that quiet interior. Warnock possessed a fine understanding of the economics of business, and during the next half-decade he led the company into some of the most productive earnings years in its history.

Some began to call this period "The Soaring Sixties," and Floor Products Operations was ready to reap the harvest. Bringing the crops into the barn, though, didn't always prove to be as easy as hoped.

In their early years rotogravure-printed floor coverings, such as Armstrong's Vinyl Accolon material, were smooth-surfaced, as their felt-base predecessors had been. By now, however, consumers responded warmly to permanent flooring goods with interrupted surfaces. That is, their surfaces were intentionally made not smooth, either through embossing (such as Embossed Inlaid Linoleum) or from the individual vinyl chips they contained (such as Tessera Vinyl Corlon flooring). Would rotogravure floor coverings also be successful if offered with interrupted surfaces?

A competitor, Congoleum, came out with a new type of roto product, a cushioned floor covering with certain elements of its design embossed. Congoleum applied for patents on the manufacturing process. Meanwhile, Armstrong was working on a product that had a similar embossed-in-register appearance but was made through another process. The company's chemists and attorneys believed that the Armstrong method was patentable because it differed significantly from that of the competition.

Congoleum received its patent, then promptly came after Armstrong, alleging infringement. The suit dragged through the courts for years. Congoleum claimed it had sole rights to embossed, cushioned rotogravure floor coverings. Armstrong, confident that its own processes did not infringe upon Congoleum's, refused to concede. Even today, Armstrong people who testified at the trial will say that a more technically proficient judge would have understood that Armstrong's process was not the same as Congoleum's and clearly did not infringe upon it.

The fact is, Armstrong lost the suit. An appeals court upheld the judgment of the lower court. The parties, after extended negotiations, settled on damages in the amount of $35 million. An attorney representing Congoleum, gloating over the victory, wondered aloud when his client would receive the money. Jim Binns, by now president of Armstrong, told him with some annoyance that it would be delivered by 9 o'clock the next morning.

When he returned that evening to Lancaster, Binns found that his promise may have been too hasty. How do you arrange a next-day delivery by 9 a.m. when it's nighttime and the banks are all closed? He called in Charles A. Walker, Jr., the company's vice-president and treasurer, and he solved the problem. On the telephone first thing the next morning, Walker connected with an officer of the New York bank who had arrived early for work. This young banker recognized the Armstrong treasurer's voice and agreed to extend the necessary loan. Binns's promise was kept on time. Long afterward, Chuck Walker still remembered with pride what one phone call had accomplished—all because it was supported by Armstrong's well-established reputation for integrity.

Adding to the farrago of frustration was the necessity to pay Congoleum a licensing fee if Armstrong wanted to continue making embossed cushioned floor coverings. The $35-million settlement was hard to swallow because of the pride of those involved, and it was a distressing sum of money. But it added up to only $16.1 million after taxes, and this amount was not regarded as material to the company's earnings when applied over all the years since the suit began. Binns dismissed it. He said, "We'll take it out of petty cash." And that was that.

It was time to move on. Armstrong had other races to run.

By 1963 the rotogravure-printed materials had taken over the floor covering market—that is, the market for sheet goods that were not intended to be professionally installed with adhesives. The painted felt-base floor coverings couldn't match the glorious variety of designs and colors being offered in roto goods. Despite the nostalgia on the part of some production people, Armstrong discontinued its line of Quaker Rugs and Floor Coverings. During their 40-year run, the plant in Lancaster had produced enough of them to stretch a 6-foot-wide sheet 12½ times around the world.

Plastics increasingly moved to the forefront of Armstrong's thinking. The multiplicity of design and construction features possible with vinyl flooring helped the company's marketing people sharpen their recognition of discrete markets that could be served by products specifically made for them. In 1964 came the introduction of Vernay Vinyl Corlon flooring, a thin-gauge material intended for the tract homes that builders were putting up across the United States.

In its March 1964 issue, *Fortune* ran a major article with the title "To Live and Die for Armstrong." It commented favorably on the company's businesses, using graphs to show how well Armstrong performed against its main competitors.

For Floor Products Operations, the following year brought one of those feel-good moments that everyone should experience from time to time. At the labs in research, at the drawing boards in product styling, at the machines humming on the production line, everything clicked. It all came together in Coronelle Vinyl Corlon sheet flooring. Coronelle was the first inlaid vinyl product with both embossing and clearly defined patterns, a combination that up to now had been available only in linoleum made through the molded process. In Coronelle flooring the consumer could choose from a wide range of new visual effects, including brick, slate, mosaic, tile, and wood simulations. Because it was made of vinyl, Coronelle offered advantages over linoleum. It featured brighter, clearer colors. It offered better wear characteristics. This inlaid vinyl product opened a whole new market area for Armstrong.

The key word here is "inlaid." In inlaid sheet flooring, the design goes right through to the backing. Contrast this, as many consumers did, with rotogravure-printed goods, in which the design is applied just to the surface of the backing, then coated with a wear layer.

Coronelle was a breakthrough product, no question about that. As with many an innovation, its introduction involved traversing a daisy field full of difficult details. In this instance, the development had taken many months. Working with vinyl mix on the production line was quite different from working with linoleum mix. While Lawrence E. "Mike" Bish in production and Charles G. Elliott in research, together with people from engineering and styling, figured out how to make the product, others in the company put together a marketing plan. In the end, producing Coronelle involved new formulations, new production-line stencils, and the reconstruction of an entire manufacturing line in the plant. Readying the product for market was an exhaustive team effort reminiscent of the introduction of Montina Vinyl Corlon four years earlier.

"We had been working on the development of Coronelle for about two years," says George Johnston. "Armstrong's top management people had the right to expect results. And our team was determined not to disappoint them."

Consumers first saw Coronelle Vinyl Corlon in 1965. Almost immediately they proved that they liked the effect. Coronelle turned out to be a huge success, even bigger than Montina. It was a modern product, in every sense of the word. But old-timers with some sense of nostalgia appreciated the fact that among the patterns offered in Coronelle was a replica, in vinyl, of the old red-brick 5352, the all-time best-selling pattern in linoleum.

Armstrong met and managed a major speed bump in 1965 when it sold its first piece of vinyl flooring to Lowe's. By this time Lowe's and other "big box" chains, or home centers as they were called, were having a real impact in marketing. Armstrong's first venture into the business came about when the wife of a Lowe's manager saw an advertisement for Montina Vinyl Corlon flooring. She told her husband, Look at this. It's beautiful, and I'd like it in my own kitchen. Why isn't Lowe's selling this?

The initial reaction from some existing Armstrong retailers was outrage. An Armstrong salesman in North Carolina received a telephone call from one of his long-time accounts: "You get Lowe's out of the Armstrong flooring business. Now. Either that, or you come up this weekend and you'll find your stuff out on the sidewalk." The Armstrong man did go to the dealer's store. Sure enough, he had tossed out all his Armstrong merchandise. But that was an early response. In fact, when Lowe's took on the line, it tended to help other retailers. Seeing Armstrong products on display at Lowe's seemed to trigger something in many consumers' minds. They'd begin to think about vinyl flooring. Then they'd go to a flooring specialty store, perhaps one that had been at the same location for years, to make their purchases.

The major home centers continued to purchase their Armstrong sheet flooring from wholesale distributors, in the usual manner. Selling tile to these home centers, however, required a new basis of sale, and Armstrong found a way to work this out while protecting its precious relationship with the wholesaler. Truckloads of tile traveled directly from an Armstrong plant to the home center's distribution center, with the wholesaler not taking physical possession of the shipment at any time. On such sales the wholesaler earned a smaller margin than he received on sales of sheet flooring. After all, for the tile sales he didn't have to do any of the selling and stocking, so his expenses were less. The point of this is that Armstrong relied so much on the wholesale distributor, and the wholesale distributor relied so much on Armstrong, that this symbiosis had to be considered in any major change in marketing. The revised basis of sale provided for the wholesaler's continued involvement in the business, while allowing Armstrong to sell to the mass merchandisers in a new way.

The product parade continued in 1966 with the addition of Cambrian Vinyl Corlon, a cushioned sheet material. It was a splendid product addition but a performance failure. Cambrian's seams tended to peak after it was installed, caused when the vinyl tautened up against the cushioning. It was another lesson to be learned. Armstrong eventually devised a way to solve the problem so it wouldn't occur in later product introductions.

Competitors were busy, too. The 1960s produced several serious challenges to Floor Products Operations. Some came out of the carpet industry. Certain manufacturers introduced a new type of non-woven carpet and began promoting what they described as its advantages over resilient flooring. They even began calling it "kitchen carpet" (a term the Floor Division never used). The idea of using carpet in the kitchen seemed preposterous to Armstrong marketing people, who for decades had been promoting smooth-surface linoleum and vinyl flooring, from which spills were easy to wipe up. The company began advertising with a "Don't cry, lady" theme to show that resilient flooring still was the easy-maintenance solution to kitchen-spill problems. The ads illustrated messages such as this: Dropped an egg on your kitchen floor? Don't cry, lady. It's okay. It's Armstrong. Logic was on Armstrong's side, and the use of carpet in kitchens never made a strong advance in America's homes.

The resilient flooring industry took a serious blow in the mid-1960s when the Federal Home Administration, which backed mortgages for homebuyers, approved the inclusion of carpet in new-home construction. Previously, a product had had to be installed permanently to receive the FHA sanction, and carpet had not qualified. The new rules meant that Armstrong in one whack lost a substantial piece of the new-home business. Another threat revolved around the use of carpet in school buildings. The Carpet Institute, an industry organization, was attracted by the huge market potential offered by schools. It published a study showing that, yes, carpet was more costly to install than resilient flooring. But because of lower maintenance costs, the Institute's study went on, over the life of the product carpet would prove to be cheaper.

Armstrong Floor Division people reacted with disbelief. Their own studies didn't agree with the Carpet Institute results, not at all. They showed that carpet cost more all the way through—in initial expense, in the cost of maintenance, and in the expected life of the product. But how to document this? The company asked the faculty of the Wharton School of the University of Pennsylvania if they would undertake an independent study of the matter. The professors said that they would do so, provided, first, that Armstrong paid for the work and, second, that Armstrong agreed to allow the study to be published no matter what the results showed. Armstrong said yes to these conditions. Its contentions were fully borne out when the impartial report came out. It showed that using resilient flooring in schools held strong economic advantages over carpet. The Carpet Institute figures had been misleading, the report showed, because they failed to give full value to the estimated useful life of resilient floors and also neglected to account for the time value of the additional expense incurred in carpet installations. The study was published in a hard-cover book, which received wide distribution. Pfft! Like that, the Carpet Institute's argument lost its steam.

Even the government seemed to be stalking Armstrong. The company received word that the Federal Trade Commission (FTC) was investigating its practice of offering volume rebates and its policies involving suggested prices for its flooring products. This serious threat seemed to strike at the very heart of the Floor Division's way of doing business. Armstrong argued that its policies had been in effect for more than 40 years, published openly and without previous challenge. In fact, twice before the FTC had reviewed and approved the Floor Division basis of sale. The FTC, however, had changed its direction. The political climate had grown chillier for business. Things were different now.

Eventually Armstrong and the FTC came together on the terms of a consent agreement. The company acknowledged no wrongdoing, but it agreed to change some of its practices. The agreement raised questions among some wholesalers of Armstrong flooring, but the Floor Division was quick to reaffirm its commitment to the wholesaler method of distribution. The company's executives traveled out to meet individually with each wholesaler, explaining the new agreed-upon requirements and reassuring each that the relationship could continue successfully. One change that did take place: The Wholesaler Policy Committee became the Wholesaler Advisory Committee.

During the 1960s, even while such challenges were being faced, Armstrong stretched out in new directions, scrambling to maximize the potential offered by its diverse markets and submarkets. It renovated and enlarged the Armstrong Manor on Lititz Pike. For 45 years, the Manor had stood as the home for marketing recruits during their training in Lancaster. Management still saw the worth of such a facility. The company attractively remodeled the house, using Armstrong products for the interior wherever feasible, and added a new wing that was three times the size of the original Manor building.

A brand-new Engineering Building found its place next to the Research and Development facilities on the Columbia Pike west of Lancaster. Somewhat resembling a box kite swung among exposed steel beams, it won several design awards because of its unusual but serviceable architecture. Like the Manor, it featured many attractive uses of Armstrong products.

Tufted carpets continued to make their presence known in the flooring industry, and some of the wholesalers of Armstrong resilient flooring showed interest in taking on lines of carpet. Understandably, the Floor Division was concerned that, if this took place, the wholesalers' attention would be diverted from Armstrong products.

One solution seemed to be for Armstrong to enter the carpet business on its own. Nobody wanted a repeat of the disappointing Deltox trial run from the mid-1950s. This time the requirements would be different. Armstrong wanted to get a fast start by acquiring an existing carpet manufacturer. This existing company should be one of medium size, one that sold direct to retailers, one that had experience with tufted carpet only, not with woven carpet.

Of the possible candidates, E&B Carpet Mills came bobbing to the surface. It was a Texas-based producer of Evans-Black tufted carpet, with yearly sales of about $24 million. Armstrong acquired E&B. In 1967 Harry A. Jensen, who headed Floor Products Operations, reassured his flooring wholesalers that Armstrong did not intend to "linoleumize or vinylize" the carpet business. The company had learned something from its experience with Deltox. E&B would continue its established means of distribution, selling Evans-Black carpet direct. It would also develop a separate line of tufted carpet, to be sold as "Carpet by Armstrong" through wholesalers.

The parent company set up a Carpet Division to handle the new products. It announced that, in addition to its tufted carpet, it would offer non-woven carpet, or needlepunch carpet as it was known in the trade, to be made at a new plant in Marietta, Pennsylvania. The company didn't scrimp. With its corporate resources behind the new business, within five years Armstrong became one of the major carpet producers in the United States.

Floor Products Operations had a new competitor, in a sense—a friendly, in-house competitor. Carpet offered a new way for long-time wholesale distributors of the company's resilient flooring to increase their sales success. These wholesalers and their salesmen could choose to work with Armstrong products, both resilient flooring and carpet, without being distracted by competitive carpet lines. Experience with this system of course soon led the major wholesalers to set up specialized management and sales organizations for each of the two lines: Armstrong flooring and Armstrong carpet.

In 1967 a second production line was completed for Coronelle Vinyl Corlon sheet flooring, which continued to gain satisfied customers across the country. Floor Products Operations quickly took advantage of the increased production capacity at the Lancaster Floor Plant, adding Castilian Vinyl Corlon sheet goods to the product mix. Made initially in 6-foot widths, Castilian became the first cushioned rotogravure-printed product recommended for permanent installation in the home. It could be installed on grade-level concrete slabs or even below grade-level, in basements. More such products would come.

This also was the year in which Excelon Tile was offered with a new "cut-in-register" design feature. It provided expanded possibilities for using this popular tile flooring to complement attractive home interiors, and it was another example of how Armstrong attempted to add value to its products.

The following year, 1968, James H. Binns was elected president of the company, succeeding M. J. Warnock. Binns, a tall, well-spoken Coloradan, had begun his Armstrong career as a Floor Division salesman. He had lived through the challenges of the Great Depression and had worked tirelessly during World War II to help the company serve the needs of the armed forces. Now he would lead it into precedent-setting new ventures that would change its corporate profile.

Since the early period of Warnock's tenure, Armstrong's top management people had been thinking of appropriate acquisitions that might enable the company to reach new levels of profitable growth. Binns agreed that this was desirable, and he came into office determined to do something about it. Diversification as an end in itself, however, was not the answer. Certain other large companies were becoming conglomerates, with product lines that ranged from farm machinery to baked goods to clothing. Binns didn't want that. He believed that for Armstrong a more sensible course was to control its diversification, with any acquisitions pointed toward helping the company become a major player in industries that had good potential for growth.

A major study of Armstrong and its strengths suggested that the company "performed very well in businesses that involved style and design, merchandising, and where its knowledge of distribution could be used to advantage. It also did well in businesses where the market rewards innovation and where the consumer is a factor in the sale." The study didn't have to mention that Floor Products Operations had

*D*uring his time as president, James H. Binns several times addressed the New York Society of Security Analysts. On one such occasion, the NYSSA tape-recorded his talk and the discussion period afterward, then had the tape transcribed. Of course Binns made numerous references to "the resilient flooring industry." The NYSSA secretary who handled the transcription was evidently unfamiliar with this term. When Armstrong people received their copy, they were amused to find frequent mentions of "the Brazilian flooring industry."

been a pioneer in every one of these areas. But Binns, whose Floor Division experience had launched his career, certainly would have recognized that Armstrong's success in flooring would be helpful if transferable to other, newer areas of concentration. He intensified the search for possible acquisitions in the home furnishings area.

If the plan for concentration in an industry with large growth potential was to work, though, Binns felt that some trimming of the sails was necessary. Within a period of two years Armstrong sold off three of its major businesses: consumer products, insulation contracting, and packaging materials. The effect on its statement of sales and earnings was significant. With these three divestitures, the company's annual sales were reduced by $120 million, more than 20 percent of the total. The money it received from the divestitures, nearly $100 million, helped finance the new shape it was forging for the future.

Armstrong was still in the process of absorbing E&B Carpet Mills, which it had acquired in 1967, the year before Binns became president. Continuing to occupy the minds of top management was the question, What else could be added advantageously? Furniture had been identified long before as a logical choice. Now it seemed even more significant. Within the home furnishings industry, furniture represented the most substantial portion. The business had grown sizably during the last few years, but relatively few companies were large enough to be considered major factors. Instead, hundreds of small, family-operated furniture companies vied for position. The opportunity seemed to be there. Binns and his team moved with characteristic decisiveness.

Studies singled out Thomasville Furniture Industries, based in Thomasville, North Carolina, as the best choice for a merger into Armstrong. Binns approached Thomasville with the proposal.

At first the family members who controlled the furniture company held out. They were not eager to be acquired. The furniture industry, however, was embroiled in a firestorm of change. They recognized that, somewhere down the line, this change would inevitably affect Thomasville if it was to compete successfully. Armstrong, with its long experience in marketing to the home furnishings industry, could offer resources not previously available in furniture. Furthermore, if Armstrong was determined to acquire a furniture company, it would do so. And if that furniture company was not Thomasville, then Thomasville would have to compete against an enhanced new rival. This line of reasoning was convincing. Thomasville's board of directors accepted Armstrong's offer in 1968.

By the end of that year, his first year as president, Binns had reached the initial step of his dream for Armstrong. He was heading an organization that, with resilient flooring, ceiling materials, carpet, and furniture, offered one of the most complete assortments of interior furnishings in the United States.

*W*hen they began using the new company slogan "Armstrong—creators of the Indoor World," the people in the company were careful to lower-case the first letter of the word "creators." They didn't want anybody to accuse Armstrong of impersonating God.

Binns typically moved fast. Once he had marshaled the facts and had made up his mind, he tended to act decisively. He became known for his creative drive, and he emphasized its importance throughout the Armstrong organization. "All of us tend to spend our time problem-solving rather than opportunity-exploiting," he believed. And he said, "Improving ROBP—return on brainpower—is the greatest challenge and opportunity for any business person or organization." Through his tenure as the company's chief executive officer, he continually urged his managers and in fact all Armstrong employees to look at their jobs with new eyes, to pioneer with innovation, to stretch beyond the ordinary. "The average performer tends to pace his effort against the general standards for satisfactory performance," he contended, "while the outstanding individual measures his progress against his own capacity."

Through divestiture and acquisition, the company had achieved the "controlled diversification" for which Binns had aimed. Now came the job of managing the new Armstrong.

One of the first places in which the public saw the coordination among the four types of interior furnishings was in advertising. The corporation adopted a new slogan, "Armstrong—creators of the Indoor World." The slogan appeared in product literature and in television and magazine advertisements. Sometimes six or seven pages of Armstrong product ads ran consecutively, for flooring, carpets, ceiling materials, and furniture, or at least some of these four.

If magazine readers concluded that they might be able to go into one superstore to buy the whole range of advertised Armstrong interior furnishings products, such a desire was understandable. The management at Armstrong had thought about this, too. Bringing such a dream to life, though, proved much more complicated than creating a slogan.

How could you organize distribution to such superstores? The various products were distributed in several different ways. This pattern couldn't be changed without disrupting existing distribution channels. Any wholesaler or retailer of Armstrong products would of course object if he felt that his business would be seriously damaged by such a move. Studies of the economic ramifications of the

Making Place 'n Press Excelon Tile, with its paper backing applied to a permanently tacky adhesive, proved to be a, well, sticky challenge for the people in the Lancaster Floor Plant. When the first run came out, the tile production manager brought in a piece to show the plant manager. The latter expressed some doubt: "Does it really work that well?"

"Let me show you," said the production manager. He stripped off the paper backing from the sample he had brought. Somehow the tile slipped from his hand and fell onto the plant manager's desk. Sticky side down. They eventually had to chisel it off. The product worked.

superstore approach suggested that enormous capital investment would be required.

In the end, the concept of the grand Armstrong interior furnishings mart faded from management attention, but that doesn't mean the effort was a waste. A lot of thought went into the idea of coordinating interior furnishings products, and that thinking produced results. One of the most important was the formation, several years later, of Corporate Markets Sales Operations. This new group brought together a team of marketing specialists who could sell any appropriate Armstrong product to such important customer groups as producers of mobile and manufactured homes, tract home builders, and national chains of retail stores. These major customers reacted well to having just one Armstrong marketing representative, rather than a succession of representatives for separate products, calling on them. Corporate Markets Sales Operations relied on the existing distribution system for each of the Armstrong marketing divisions whose products it sold, and this undoubtedly helped smooth its way in getting started.

Even with so much corporate attention being given to the Indoor World concept, Floor Products Operations continued a year of intense activity in 1968. In the Lancaster plant, the giant rotary machine for producing certain types of sheet flooring was dismantled after 44 years of use. That same year, the Floor Division sales organization landed the contract for flooring in the World Trade Center's twin towers in Manhattan. The client selected Imperial Excelon Tile, which by now was established as the flooring that commercial building specifiers tended to think of first. What made the giant sale a success, though, was Armstrong's finding a way to meet competitors' bids with competitive pricing.

Increasingly Armstrong's flooring people strove to meet the needs of discrete submarkets with products designed specifically for each one. It helped that the company's marketers were becoming better two-way communicators. "At first when I joined the Armstrong marketing organization, we all thought we knew something," remembers Alfred B. Strickler, Jr., who would become vice-president and general manager of Floor Products Operations. "We didn't share too much. We didn't ask advice. Later, though, we gradually began to listen to our wholesalers, our retailers, our consumers. We were surprised at how much we were able to learn from them, once we opened our minds to this."

In 1968 Imperial Accotone flooring came center stage for a bow. It was an embossed and cushioned type of rotogravure-printed material, offered in 6-, 9-, and 12-foot widths. Intended as an upgrade product for use in the home, it was priced at a higher level than Vinyl Accolon, but the Imperial product offered significant styling and other advantages over the older product as well.

That same year the company brought out its popular Castilian sheet goods in a 12-foot width. The new size meant that the rotogravure product, intended to be adhered permanently in place rather than loose-laid, could be installed seamlessly in a typical room. Aimed especially at the do-it-yourselfer, it was sold through mass merchandisers such as Lowe's. It was extremely successful.

Floor Products Operations continued its search for proprietary new products, those that would outstrip competitors' capabilities, but the innovations didn't stop with products. In 1968 it announced a new way to install resilient flooring: the Perimiflor installation technique. For the vinyl floors to which it was applicable, it was revolutionary. Flooring installation mechanics in the past had struggled with removing an old resilient floor and its adhesive before putting down a new flooring. Perimiflor made this step often unnecessary. The flooring products with which it was used could be simply stapled around the perimeter of a room, right over the old floor if it was smooth and flat. In replacement jobs, this capability represented a saving in time and money for both the installer and his customer.

During 1968 the molten lava of new products continued to spew forth from the Armstrong volcano. Some of these were successful. Palestra Vinyl Corlon sheet material was introduced in .090-inch gauge for the commercial market. An effect resembling painted tile lit up the patterns offered in Castilian, a cushioned rotogravure product intended as a permanent flooring. Place 'n Press Excelon Tile offered new convenience for the do-it-yourselfer. To install it, all he had to do was peel off the backing, then stick the tile right to the subfloor. No more messy adhesives with which to contend.

Then there was Easy Street sheet flooring. What led to its introduction provides an interesting behind-the-scenes look at how the company's Floor Products Operations made decisions in those days of excitement and opportunity. Duncan B. Tingle, vice-president and general manager of the operations, brought his marketing people together with representatives of production, research and development, product styling and design, and engineering to review what was going on in the marketplace. In the resilient flooring portion of the industry, rotogravure-printed materials were coming on strong. In carpet, consumers were increasingly attracted to a low-cost material that obtained its design and color through silk-screen printing. (In fact the carpet industry uses this method even today.) One can imagine Tingle saying something like this: Does Armstrong have something to learn here? Can we increase the styling options that we offer to consumers by bridging the gap between roto products and this screen-printed carpet? In other words, can we apply this printing method to resilient flooring?

This was not a new subject for the company's styling people. They had already run tests. They assured Tingle that, yes, it could be done, and they were enthusiastic about the results that could be achieved.

The team discussed the subject at length, then each member went his own way to work on the many details that had to be considered. Finally, the decision was made. Armstrong would launch a new venture, making screen-printed flooring in 12-foot widths. It would combine the smooth surface of resilient flooring with the visual effects currently available only in carpet. The printing inks or dyes would infuse themselves right into the vinyl, just the way they did in carpet.

The 1969 annual report glowingly described Easy Street as an "easily maintained cushioned vinyl floor [that] combines some of the most desirable features of carpet and conventional resilient flooring; it offers a textured appearance, is quiet and comfortable underfoot, easy to clean, light and bright in color, and can be installed without seams in most rooms of the home." Armstrong marketing people assured each other that this product offered a lot that was desirable. It seemed to be on target—until it entered the marketplace. Then it sank to the bottom of the ocean and just lay there. It turned out that consumers preferred the more sophisticated designs possible with the rotogravure process.

"Easy Street was a great product in many ways, but its screen-printed visual did not match up to the fine detail achievable in rotogravure," says George Johnston, a marketing manager of the time. "We made a calculated gamble with this product, betting on both directions, and we did it with our eyes wide open. We felt that we couldn't afford not to try it. It was a courageous decision, because we spent a lot of money developing Easy Street. In the end, this one didn't drive home any runs. On the other hand, the attempt didn't hurt our business. We had too many other things going on, and we were strong enough to deal with something like this."

The stateside marketing people of Floor Products Operations were not the only ones who catered to the opportunities in discrete markets. Armstrong's international marketing people also were recognizing distinctions in their markets. Their markets differed not only from those in the United States but also from country to country. In 1969 Product Styling and Design established the position of research and international stylist to study and respond to the varying needs of consumers outside the United States.

In 1969 Armstrong undertook the largest program of investment spending in its history. The parent company and its subsidiaries invested more than $64 million to build, expand, and improve their manufacturing, warehousing, marketing, administrative, and technical facilities. That amount represented a 45 percent increase over the previous year in capital investments. Clearly, Armstrong saw a series of green traffic lights ahead. It wanted to be ready for the opportunities of the coming decade, especially those offered by the profitable resilient flooring side of the business.

By the end of the following year, 1970, all of the Product Styling and Design organization was settled into its new building. Moving to the Columbia Pike west of Lancaster, the group joined Research and Development, Central Engineering, and Central Purchasing at a 600-acre campus known as the Armstrong Technical Center. The new product styling structure, resplendent with novel architectural features, was dominated by a large sloping wall on one side—the north side, so the stylists and colorists could work with the best natural light available. At last they had an environment worthy of the fine work they continually turned out.

The product research organization already was in place at the Technical Center. It was being headed by James E. Hazeltine, who in 1970 had been appointed director of research and development. At one time, Hazeltine would recall, the marketing divisions within Armstrong would "suffer" R and D people, whom they thought might be spending too much time pursuing pure research and not enough in creating products that had a good chance for success in the marketplace.

Now, under the leadership of Hazeltine and others, the researchers became much more sophisticated, more a part of the team than they had been earlier. They moved toward a better balance between fundamental and applied research, with a ground-zero recognition that research can and should be an integral part of marketing, in its broadest sense of making available products that meet customers' needs.

The Floor Division in this year sold several new products. One of the more successful was Cushion Coronelle Corlon sheet flooring. It offered embossed-in-register designs. They included an old favorite carried over from Embossed Inlaid Linoleum's pattern 5352, but now with the added feature of cushioning.

A product breakthrough, and homemakers rejoice, 1970–1995

Of notable significance to the future of Floor Products Operations was a product that became a star in the crown of Edgar A. Yale, the vice-president and general manager of Floor Products Operations. This one started in a classic way, with market research.

A study of consumer preferences identified three jobs that were considered especially onerous and unpleasant by homemakers: cleaning the oven, ironing clothes, and scrubbing and waxing floors. Self-cleaning ovens had taken care of the first of these, permanent-press fabrics the second. The third, the one involving floor maintenance, remained a chain around the homemaker's ankles. Oh, it was true that some flooring manufacturers claimed of their products, "You never have to scrub these floors." To that Armstrong people snorted, "Sure, you don't have to scrub any floor if you don't mind having a dirty floor." The fact is, a true no-wax floor had not yet appeared above the horizon.

For several years Yale had been meeting with a team of product research specialists. He often would cite the consumer study, mentioning that it pointed the way toward an enviable opportunity for Armstrong. His message was clear: We must develop a no-wax floor, and we must do so before our competitors.

The research budget was adequate to the task, and the researchers went to work. In 1970 Yale and his team proudly displayed the result of their efforts. It was named Solarian flooring. Armstrong regarded it as the world's first no-maintenance floor. Its surface, called Mirabond, was a urethane composition, not vinyl. The company's research people had come up with a radically different approach by using urethane, which obviated the need for waxing. It was a winner.

At last the homemaker could be freed from the burden of waxing her floor. All she had to do was look for the name Solarian. As she rejoiced in her kitchen, Armstrong marketing people rejoiced in Lancaster. The Solarian name graced many an Armstrong product in the latter third of the twentieth century, and the no-wax feature opened new sales doors every day for the company.

Since the mid-1960s certain retailers of Armstrong products had been identified as Floor Fashion Center dealers. To qualify for this title they agreed to display Armstrong goods in racks that their customers could use in selecting their purchases, rather than in rolls standing on end. In 1970 this program underwent a substantial upgrading. The basic purpose remained the same — to focus the attention of both consumers and retail salesmen exclusively on Armstrong products — and the name Floor Fashion Center was retained. A retailer who wanted to sign on now had to agree to stock and display the full Armstrong line, offer assistance in decorating, and assure customers that it could provide professional installation. Moreover, to participate the dealer had to pay a fee of $1,500 and had to commit to following the high standards being established for Floor Fashion Centers. A lot was being asked of this dealer.

In return the Floor Fashion Center dealer received unprecedented benefits. They included special display units, along with training for his employees in such areas as interior design, management, and selling skills. National advertising promoted the Floor Fashion Center stores, and local advertising identified such stores in each community. Armstrong at this time had a huge, broad-based product line.

Now certain exclusive products would be offered to Floor Fashion Center outlets, products that were not available through other types of retailers.

Dealers responded energetically. Over the next couple of years, scores of retailers across the country signed on to the program. By February 1973 Floor Products Operations was able to bring together more than 1,800 Floor Fashion Center retailers in Lancaster for three two-day meetings, back to back. The meetings incorporated certain portions of the wholesalers' convention that had been held in December 1972, including entertainment segments, and that recycling reduced the script-writing somewhat. Bringing in this many Floor Fashion Center dealers over such a short time, however, meant overcoming logistical problems aplenty. Could the Armstrong airplanes carry enough passengers? Were there sufficient hotel rooms in and around Lancaster? How, where, and what would the guests be fed?

It all worked out. Edgar Yale welcomed the retailers. George Johnston served as master of ceremonies for the three meetings. The Floor Fashion Center retailers had the opportunity to tour Armstrong's styling, research, and production operations and to ask their questions. They were truly on board now, more than ever before. At the end of the meetings, the Floor Division felt that it had found an answer to the consumers' question that had been nagging it for years: If I want to buy an Armstrong floor, how do I know which store to go to?

A half century in business is a milestone seldom reached. By 1971 Armstrong had long surpassed it in the flooring business and was revving its engines for much more ahead, but the company took time to recognize a special event occurring that year. At the wholesalers' convention, representing the whole conclave of distributors, four wholesaler representatives presented the company with a striking bronze plaque. It read:

In recognition of the Fiftieth Convention
of Armstrong Floor Division Wholesale Distributors

Commemorating Armstrong Cork Company's dedication and service
to the wholesale distributor, their leadership in the flooring industry
and in the field of wholesaler/supplier communications,
the honesty and integrity displayed in every business association,
and the close personal relationships maintained between
the people of Armstrong and their wholesale distributors.

Presented by the wholesale distributors of the
Armstrong flooring line at the fiftieth convention.

December 7, 1971   Lancaster, Pennsylvania

Jim Binns, president of Armstrong, accepted the plaque on behalf of the company. Presenting it were Morris A. Cox, president of William Volker & Company; Frank G. Hoylman, president of Empire Carpet Corporation; W. S. "Spence" LeeKing, president of Burnham Stoepel & Co.; and John N. Marston, chairman of the board of J. J. Haines & Co., Inc. Interestingly, their four wholesale distribution companies had all handled the Armstrong line since the first wholesaler convention in 1917.

The fiftieth convention held another unforgettable highlight for the wholesaler delegates. It was a surprise appearance by Neil A. Armstrong, the astronaut who in 1969 had been the first man to set foot on the surface of the moon. He concluded his remarks to the audience with words along these lines: "You Armstrong wholesalers, be sure to do a good job. I can tell you, there are no wholesalers on the moon. So get in line. You can be the first!"

Asphalt tile, which had been a part of the Armstrong line for more than 40 years, was discontinued in 1972. Its loss went unnoticed by almost everyone, as by now the asphaltic products were being rapidly replaced by the more versatile tiles of vinyl composition. This evolution was especially true at Armstrong, where Excelon Tile continued its commanding presence in the marketplace.

The company could now produce embossed-in-register sheet flooring, adopting the word "Designer" for its products that included this new feature. In 1972 a new Sunstone effect was added to Designer Solarian no-wax flooring. Another new product was Quiet Zone, a sheet flooring intended especially for use in hospitals and other medical facilities.

In the January 1973 issue of *Modern Floor Coverings*, an industry trade magazine, appeared an article based on an interview with George Johnston. Perhaps nothing else from that period vivifies the state of the resilient flooring business quite as well as Johnston's comments:

> "Now we're coming into a new age of resilient flooring—the Age of Function. We are really trying to give the consumer more than utility and more than esthetics. We're trying to create new functions for the things she really wants and demands.
>
> "In the mid-1960s, market research indicated that the consumer wanted floors that were quieter and more comfortable, that took drudgery out of day-to-day housework, that had fewer joints or seams, that were easier to install—all this in addition to fashionable, contemporary design and colors that fit in with current home furnishing trends. We, as an industry, are now able to meet these demands."

Johnston went on to amplify his statements. He said,

"Foam materials, for instance, enabled us to produce cushioned vinyls and cushioned rotogravure vinyls that are inherently more quiet and more comfortable than previous products.

"We concentrated hard and long on the development of no-wax products. They caught on because they are care-free. They satisfy the demand for less maintenance.

"Seamlessness is another example of this Age of Function. First, we were able to provide 12-foot widths in rotogravure materials that were easy to install and handle. In addition, a lot of the new styling in service-gauge vinyl asbestos tile now gives a seamless appearance when installed.

"Installation itself has been vastly improved, both for mechanics and for do-it-yourselfers. Self-stick tiles, flexible sheet materials that are easy to handle, and pre-packaged rugs have all had a tremendous appeal for the do-it-yourselfer. For installation men, there have been a number of new techniques. Perimeter bonding, for example, enables easy installation of some new materials over old floors. Tile-on systems eliminate the need for tearing up and sanding the old floor before installation.

"Today I think we're right on target with what the consumer wants in terms of function, and we're able now more than ever before to meet the constant demand for new visuals, textures, designs, and colors. That need doesn't change, for this is more and more a fashion business, not unlike ready-to-wear or automotive."

Is there any doubt that, in his remarks, George Johnston was handing to the umpire the line-up of advantages offered by his own company's product assortment?

That same year, 1973, Armstrong's classic, can't-live-without-it pattern 5352, which had first become widely known in the early days of embossed linoleum, joined the Designer Solarian line. This famous pattern now boasted a no-wax surface.

It was good that 5352 had found a home in a product line other than linoleum. On August 10, 1974, Armstrong rolled its last square yard of linoleum off the production line. And yes, the last pattern it produced was 5352.

The plant in Lancaster owed its very existence to linoleum, and the plant had been steadily turning it out since 1909. The people at Armstrong took time out for a nostalgic look back at the product that had meant so much to them. During the 65 years it had been producing linoleum, the company had made 394 million square yards through the rotary process, 332 million square yards through the embossed inlaid method, and 231 million square yards through calendering.

Those figures add up to 957 million square yards, enough linoleum to reach the moon in a path 6 feet wide and then circle it four times.

As for the all-time best-selling linoleum pattern, 5352, the plant had made enough for a 6-foot band to stretch halfway around the earth. From 5352's introduction in the early 1930s until the end of its run in 1974, the Lancaster plant made 42.25 million square yards of pattern 5352.

For the American family, linoleum was a bargain flooring from the start. In 1915, for example, about half a decade into its manufacture, an "economy" type of Armstrong linoleum sold for 36 cents per square yard at retail, while premium grades of linoleum sold for prices ranging from 56 cents to $1.12 per square yard. About 60 years later, when the company closed out its production of linoleum, the approximate price at retail was only $6.25 per square yard.

The November 1974 issue of *Armstrong Logic*, a publication circulated to some 60,000 retailers, flooring installation mechanics, and wholesalers and their salesmen, carried comments by James Binns on the gentle death of linoleum:

"The word 'linoleum' has become a blanket term in the American vocabulary. It's often used to refer to any kind of resilient floor. Linoleum was, and still is, a good product, but it had been on the market for 65 years, and that's a bit like marketing continually improved versions of the Model T. The end had to come sooner or later.

"The term 'linoleum' will probably be in the dictionary centuries from now, though, and that's about the greatest testimony to a flooring product and its widespread acceptance that I can conceive of."

An interesting historical coincidence surfaces here. Armstrong found linoleum dispensable during the same decade in which the slide rule, which had remained virtually unchanged over its 360-year history, was obsoleted by the hand-held calculator.

The business rolled on without linoleum. The plant began making Fourscore flooring. This product was intended for mobile homes, and it could be perimeter-glued for quick, easy installation. Such specialized mobile home products were being sold by another division within the company. The Floor Division had its own new products to offer. It launched Sundial flooring, a rotogravure-printed material. Sundial had a Mirabond wear layer, as did Solarian inlaid vinyl sheet floors.

The City of Lancaster, which received its borough charter from King George II of England in 1742, is one of the oldest inland cities in the United States. Like many another municipality of such years, it was showing signs of decay, with the center-city areas beginning to collapse in on themselves. James Binns was concerned about this and wanted to do something to reverse the aging process. Others felt the same way. In 1974 the company made an announcement that would have enormous impact on the downtown area. Together with National Central Bank (later to be known as Hamilton Bank, then as First Union Bank, then as Wachovia Bank), it would take over a failed urban rehabilitation area on the west side of the second block of North Queen Street. Armstrong, the announcement said, would erect two buildings in that block: a 70,000-square-foot office building and an 80,000-square-foot Interior Design Center. Though completion of the project was still two years away, the effect on Lancaster's citizens was contagious. This and other projects taking shape in the city would provide the biggest economic stimulus Lancaster had felt in years.

When the move to downtown Lancaster occurred, it was a fitting cap to the community's celebration of the nation's bicentennial observance. Over one weekend, more than 300 Armstrong men and women relocated to the new office building, named Armstrong House Lancaster Square. All of a sudden, the company infused the downtown area with people. At lunchtime they spread through the area, seeking places to eat and shop. It was a jolt that helped to revivify center-city Lancaster.

Adjacent to the new office building, the company occupied its new Interior Design Center. Here, in towering studio spaces not unlike Hollywood sound stages, the company's interior designers held sway. They combined their talents with those of cabinetmakers, lighting specialists, and photographers to create the room interiors featured in Armstrong magazine advertisements. The beautiful, colorful, idea-filled rooms that sprouted from this building, generally featuring recently introduced flooring products in attractive home settings, played an important role in the Floor Division's marketing program. To the consumer, these rooms typified Armstrong and its products as probably nothing else did.

Under the leadership of Edgar Yale, vice-president in charge of Floor Products Operations, and Alfred Strickler, general sales manager of the Floor Division, Armstrong continued finding innovations that could make its products more appealing to the consumer. In 1975 it brought out Tredway Cushioned Vinyl flooring. Tredway combined the 12-foot width, which meant that it could be installed in most rooms without a seam; cushioning, which added underfoot comfort; and the Perimiflor bonding technique, which meant easier, less expensive installation. The company still found success in developing products with proprietary advantages.

Over the next couple of years the new-products parade included two tiles of note. In 1976 no-wax Solarian Tile came to the market. The following year Stylistik Vinyl Tile debuted. This was a no-wax tile that was formulated from the beginning as a tile, rather than being cut from sheet goods. Stylistik had a Duracoat finish, which was the name Armstrong gave to its no-wax surface in tile products.

But Stylistik was a different kind of product, made through an innovative new process. Its development grew out of a competitive problem that was increasing in importance. Flooring tile manufacturers in Taiwan had begun shamelessly copying Armstrong designs and patterns, then flooding the market with these knockoffs, pricing them at less than the original Armstrong goods. How could the company compete successfully?

Armstrong was determined to find a way to lower its production costs for tile so it could compete on a product-to-product basis with the Taiwanese imports. Somebody came up with an idea. What if you had a standard, neutral-colored blanket as a base for the tile, then applied the pattern separately? That way, you could reduce costs by using the standard blanket and still achieve virtually any effect you wanted in terms of design and color. Richard A. Graff, general production manager, was given the job of finding a means of producing tile under this new procedure. Trials showed that it would work, with a printed pattern applied to the blanket, then with a clear Duracoat wear layer applied to the surface. This led to the reopening of the former carpet yarn plant at Beech Creek, Pennsylvania, where the tile patterns were now printed.

Armstrong began copyrighting its Stylistik designs. The legal procedure enabled the company to petition customs officials to quarantine any Taiwanese knockoffs, to prevent ships from unloading the faux Armstrong patterns onto the dock. That helped, too.

The Stylistic experience convinced Armstrong flooring people that they could compete against rivals from anywhere in the world. Armstrong had the research and development, advertising, distribution, financing, and other programs in place, and these resources provided a strong advantage in the U.S. marketplace.

So successful was Stylistik that almost immediately it was placed on allocation. The plant in Lancaster sold out, and in its first year of making the new tile product the plant at Kankakee had to double its production.

In March 1977, Armstrong managers from across the globe gathered in Lancaster for a meeting. Television personality Dave Garroway, formerly of NBC-TV's "Today" show, served as master of ceremonies. The audience received a surprise when James H. Binns was announced as president of Armstrong World Industries, Inc. It was the first time that those attending learned of the impending corporate name change. The name Armstrong Cork Company, which had been in place since 1895, was considered out of date (cork by this time represented less than half of 1 percent of the company's raw materials purchases), and the new name better represented the kind of corporation Armstrong had become. The company had spent millions of dollars and years of concerted effort establishing "Armstrong" as a symbol consumers could trust, though, so those who made the decision were careful to retain that well-recognized name of the company founder in the new corporate designation. Because of legal tie-ups, the corporation did not officially become Armstrong World Industries, Inc., until May 15, 1980.

In 1977 Armstrong's corporate sales exceeded the billion-dollar mark for the first time. It would not be the last.

Effective at the start of 1978, Jim Binns became chairman of the board. During his 10 years as president, the company had undergone significant change. Though its focus on resilient flooring had never been neglected, Binns had led Armstrong to make a number of tectonic-plate–like decisions at the corporate level. He did so, however, with an interesting philosophy: "A decision isn't necessarily right or wrong at the time it is made. What makes it right or wrong is whether it works or fails to work. The real key to a good decision-making batting average is implementation. If you set out to make a decision work, with the right kind of energetic and imaginative follow-through, you increase your chance of success by a thousand percent."

Harry A. Jensen succeeded Binns as the company's president. The personable Jensen, originally from Iowa, was known as a skilled communicator. Like Binns, he had begun his career as a Floor Division marketing representative. He knew the flooring business well, and during his five years as president he led the company in adopting many an innovation developed through enhanced technology. As an example, in his first year the flooring plant at Lancaster began a five-year business systems development project aimed at computerizing all phases of its managerial and recording operations.

It was during this period that Edgar Yale and J. Ross McCray, general production manager of the operations, took action to do something about a problem they had been discussing for some time: the need for more warehouse space for flooring products. The typical manufacturing plant had its warehouse situated in the center of things, as was the case at the Lancaster Floor Plant. Yale and McCray decided to do something different. They directed the construction of a 600,000-square-foot sheet goods warehouse at Spooky Nook Road, near Landisville. Now the wholesalers' trucks could pick up their orders from a modern facility with a full bank of truck docks.

Another important technical addition came through in 1978. At Product Styling and Design, a Scitex computer, one of only a handful in the world with its advanced capabilities, was brought online to assist in the creation of new designs. It added an important dimension to the stylists' work, and, so far as Armstrong people knew, no competitor had anything that could approach it.

Technology also helped in the development of new products. The most notable of them that year was Solarium Supreme Vinyl Corlon flooring. Along with a rotogravure-printed image, it brought together some of the most appealing features offered in sheet goods, including a long-lasting no-wax shine, cushioning for underfoot comfort, through-grain designs such as those found in inlaid vinyl

*S*ome of the new wholesalers had surprising backgrounds. In San Francisco and Los Angeles, for example, they were Budweiser distributors. They transported their initial Armstrong flooring inventories to their new warehouses in beer trucks.

floors, and Interflex (perimeter-bonded) installation.

The Flooring Installation School moved in 1979 to a new, larger location adjacent to the floor plant. Marking its 56th year, the school noted that it had trained nearly 46,000 flooring installers to date.

Then, with no warning, came one of those moments that can move a corporation like a landslide. William Volker & Company had been one of Armstrong's distributors right from the beginning. By this time Volker had branches in 28 locations, and something like 20 percent of the Floor Division's total sales flowed through these distribution points to retail dealers throughout the West. But a carpet manufacturer, Mohasco, had acquired Volker several years before. One day in 1980 Harry Jensen, as Armstrong's president, received a telephone call. Mohasco, he learned, was liquidating its distribution business, and right away.

At Armstrong this news was potentially paralyzing. Clearly, a Heimlich maneuver was needed, and fast.

Over the next few days, Jensen led the company's flooring organization in laying out a systematic changeover that Mohasco would find acceptable. His basic idea was to find replacements for the Volker wholesaler points, then to transfer the inventory to the new locations. It took an incredible amount of legwork to identify these new distributors, but in less than nine months, the process was wrapped up. Most of the people who had been with Volker's resilient flooring organization stayed on with the new distributors, and their experience helped to provide a seamless transition.

The miracle of all this, Jensen would comment later, is that Armstrong had such an admired wholesale distribution system that it became relatively easy to find replacements. Not only had a crisis been averted but also, thanks to the 70-year relationship between Volker and Armstrong, it had turned into an opportunity for growth through new distributors.

Armstrong was having to deal with another landslide as well. This one went back a few years, and it would not be so easy to dispose of. It centered around asbestos.

About 10 years earlier, the company had grown concerned about a number of lawsuits that alleged injury or illness resulting from asbestos-containing insulation products that Armstrong had made to government specifications, especially during

World War II, for use on Navy ships. By 1979 the costs of litigation related to asbestos amounted to about a million dollars a year. In ensuing years, as the legal expenses took off and as the company began dealing with lawsuit settlements, the costs rose to $10 million in 1981, then $13 million in 1982.

It should be noted that the suits revolved around insulation products, not resilient flooring. The company had incorporated asbestos into two types of its flooring products, also, but it was not considered a risk in those. In vinyl-asbestos tile, the asbestos was encapsulated—sealed in—and asbestos in Hydrocord backing materials for sheet flooring was covered over with vinyl. Unless the consumer or the flooring installer abraded the flooring, a practice Armstrong said should not be undertaken, such products were safe to use.

At one time asbestos had been regarded as a raw material for saving lives. It was used in flame-resistant suits for firefighters, for example. Asbestos was incorporated in many buildings, even in the Pentagon. By the mid-1970s, though, it had earned

*C**rosswalk sheet flooring was introduced in 1982. It was another example of an Armstrong innovation for a discrete submarket. Intended for use in industrial buildings and for entryways and pedestrian ramps within commercial and institutional structures, Crosswalk featured orderly rows of non-slip discs set into a vinyl base.*

Armstrong research people had developed this product as a non-slip flooring for mobile and manufactured homes. Eric Berman of the advertising organization came up with the name "Crosswalk," which everyone agreed was just right for a product of this type. A few weeks later, Berman received a telephone call from Gary A. Cross, a Floor Division marketing manager. Cross said, We like this product, and we intend to introduce it at the wholesalers' convention in December as a new addition to our line of commercial flooring. But you'll have to find a new name for it. We can't call it Crosswalk.

"Why not?" Berman asked. "It's the perfect name for this product."

Cross replied, Because I can't stand up in front of a convention audience and introduce a product that they'll think I named for myself. Can you imagine the reaction I'd get to that?

Berman stood fast. Eventually he and others were able to convince Cross that the name was too good to discard. With a witty and lighthearted convention script, it was unveiled to the audience under the name it retained: Crosswalk.

a dismal reputation.

James E. Hazeltine, who served as director of research and development from 1970 until his retirement in 1981, remembered the reaction among the company's research people when the first reports about the carcinogenic aspects of asbestos appeared. As early as 1952, he said, these researchers strove to remove asbestos as a raw material in tile floors. They were driven not by health reasons at first, as the dangers of prolonged exposure to the substance had not yet been recognized. The R and D people wanted asbestos out of the picture for cost reasons. If a way to replace it with limestone could be perfected, that would mean less pigment required, shorter mix cycles, less wear on rollers and rotors in mixers, and a shorter learning curve for production teams. Through the years, they made encouraging progress, but when the health risks associated with asbestos became known, Armstrong people intensified their efforts. By 1981 the research teams achieved complete success in tile. The Floor Division field organization received word that all the tiles leaving all four of the company's tile plants were now totally asbestos-free. Then asbestos was eliminated from the backing for sheet floors as well. Over time, Armstrong succeeded in removing asbestos from its non-flooring product lines also, but the asbestos liability suits continued to mount.

In addition to asbestos suits, Harry Jensen dealt with other big issues early in his five-year tenure: social upheaval caused by the Vietnam conflict, increased governmental regulation, and at times double-digit inflation. The resulting recession slammed Armstrong and other American companies. Some didn't survive. Armstrong did, but its net earnings fell off in 1980, 1981, and 1982. Then in the second quarter of 1983 profits took an upturn, shortly before Jensen's retirement as president. He became chairman of the board. Joseph L. Jones succeeded him as president.

Jones, a courtly Virginian who had served as an Army officer in World War II, was the first person to head Armstrong since Henning W. Prentis who had not begun his career as a flooring salesman. Hired as an accountant, he had quickly moved into production planning, then into production management with flooring products, industry products, and building products. He had served as the original vice-president in charge of Carpet Operations. Then he served for five years as executive vice-president of the company. He brought to his new position an unusually diverse background.

When he became president in 1983, one of his first steps was to publicly disclose his corporate strategy:

1. To build on the existing strengths in our core businesses.
2. To continue searching for ways to expand into related businesses through technology that is either developed in-house or acquired.
3. To attempt to acquire companies in related businesses.

4. To continue our willingness to dispose of businesses that do not adequately support our corporate objectives.

This new expression of a corporate strategy was published for everyone to see, those outside the company as well as inside. It would have its effect on Floor Products Operations. So would another major development undertaken soon after Joe Jones became president: the implementation of a formal quality management program.

John H. Moore, who had gained valuable experience as an industrial engineer, brought the idea of enhancing quality awareness to the attention of corporate management. Moore expanded on how the idea could be introduced throughout the company, and top management bought into the program with fervor.

Armstrong people believed in quality and lived by it every day—quality in their work output, in the products they made, in the way they served customers. This program took the concept much further. In the mid-1980s more than 400 of the company's managers traveled to the Crosby Quality College in Florida to learn a new way of approaching the subject. More than 4,000 salaried employees took part in a 30-hour course on quality taught by trained Armstrong men and women. The lessons were adapted for production employees in the manufacturing plants and for marketing people in the field. Eventually every employee was a part of it, including those outside the United States. Armstrong employees now worked within a system aimed at making quality specific and measurable for everyone.

Quality management was summed up in a new policy statement that many employees hung on their walls alongside the four Operating Principles that had been committed to writing at the time of the company's centennial observance. The quality statement read:

> *We are committed to quality performance. As an organization—and as individuals—we will continually seek out the specific needs of those who depend upon us. We will then consistently satisfy those needs by doing everything right the first time.*

Perfection was the goal now. The bar had been set as high as possible. Floor Products Operations was as eager as any other part of the Armstrong organization to do its part in meeting the new criteria.

In the president's chair, Jones wasn't through with his own ambitious plans for the company. As a corporate objective, he laid out a plan to achieve after-tax profits amounting to at least 10 percent as a return on assets each year. Floor Products Operations and the other operations were charged with setting up strategies to reach specific, measurable goals. Business units were identified within the company, every

To make its production people in the plants know that it was serious about quality management, Floor Products Operations tightened down as it never had before. This run of tile is off color? Junk it. But it's off only very slightly. Doesn't matter. Junk it. A few months later, the production people encountered a similar problem with sheet flooring. Junk it. Let's do it right. People on some of the production lines had been paid based on the amount of product shipped from the plant. Now a system had to be worked out so they could be paid even if the inspector stopped the production line to correct a flaw in the product. That took some doing, but Armstrong found a way to make it work. The improvement in quality was measurable.

such business unit defined by its markets, its product line, its competition, its methods of distribution, its mission, and its management. Each one was examined with an eye toward the direction it could move and what resources and personnel were needed to help it reach its goals.

Measuring the return on assets was a refinement of Armstrong's familiar idea based on the return on capital employed (ROCE). The ROCE concept had served the company well. Concentrating on capital employed alone, however, sometimes made the company's managers too cautious about investing in worthwhile projects because doing so tended, initially, to lower ROCE. Adopting the return on assets concept was intended, among other ends, to overcome this problem.

Over the next three years, the company's sales increased by almost half. Earnings nearly doubled. The objective of a 10 percent return on assets was almost reached in 1984 and was topped in 1985 and 1986. After coming through the recession, Armstrong was back in the saddle and ready to ride.

For years the company had been producing adhesives used to install its own flooring and other types of products. With demand now outstripping supply, more capacity was needed. One solution was to purchase an existing successful adhesives company. In the mid-1980s Armstrong acquired W. W. Henry Company, a leading producer of adhesives for flooring and other building applications. The California-based concern, which had a belt of five plants stretching across the country, proved to be a valuable addition to the Armstrong family.

In 1983 Armstrong introduced several new flooring products. Among them were two especially worth noting. The first was Medintech vinyl flooring, an unbacked sheet material especially designed for hospitals, other medical facilities, and "clean room" applications. It had outstanding resistance to stains, acids, and chemicals. Furthermore, its seams could be sealed tight, either chemically or with heat, to prevent dirt and spills from penetrating its surface.

The second 1983 introduction was Glazecraft Tile, a premium-priced no-wax vinyl material. The company's pattern book described it, with quiet modesty, as "the finest no-wax vinyl tile floor Armstrong has ever made."

They were followed the next year by At Ease vinyl sheet flooring. It was a cushioned rotogravure-printed material made in 12-foot widths, so it could be installed in a typical room without any seams. Interestingly, At Ease was an adaptation of flooring types gaining currency in Europe. That is, it was a "lay-flat" type, which needed no adhesive to stay in place. Armstrong described it as "the easiest do-it-yourself floor ever." Also, it featured an innovation known as Rear Guard protection, which retarded mold, mildew, and bacterial growth even on the back side of the flooring.

Armstrong's 75th year in the flooring business was the spark that illuminated 1985. The occasion did not go unremarked by Floor Products Operations, but peering backward didn't occupy too much of anyone's time. In truth, events continued to move so rapidly that reminiscing never became as popular as looking to the future.

The Floor Division invited to Lancaster each of its wholesale distributor's key decision-makers, such as the president, the owner, or the general manager, along with the Armstrong district managers who served them. From Alfred Strickler, group vice-president for Floor Products Operations, and Dennis M. Draeger, vice-president and general manager for sales and marketing in the Floor Division, the wholesaler representatives heard some tough but realistic talk: "Your business is going to grow 30 percent in the next few years. We want you to come back to us within the next month and a half. Show us how you're planning to handle this added business. Where will you get the people? Where will you get the additional warehouse space you'll need? Where will you get the financing? How will you invest some of the money you're going to make to help your business grow even further?" The meetings led to some changes in distributors, but those who stayed in the game knew they would be rewarded if they were ready for what was to come.

Technical advancements were in the forefront, leading not just to new products but also to new production methods and distribution improvements. A program for computer-aided design (CAD) was inaugurated; this CAD system permitted many aspects of building and production-line design to be augmented by the computer's electronic capabilities. At the tile plant in Jackson, Mississippi, a modern new production line and warehouse were put into place to assure improved service to customers. The other tile plants were also upgraded. Further modernization took place at a plant in Beech Creek, Pennsylvania. Once used to make carpet yarns, this plant had been reopened in 1977 with a new purpose: to produce high-definition printed surfaces for certain flooring tile products. The flooring plant at Lancaster received an advanced computerized order system.

The Lancaster plant also began more fully utilizing the capabilities offered by spectrophotometric color control. Developed by Applied Color Systems, a New Jersey company that Armstrong had acquired in the early 1980s, these capabilities permitted designers and colorists in resilient flooring, paint, fabrics, and other fields to match and coordinate colors so that they could be duplicated with unerring precision at other locations. Did a maker of kitchen appliances, a draperies manufacturer, and Armstrong want to come out at about the same time with products all of which accented a specific celadon green? The Applied Color Systems technology made this possible.

The changes affected the flooring business at the retail level, also. The well-established Floor Fashion Center stores received a facelift. New standards went into place for participating retailers, they received new display units, and their customers could now use the first credit cards ever sponsored by a manufacturer of flooring.

Up to now, Lancaster was the only Armstrong location in the United States that made sheet flooring. But several developments began to tug on the sleeves of the company's management people, demanding attention. First, sales of rotovinyl-printed materials continued to grow, while those of inlaid vinyl flooring began to tail off. More capacity was needed to meet the demand for the roto products, and it made sense to add capacity with the most modern equipment available. Second, the company now shipped about 40 percent of its Lancaster-made sheet goods to destinations west of the Mississippi. Third, inasmuch as Lancaster was the sole producer in the United States of sheet goods, management recognized that, if they chose to, the unions representing hourly paid employees could shut down sheet-goods production in a blink.

Once again top management showed its willingness to make a heavy investment in a promising new venture. In 1985 Armstrong revealed plans for a 300,000-square-foot manufacturing facility in Stillwater, Oklahoma. It was to be Armstrong's first sheet flooring plant west of the Mississippi, and it was to produce rotogravure-printed vinyl products. The Stillwater plant went into production in the late 1980s.

As you count up the significant events that rang the bell in 1985, you find that the 75th anniversary of Armstrong's entry into the flooring business was quite a celebration after all!

The bell was still reverberating the following year. Of the several new flooring products that entered the Armstrong mix, two deserve singling out. One was Popular Choice sheet material, made in both 6- and 12-foot widths. It was made with a

Armstrong Flooring Through the Years

Embossed Inlaid Linoleum
Pattern 5352 (best-selling pattern)

Sundial Solarian

Designer Solarian

Tessera Corlon

Coronelle Corlon

IMAGES REPRODUCED BY JOHN M. HORNBERGER, ARMSTRONG STAFF PHOTOGRAPHER

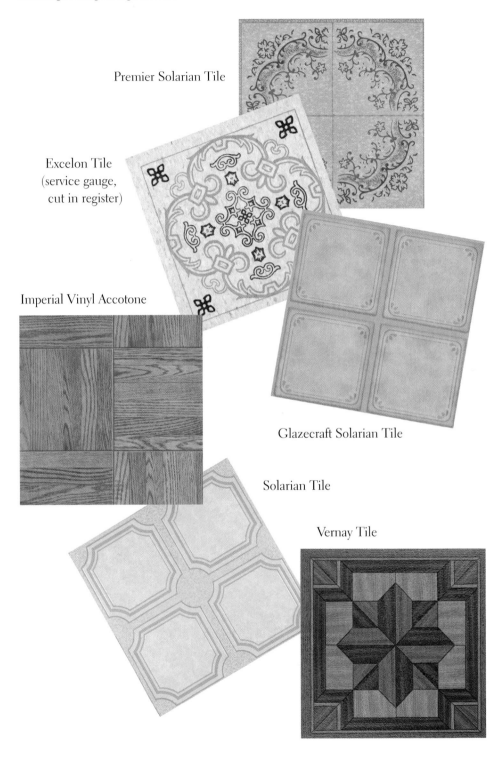

Premier Solarian Tile

Excelon Tile
(service gauge,
cut in register)

Imperial Vinyl Accotone

Glazecraft Solarian Tile

Solarian Tile

Vernay Tile

REFLECTIONS OF GRANDEUR. *True luxury is found in this home, from the floor up. The foyer overlooks scenic splendor. Inside the home, the theme is maintained through the quiet understatement of Solarian Supreme flooring. It's a sheet material, here in a design that resembles tile—and it doesn't have to be waxed.*

RUSTIC BUT RICH-LOOKING. *The heavy wooden uprights taken from a barn that was being dismantled, along with the stone fireplace, suggest country living. But this great room, with its conversation pit, is modern in every sense. Effectively tying together its decorative elements is a Montina Vinyl Corlon floor with arched insets.*

MORE THAN BEAUTY ALONE. *When Armstrong introduced a true no-wax flooring, it named the result "Solarian." That's the name many homemakers learned to look for when they wanted to make their lives easier. Designer Solarian flooring provides a glowing foundation for the handsomeness of this kitchen with dining alcove.*

AN UNCONVENTIONAL SHOWPLACE. *Here's an interior
that would lead you to say to a visitor, "Wait. I want to show you my
bathroom." It's that attractive. But it's an entirely livable room, too.
Lots of light, in the event you want to read in the bathtub. And the floor?
It's no-wax Designer Solarian II, so it's an easy matter to sponge up spills.*

ENTER HERE FOR ELEGANCE. *Through the years, as production
techniques advanced, Armstrong flooring designs became more detailed,
more sophisticated. In this bungalow sitting room, a nicely understated
styling in Sundial Solarian sweeps the decorative theme through the
entire interior. The result is to make a small space seem larger.*

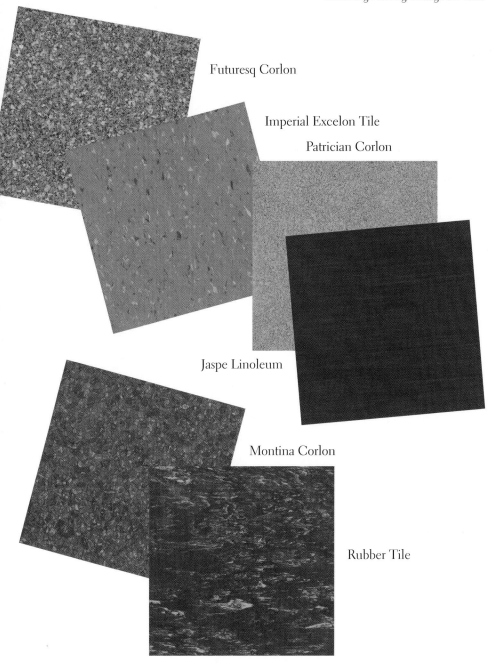

Futuresq Corlon

Imperial Excelon Tile

Patrician Corlon

Jaspe Linoleum

Montina Corlon

Rubber Tile

READY TO DO BUSINESS. *Commercial Corlon flooring in the Sandoval design effect helps this reception area establish a businesslike environment. Its neutral tones provide a framework for the splashes of color in the seating area beyond the desk. The sheet flooring is easy to maintain, too, even in heavy traffic areas.*

LOTS OF CLASS IN THE CLASSROOM. *Imperial Excelon Tile provides a long-lasting floor in a schoolroom for typing students. When Armstrong introduced this innovative product, it distributed samples with concentric circles milled out in increasing depths to show that the Imperial pattern went all the way through the tile.*

INDOORS OR OUTDOORS? *The light pouring in through the window-walls makes it hard to tell at first. The ferns and hanging plants add to the greenery-laden atmosphere. Can't you imagine how pleasant a meal would be in this setting? The Glazecraft Tile flooring is just right for the room. It's also durable and easy to keep clean.*

A PATTERN TOO GOOD TO IGNORE.
In Armstrong's Embossed Inlaid Linoleum (right), pattern 5352 was the best-selling pattern in the entire flooring industry. By far. When later, updated types of flooring came along, such as the Colonial Classic Designer Solarian shown below, consumers could still obtain the classic look offered by 5352.

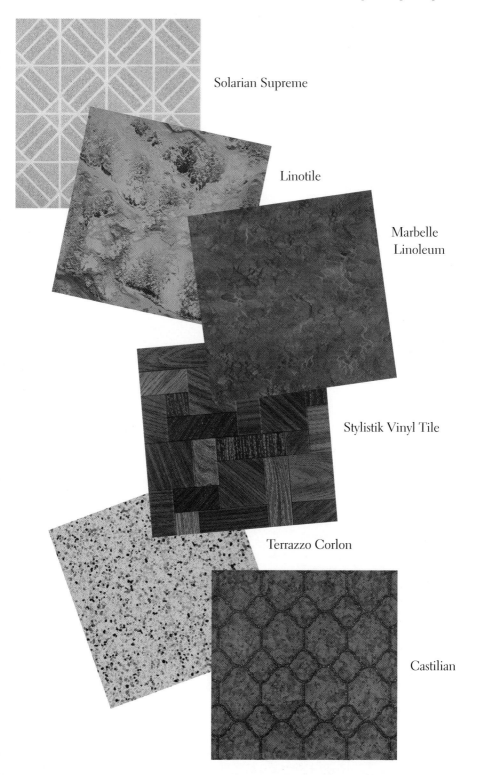

Solarian Supreme

Linotile

Marbelle
Linoleum

Stylistik Vinyl Tile

Terrazzo Corlon

Castilian

PRODUCTION UNLIMITED.
The Lancaster Floor Plant, largest of Armstrong's manufacturing facilities, dominates this 1974 aerial photograph. In the center foreground, facing West Liberty Street, is the general office building, at that time the headquarters for the company as well as for Floor Products Operations.

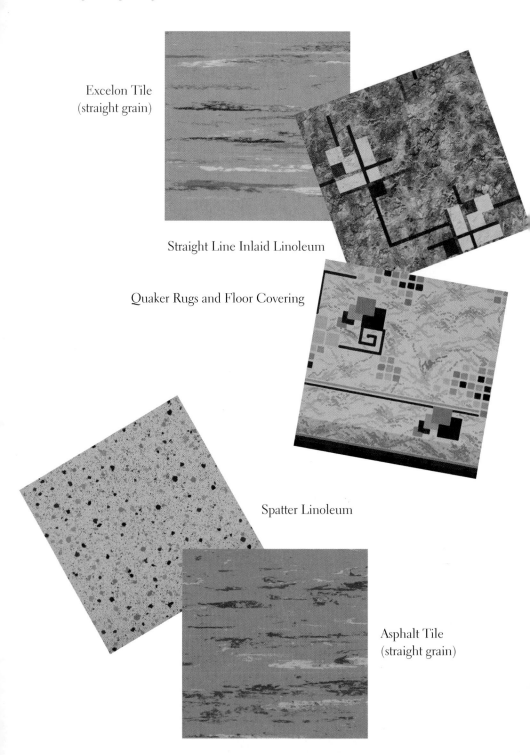

Excelon Tile
(straight grain)

Straight Line Inlaid Linoleum

Quaker Rugs and Floor Covering

Spatter Linoleum

Asphalt Tile
(straight grain)

rotogravure-printed design and a no-wax wear layer. What made it distinctive, though, was its surface, featuring "differential gloss, differential texture." As you moved your eyes or your hands across the flooring, you encountered varying degrees of shininess and tactility. The nubbly, interrupted surface that had replaced a mirrorlike smoothness, first in Tessera Vinyl Corlon, had reached full maturity. By now, consumers not only accepted the interrupted-surface materials, they reacted enthusiastically to them. Way back in 1958, Pop Foster had been right.

Another introduction of the mid-1980s was a tile flooring, Pavimar precast marble tile. Armstrong was stretching out beyond the world of vinyl. Made in a 3/16-inch thickness and in a 12 x 12-inch size, Pavimar was a bonded marble tile with a luxurious polished finish. Marble stones constituted more than 50 percent of its composition, and the visual appearance offered a rich depth of detail normally found only in natural marble slabs.

Pavimar was the offspring of a 1982 joint venture involving Armstrong's Floor Division; Lone Star Industries, a cement manufacturer; and Shell Oil Company. The companies brought together their know-how in various fields to make use of polymer concrete technology. The joint company, named ArmStar, with Armstrong's S. Todd Lewis as president, had a plant at Lenoir City, Tennessee. The plant manufactured Pavimar and, later, Armstone, a similar product intended for commercial buildings. Polymer concrete appeared to offer rich potential for products in several areas. Little came of the venture, ultimately, but it demonstrated Armstrong's willingness to invest in new ideas.

At the beginning of 1987 Richard Flanders Smith retired as vice-president and director of product styling and design, and elected to succeed him in this position was Wendy W. Claussen. She became the company's first officer who was a woman.

Later in that year Armstrong tile flooring had a chance to show its stuff with the inclusion of an unusual raw material. Century Solarian Tile was made in 3/32-inch gauge, 12 x 12-inch size, and it had the Solarian no-wax surface with a self-adhering backing for easy installation. It offered something more as well: a high-fidelity rotogravure image with what the company described as built-in quartz crystals for "a glittering, jewellike look."

During 1988 William W. Adams became president, succeeding Joe Jones. Adams, an articulate Iowan of unquestioned integrity, began his Armstrong career in advertising, then moved on to positions of increasing responsibility in areas that included Building Products Operations, International Operations, and the President's Office. Under his leadership as president, the company fought off a hostile takeover attempt by the Belzberg family. The battle raged for two and a half years, but Armstrong successfully retained its independence.

In 1988 Suffield Commercial Classic Corlon sheet flooring joined the Armstrong line. It had a 50-millimeter wear layer and was intended for use in commercial and public buildings. Its main claim to longevity, though, was that it was made to be put into place with the Securabond installation system. Its seams could be bonded chemically to eliminate cracks that could accumulate water, dust, or dirt.

The company continued to add niche products from time to time. Though their contribution to volume may have been small, they helped round out the product line for specialized submarkets. In 1989 two such niche products emerged. The first was SDT Tile. It was essentially Premium Excelon Tile with a static dissipative feature added. The second was Step Master flooring, a 1/8-gauge, 12 x 12-inch tile that was slip-retardant. It was designed to be used with other 1/8-inch tiles in the commercial flooring line.

About this time the Floor Division developed "recommended installation systems" for its broad range of products. In its pattern book for 1990, as an aid to both consumer and dealer salesman, it included a chart showing every type of flooring sold at retail. For each it listed detailed instructions showing the most desirable type of installation to use, including the recommended adhesive.

By the following year the consumer could find Armstrong flooring products defined as "good, better, or best" in certain qualities. For example, the Solarian Supreme Pearl Glaze collection was given a rating of "best" in easy care, resistance to household stains and traffic stains, scuff resistance, and damage resistance. The product was rated "better" in indentation resistance. Such ratings were shown in the pattern book and on retail showroom displays and helped consumers educate themselves in which was the best Armstrong product for their specific needs.

In 1992 came two additions to the line of tile flooring. The first of these was Serene Solarian Tile, made in .080-inch gauge, 12 x 12-inch size. It had a urethane no-wax wear layer and an embossed image. To help it appeal to the do-it-yourselfer, it was self-adhering. The second was Companion Square Premium Excelon Tile. Made for use in commercial and public buildings, it was 1/8 inch thick and was made in the 12 x 12-inch size. This product, like the original Imperial Excelon Tile, had through-pattern construction; the design elements went all the way through the tile. Armstrong still used samples with cutaway concentric circles to demonstrate this feature.

George A. Lorch, another Virginian moving to the top rung of the ladder, succeeded William W. Adams as president of Armstrong in 1993. During his seven-year tenure, Armstrong stretched in new directions as the dynamics of the marketplace changed significantly.

A subtle, slow slide begins

Think of the years between the end of World War II and the early 1990s. For Armstrong's Floor Products Operations they were marked by a procession of outstanding product introductions: Spatter Linoleum. Futuresq Vinyl Corlon. Tessera. Montina. Imperial Vinyl Accolon. Coronelle. Cushion Coronelle. Castilian. Solarian. Designer Solarian. Sundial Solarian. Solarian Tile. Premier Solarian Tile. Imperial Excelon Tile. Place 'n Press Excelon Tile. Perimiflor. Stylistik Tile. Glazecraft Tile. Vernay Tile. At Ease. Solarian Supreme. Designer Solarian with Interflex installation. The names roll down through the years like those of major league players being called out at an all-star game.

Each of these products stood within a nimbus of its own. Each was an innovation recognized as a substantial departure from anything previously known in flooring. Each was a proprietary Armstrong product unlike anything competition had devised. And each contributed to the unmatched success achieved by the company's flooring business during this period.

As the twentieth century drew to its close, the new-product parade continued. But somehow it was different now. Instead of all-stars, the products added to the line tended toward the quotidian. Good performers, to be sure, but not record-breakers. They were mostly additions to an existing pattern line or were products that incorporated new combinations of features that had made their marks in earlier introductions. Maybe the string had run out—or at least had begun to fray.

For the better part of a hundred years, Armstrong's flooring business had been the star performer in a hit parade of its own making. Success followed success, almost without interruption. Now the business was beginning to show wrinkles and liver spots, though no one at Armstrong was as yet willing to acknowledge that. Not publicly, at least.

This chronology takes us into 1995. The year was chosen with a purpose, as it marks just half a century from the end of World War II. It allows us to end the story of Armstrong flooring on a happier note than would have been the case if we had extended it by 10 years or so.

By the end of 1995 the resilient flooring business at Armstrong had witnessed the passing of its springtime. Will it ever return? It's hard to say.

But scores, hundreds, thousands of people look back with pride on the years following World War II, years during which the company's flooring business grew gloriously—and profitably. They had been part of this profitable growth. And all of them, in one way or another, contributed to it. Really, it would not have been possible without them.

They were people from the company's top management, who of course exercised overall control. From Research and Development. From Product Styling and Design. From Central Engineering. From production organizations, including the thousands of men and women who took pride in being employed in the company's factories. From Advertising and Marketing Services. From other staff organizations, including but not limited to human resources, industrial relations, finance services, marketing research, legal services, industrial engineering, and data systems. From the wholesalers who distributed the company's flooring line. From the retail dealers and contractors who handled Armstrong flooring products so effectively (and made a lot of money doing so). From those in Armstrong's marketing organization, who worked with all these others and brought them together as one strong-driving team. And, most important of all, from the consumers who bought the products—because in business, as the saying goes, nothing happens until a sale is made.

PART III

The People Who Worked the Magic

Their Stories in Their Words

Fom its inception, this book was never intended to be a mere chronology. The history of Armstrong flooring's glory years is much more than a recitation of events and dates. Rather, it's a story of the people, as individuals and teams, who worked successfully to turn aspirations into reality.

You can better understand Floor Products Operations' success through the years if you tune into conversations among representatives from various Armstrong organizations. Listen as they reminisce about significant events with which they were involved.

Research: Changing 'impossible' to 'I'm possible'

Research and development. Its responsibilities included not only the development of material formulations but also process development, testing, and troubleshooting.

It's a land of test tubes and Bunsen burners, right? Well, yes, but it became so much more than that. At Armstrong, along with the use of ever more sophisticated equipment, research broadened its scope through the years. While it continued as the point of origin for major new product and manufacturing developments, it also improved its ability to adapt to good use the ideas it picked up from outside its own organization.

In the early days it operated in its own enclave, literally contained within the boundaries of the Lancaster Floor Plant, in what had been known as the "wire mill" part of the plant. Once it attained status with its own modern facilities west of Lancaster, it grew in stature. It was more than a physical move. It marked an attitude change as well. Under the leadership of James E. Hazeltine, the research people developed a greater sensitivity to marketing needs and ultimately joined with the company's marketing efforts in a vital way. What products does the consumer need now? That became the question. The team continually found answers, even in instances when the consumer might not have known what she needed until the new products entered the marketplace.

The way was not always smooth. Research people sometimes met resistance, even at the highest levels of the company, when commitments to breakout opportunities were required. Robert W. Snyder remembers with a smile Kenneth O. Bates, who at the time was executive vice-president of the company: "When Ken Bates was nodding, it didn't always mean he was agreeing with you. It just meant that he was hearing you. This could be misleading, because when you got to the point of your request, you might suddenly find him shaking his head 'no.'"

The company's research people had to adapt their work to meet unexpected challenges. For example, linseed oil, a major component of linoleum, became hard to find in the 1950s and early 1960s. When it was available, price fluctuations for this raw material complicated budgeting for production costs. The researchers developed a way to replace linseed oil through the esterification of tall oil, a by-product of the paper industry. The innovation saved the company a lot of money.

For the resilient flooring business, time and again the company's research scientists came up with new approaches for solving problems. William E. "Bill" Irwin well remembers the staining that affected Armstrong's earliest types of plastic flooring, especially Terrazzo Vinyl Corlon in 1955. "The styling people always wanted white, white, white in the patterns they were coming up with," he says. "But to achieve this, you need careful control of plasticizers and stabilizers." Complicating the situation was the discovery that several different kinds of staining were contributing to the problem. Even bacteria could cause a pinkish stain in some Terrazzo patterns. The people at R and D jury-rigged a revolving wheel that simulated rubber-soled shoes walking across flooring test panels. Through this they demonstrated that rubber could stain a floor through aromatic amines. These chemicals were used as stabilizers in tires and other rubber goods and could be tracked into a kitchen from the garage or driveway.

In time the research scientists found solutions to all the staining problems. It was not as glamorous an assignment, perhaps, as creating a sparkling new type of flooring, but it was vital to the future of Armstrong's vinyl flooring business.

W hen Tessera Vinyl Corlon flooring was under development, Bob Snyder says, some people in marketing were disturbed by its uneven "interrupted surface." He adds, "For months we tried to make it with a flat surface. But then we gradually came to recognize that the nubbly surface could be sold as a product advantage. So we came up with an embossed roller that could be used to provide such a surface to other, non-Tessera products. By then everybody liked it."

Bob Snyder shakes his head as memories take him back through the major conversions that saw Armstrong move from linoleum and asphalt tile, products made with natural raw materials, to vinyl flooring, produced with manmade materials. "Converting linoleum production to plastics in the Floor Plant was easiest on the stencil equipment," he says. "But on the calender and rotary processes it was much more difficult. We needed to make new types of equipment or to make major adaptations on the existing equipment."

Snyder is given the credit for developing an "oscillating blade" for use on flooring production machinery. This device, which made possible precision feeding of vinyl particles onto a blanket passing below, is justly renowned within Armstrong's research corridors because it proved to have so many uses. Mounted above a calender roll, the blade moved back and forth to varicolored particles flowing evenly. The blade was first used on a tile production line at Lancaster. Later, it was adapted and improved for use in the plant at Kankakee.

The oscillating blade was simple in concept but mighty in potential. Imperial Excelon Tile could not have been produced without it, for the blade made possible the Imperial design without striations. Later the technique was adapted for use in making sheet vinyl flooring and for the luxury vinyl tiles made at the plant in Braintree, Massachusetts.

Maybe Edgar A. Yale, vice-president and general manager of Floor Products Operations, was the one who indirectly suggested the need for the oscillating blade. Maybe not. Nobody remembers for sure. He certainly had a major influence on new products and processes coming out of the research staff. "Ed Yale would trigger more ideas!" says Bob Snyder. "He'd come out to my office and hold up a drawing of some sort. He'd say, 'I wish we could have something like this.' And we'd be off once again, searching for a new idea and how to make it work. He was a real contributor to what we were attempting to do."

Burt F. Hofferth was involved in the company's entry into rotogravure-printed materials. "Later, attitudes were considerably liberalized," he says. "But in those days, in the late 1950s, we were encountering a rather conservative corporate culture regarding some new ventures. It was this conservatism that delayed our entry into roto." It was true that other manufacturers' rotogravure products were having some difficulties, including delamination. Those deficiencies made it easier for the Armstrong nay-sayers to say nay. It's a cheap-looking product, they would comment. Who'd want it, anyway? With our products, the color goes all the way through to the backing. With that roto stuff, it's only a surface printing, and it'll wear off.

By 1959 Sandran, a competitor, had sold 30 million square yards of 9-foot-wide rotogravure-printed floor coverings. A splinter in Armstrong's heel was the slogan Sandran brandished in front of anyone who'd listen: "Sixty by '60." That was their goal: to sell 60 million square yards of their product by the following year. Then Mannington Mills, another competitor, announced that it was adding a 12-foot-wide rotogravure printing press. The move added further pressure on Armstrong to do something.

"When we finally got into it," says Hofferth, "we did it right. Maybe we were three years late in entering the roto business, but eventually Armstrong led the industry."

And Sandran never did reach its goal of "Sixty by '60."

D. Dwight Browning, during Armstrong's difficult early days of producing Vinyl Accolon rotogravure floor covering, triumphed with an important break-through. He developed a white coating for the raw felt, 12 feet wide, that was used as a carrier for the product as it glided through the printing rolls. This coating, which saturated the surface of the felt, allowed the precision rotogravure images to be printed without skips.

Another research scientist of the time, Charles D. "Charlie" Elliott, thinks back to the development of Tessera Vinyl Corlon flooring, which was introduced in 1958. "At first the Lancaster Floor Plant made Tessera through a rather slow stop-and-go process. That might have been all right had this product been used only for commercial buildings, which was the original purpose. But when consumers began wanting it for their homes, we needed more output, and fast. The research began on a new way to make Tessera, and that's what led to the rolling press."

Linoleum sold at retail, typically, for $5.95 a square yard. Futuresq Vinyl Corlon had been introduced in 1957 at $7.95 a square yard, then Tessera a year later at $8.95. After that came Montina Vinyl Corlon sheet flooring. This propri-etary product entered the marketplace with a suggested retail price of $10.95 a square yard. "Nobody had thought we'd ever reach such a point," says Dwight Browning.

Browning, who went on to head the Research and Development organization, recalls the pressures of the early 1960s, when preparations were under way for the initial production of Montina: "This was our first product with a factory test that was costing more than $100,000. There was no starting over. With that kind of expenditure, our top management people had a right to demand success, and they did. We had to make it work."

Charlie Elliott adds, "At the suggestion of [general production manager] Ross McCray, the production people purposefully overestimated the costs of manufac-turing for Montina. Then, when we were able to bring down these costs through production efficiencies, the marketing people in the Floor Division found that they were working with greatly increased margins. They liked that."

In reviewing Armstrong R and D, consider the unusual career of Clarence D. "Slats" Barlet. He joined the research organization in 1955, at first working with adhesives and then commercial flooring maintenance products. Eighteen years later he moved over to the company's Central Purchasing organization, where he used the experience gained in product research to help overcome a growing problem with raw materials shortages. The problem became most acute with a shortage of vinyl chloride monomer. Interestingly, Armstrong did not use this product, at least not directly, but the company did use vinyl chloride polymers, and these polymers were made from the monomer by Armstrong's chemical-company suppliers. The dearth of vinyl chloride monomer meant many a trip for Barlet. He traveled to various parts of the United States, even to Europe and Japan, to line up shipments of the monomer to chemical processing plants owned by Borden and Union Carbide that were to supply his company with polyvinyl chloride. When he purchased the monomer, Armstrong owned it, and Armstrong tracked it all the way through until the needed product was shipped to the Lancaster Floor Plant. "Those were tough times," Barlet remembers. "But it wasn't all bad. We were buying plasticizers, resins, stabilizers, fillers, and other raw materials, as well as monomers. Before it was through, we learned to know the suppliers much better. And we developed a tighter-knit purchasing and production team."

Slats Barlet returned to R and D eventually, but first he had one more career stop to make. In 1977 he moved directly to Floor Products Operations to serve as manager of new product development. It was the first time such a position had been established. During his three years there, Barlet served as liaison between marketing, research, product styling, production, and any other organizations necessary to facilitate the growth of propriety new products. It was out of such cooperative efforts that Stylistik Vinyl Tile was developed, to be introduced in the late 1970s.

At R and D in those heady days, creativity was a key to progress. The research scientists accepted creativity wherever they found it. Sometimes it came from a lightbulb that went off over your head when you were seeking a solution to a problem, then discovered that you could adapt an idea you had seen elsewhere. You had to keep your mind open for these inspirations.

This sort of "Eureka!" experience hit John H. "Jack" Young one day in the early 1970s as he grappled with a problem in the production of Excelon Tile. It was an important moment for the product, and Young had been told that, to stay on schedule, the process had to be working within two weeks. The trouble was that the vinyl mix, heated and elastic, tended to stick to the metal parts of the machinery as it moved down the line. That jammed up everything. What to do? Jack remembered seeing ovens moving dough through a line when he had visited a Lancaster bakery, and the similarities in the processes caused his synapses to begin sparking. He telephoned his friend at the bakery and asked, "Why doesn't your dough stick to the hopper in your ovens?" "Oh," he was told, "we use Teflon-coated screens. That way, we don't have to worry about sticking." Teflon! That proved to be the answer. Jack Young went to the same Chicago source that provided the Teflon grids for the bakery. The source coated Armstrong's screens for a charge of just $15 apiece. The project moved on from that forehead-smacking moment. The ultimate result was that Armstrong was able to discontinue its line of asphalt tile in favor of a vinyl-content flooring with much better qualities.

Another time, while working on a variation of Excelon Tile in 1975, Young found that the traveling belt of material tended to sag and become distorted as it moved through the production line. This deformity meant that the finished pieces would not have the desired perfect squareness, and of course that would be a problem when it came to laying the tile at the construction site. Several traditional methods were tried. None did the job.

Then one day Young was at a Lancaster swimming pool. There he saw something that seemed to offer a new approach. It was a water slide. As he watched the bathers shrieking and splashing their way down the slide, Jack began making mental sketches of his new idea. At the research lab, he wasted no time in trying it at the pilot plant. It worked! Soon water slides were in place at all four of Armstrong's U.S. tile plants, and they became a new, distortion-free way of transporting the Excelon Tile belt through the production process.

Jack Young sums up his long career as an Armstrong research scientist with a happy thought: "When you get good, you get better. Then you get still better. Then you get excellent."

His words could stand as a motto for the company's research and development people. Over and over again, they found the ways to surmount the abatises of the impossible and turn them into advances for Armstrong.

Styling: So you'd invite Armstrong flooring into your home

It doesn't much matter how durable your flooring is. Or how scratch-resistant or fade-resistant or stain-resistant. Or how easy it is to install. It may not even matter how much or how little it costs. All of these factors can have importance in a buying decision. But in the end, what it comes down to is this: If the consumer doesn't like the looks of your product, she doesn't want it in her home.

That's where the people of product styling and design came in.

These men and women were artists, but they were artists with a purpose. Their mission was to visualize a flooring design that would appeal to customers, then to develop the pattern colors that were appropriate for that design, then to put together prototypes that could be reproduced on the production floor. Along the way, using the latest available techniques, they worked with their counterparts in research, engineering, production, and marketing to help transform those designs and patterns from dreams into reality. Whether the products they created moved off the retail sales floor into the consumer's kitchen was the ultimate measure of

*T*he most famous pattern that ever came out of Armstrong styling was the red brick effect designated 5352 in Embossed Inlaid Linoleum. It was introduced in 1932, and for years it was the best-selling pattern in the entire flooring industry. By far. In 1957 the managers of product styling tried to locate the man who had come up with this pattern a quarter of a century earlier. They wanted to recognize his contribution to the company's success, to bring him to Lancaster for a celebration of some sort, to give him a plaque or some other lasting memento of what he had done. But they couldn't find him. Soon after designing pattern 5352, this man had left Armstrong. He felt all washed out, he explained at the time, with no more designs left in him. He had relocated to Vermont, or perhaps New Hampshire, and reportedly had become a watch repairman. That was all that anyone at Armstrong could find out about him. He had moved on, leaving no tracks. Probably he never found out what an industry legend he had created in pattern 5352.

how well they succeeded.

Think about this. Just about everything we buy has an element of design in it. An automobile. Clothing. A kitchen appliance. With some of our purchases, such as a stapler or a socket wrench or a bundt pan, we give little thought to it. But somebody, somewhere, designed that item. Designed it well, or not so well. Even when we don't think about it, we are influenced by its design. That's true of flooring, also, whether flooring for the home or for a commercial or public building. Armstrong designers were on the front lines every day, trying to come up with the effects that would rest comfortably on the mind of the consumer.

Did they succeed? Spatter linoleum. Styletone in Quaker floor covering. Futuresq. Tessera. Imperial Excelon Tile. Vinyl Accolon. Montina. Castilian. Coronelle. Sundial Solarian. Designer Solarian. Stylistik Tile. Glazecraft Tile. The list of products goes on and on, and every one of them is a credit to the people of the company's product styling and design group.

The stylists knew from the start that their creative efforts couldn't be totally unfettered, that they were pointed in a certain direction. The need to originate designs and patterns that the consumer would buy was a constant challenge. James J. "Jim" Riley explains it this way: "You want to have people saying, 'I like that. I want that.'" The successes, and there were many, proved extremely rewarding. "The best thing was the response," Riley says. "It was a great feeling to see a row of top-selling patterns, and yours was there."

At Armstrong, product styling and design started in the Lancaster Floor Plant, in a reconditioned crate shop. It was not the most ideal setting. The stylists in those days came off of the factory floor, mostly. Richard Flanders Smith, who was the second college-trained stylist hired by Armstrong and who later headed the product styling and design organization, became the driving force for a new facility at the campus on Columbia Avenue.

The new product styling and design building, occupied in 1970, had been designed from the beginning for its special purpose. One wall was made almost entirely of glass. This wall faced north, to take advantage of what artists traditionally regard as the most dependable natural light. It was the most advanced styling facility in the industry, and it provided Armstrong with an unparalleled opportunity to display fashion in flooring.

Along with the new building came new techniques. The company's product styling people were quick to pick up the latest advancements—the use of digital technology in a photographic laboratory, for example, which was under the direction of Randall E. "Randy" Stewart. Digital technology made it possible to endlessly repeat a design idea, or to enlarge or reduce it, or to reverse its image, or to purposefully distort it. "Eventually," recalls Jim Riley, "we developed a system through which we could scan a color, then give production people an actual mathematical formula to follow. That helped to assure colors in the finished product that didn't deviate from the originals."

Hubert J. Fitzgerald adds, "We set up a computer to organize and systematize all the colors. It took a year to put this into place. But once we had it, it worked in all our plants. Now they knew which pigment to use, in what precise quantity, to produce each color in a given pattern."

Styling produced prototypes of the finished patterns, and these prototypes became the masters that were to be matched on the production floor. It wasn't just color that was to be matched. "A flooring effect called Portofino sometimes put us at odds with the folks in production," says Abram Rudisill. "We felt it was necessary that this product, which involved four-color printing, be kept in absolute register. But the plant people were expected to come up with good yields, and they didn't like to slow everything down while perfect register was achieved." It was a healthy tension, as was so often the case.

Designs and patterns coming from Armstrong may have been out in front of consumer tastes from time to time. After all, Armstrong helped to create these tastes. The designers had to be alert to what was going on in the marketplace, too. Rudisill says, "Harvest gold, avocado, copper. Those were appliance colors. We'd have to consider them, especially for flooring that was to be used in the kitchen. Within our organization was a color marketing group that monitored color usage in automobiles, appliances, wallpaper, and draperies. Out of this came our design and color forecasting activity, headed by Tom [Thomas Hills] Cook, and that took us to a new level." Now the Armstrong stylists could with greater accuracy predict what colors consumers would be favoring five or ten years in the future.

What would the consumer buy? One year, the people in marketing wanted to introduce rotovinyl-printed products with "position glitter"—that is, with sparkling metallic highlights precisely placed in the pattern. Styling could design such patterns. No holdup there. But that wasn't the problem. How could they be made on the production line? It was tricky. Hubert Fitzgerald tells the story: "Two or three of our people went to lunch in New Jersey with a man who wanted to sell us glitter. The Armstrong people included Tom [Thomas W.] Smith, a chemist at R and D, and Jack [John W.] deGroot, a chemist at the floor plant. The glitter salesman, hearing that we couldn't figure out how to apply his product, said, 'Oh, here's how you can do it.' He drew a rough sketch right on the tablecloth. It was amazing. Tom and Jack looked at each other, then rolled up the tablecloth and brought it back to Lancaster with them. They showed it to the people in the floor plant and said, 'Here's the answer.' It worked. This was the best lunch we ever bought for anybody!"

Thinking back over all the dazzling effects that the product styling and design organization created through the years, Abe Rudisill allows himself a slight smile. He says, "When you consider that this whole thing started in 1909 with plain brown battleship linoleum...."

Engineering: Coming up with a concept, carrying it to reality

It's self-evident that a product such as Armstrong resilient flooring couldn't be marketed until it was made. That's where the men and women of production came into the picture. But there's one team of people who had to do their work first. They were the engineers, and they were what Armstrong called a staff organization (as contrasted with production and marketing, which were line organizations).

At Armstrong the Central Engineering Department had the responsibility of making sure that discovery, creativity, and meeting consumer demand were aided, not held back, by production capabilities. Most of the department's activities were involved not so much with revolutionary new products as with the less romantic but far more important job of keeping the manufacturing wheels turning.

On any given day the engineers might be called on to help in the selection of a new plant site, to design and direct the construction of a new facility or the expansion of an existing facility, to develop a new manufacturing process and the machinery for it, or to undertake a cost-reduction project. When the company's capital investments were involved, the engineers were on the front lines. The ability to move fast and faultlessly became their practiced hallmark.

"Our job was implementation," says Donald H. Betty, who headed Central Engineering. "We might receive a request, such as 'We want a new facility to make tile.' We would establish a project to meet that need. And we would assign one of our people to the job as a project engineer. From that moment, it was this man's responsibility, with the team he put together, to see the job through."

Edgar C. Fearnow, who was assistant director of Central Engineering, comments, "One of the smartest approaches we adopted was to set up project engineers. A committee can't really do anything. A single person can. That's why we wanted to have one person in charge, throughout a project."

Most of the project engineers at Armstrong were mechanical engineers or chemical engineers. As they managed the project, they coordinated the work of others. The team might include electrical engineers, fluid engineers, architects, and others. Each contributed from his own area of specialization.

Along the way, the project engineer would generate M-requests—money requests—to finance the project. "We made the estimates. We spent the money. We controlled the money," says Don Betty. Before flooring expenditures were made, the M-requests of course had to run the gauntlet of approvals from Floor Products Operations management. If the request for funds was for a high enough amount, even the President's Office had to approve it.

"Once M-requests reached the level of the President's Office, I don't remember a single one that was ever turned down," adds Biddle A. Whigham, who served as project engineer on a number of major undertakings during his long career with Armstrong. "They were so well thought out." Whigham also recalls that a certain skill, based on experience, went into writing an M-request. "Always, always, from the very start of a project, the question was, 'What's this going to cost?' Once the dollar figure was written into the M-request, it was there forever. So we learned to build about a 10 percent contingency fee into the cost estimate, and also to express estimates in terms of ranges. That helped us get through some of the unexpected problems that might arise during completion of a project."

An M-request, like the project it represented, was assigned to a specific category, such as capacity enhancement, cost reduction, maintenance, new product manufacture, or environmental improvement. In the case of a new production line, the project engineer would obtain the money, have the line built, and get it running. Once the job was completed and the new line had been running for a reasonable period of time, the project could be closed out. "The project engineer would initiate what was known as a 'project closing request,'" says Ed Fearnow. "It went through all the same levels as the initial M-request. A signature on the closing request meant, 'I am satisfied that this project is completed.' Now it could be fully turned over to the production people, and the project engineer was free to move on to another job."

Fearnow was there during the interesting, and often difficult, period when Armstrong flooring products changed from those made from natural raw materials, such as linoleum and asphalt tile, to those made with petrochemicals, such as vinyls. "The turmoil of change, that's what it was. And it extended from the early 1950s until Central Engineering moved out to its new building on Columbia Avenue in 1964," he says. "The shortage of rubber in World War II had led to immense developments in the petrochemical industry. Then in 1950 the move of Armstrong research to its own facilities on Columbia Avenue proved to be a milestone in the company's growing interest in petrochemicals and plastics. We all recognized that materials research would be essential in the future development of flooring. A part of the transition was a better cooperation between the engineers and the research people."

From such cooperation came pilot plants in the development end of research and development. Together the engineers and the research scientists worked out the requirements, then the engineers installed the pilot plants. The results from these small-scale production lines at R and D suggested improvements that could be made on the full-size production machinery installed in the manufacturing plants. "Not only did the pilot plants save time and money," says Ed Fearnow, "but also having them meant that we didn't need to tie up production machinery in the plants while we worked out how to make new products."

With the pilot plants, sometimes it was possible to design "plug-in" production lines for the manufacturing plants, Fearnow adds. Certain pieces of equipment could readily be added or taken out of a production line, providing greater flexibility in making various kinds of products.

"Continuous process improvement," says Robert J. "Bob" Stewart. "Those three words sum up what we engineers were aiming for.

"From 1953 on we went through a time of extensive transition. Some of the changes included running a continuous sheet in operations that previously had been stop-and-go, bulk handling of raw materials, automatic weighing of raw materials, automatic packaging, tile counters, automatic charging of mixers, automatic palletizing, automatic warehousing, computerized inventory control, and other technical innovations to the process." The changes continue to this day, Stewart says.

It was Biddle Whigham who served as project engineer on the development of Imperial Excelon Tile, the through-grain product that proved to be so important in Armstrong's marketing of flooring for commercial and institutional buildings. "Things went slowly at first when regular Excelon Tile came in," he says. "The company was feeling its way and was reluctant to commit sizable assets to this new product. But then a second tile production line went in at Kankakee in 1957. It was a great success, thanks to the use of an oscillating blade that R and D had developed. This blade went into the nip of the mill rollers and was used to dispense chips

I wrote the M-request that would allow us to make Imperial Excelon Tile at the Kankakee Plant," says Biddle Whigham. "It was for about $500,000—a lot of money. I went over it with the general production manager [for Floor Products Operations]. He okayed the M-request, but he signed it in pencil. Next it went to Curt [Curtis N.] Painter, who at this time was vice-president and general manager. For some reason, he declined to approve it. When it came back to me in the company mail, I found that the general production manager's signature had been erased! Later on, after modifications, the request did go through. But with that project the biggest problem I ran into was in getting a new conference room established for the Kankakee plant. 'The conference room will be at the south end of the building. Will there be enough north light? Will the room have space enough for rolling racks, so we can lay up samples?' Sometimes it's hard to predict how small matters like that can become major stumbling blocks."

of color over the blanket of material passing below. The sales of that product led to the addition of a No. 2 line at Lancaster. Also successful.

"Then in 1958 Imperial Excelon Tile came in. Kapow! It was an Armstrong exclusive, and it blew the lid off the commercial tile business." What made Imperial so popular was that the design went all the way through the tile. You wouldn't wear it off the surface, even in heavy-traffic areas. Architects, building owners, contractors, maintenance people all loved this feature.

"At first Imperial Excelon Tile was made only at the Kankakee plant," Whigham points out. "Later, as the sales began to grow, its production spread to all U.S. tile plants, including Lancaster, and eventually even to those in Canada and Australia. And I like to think about this. When Kankakee began making Imperial, on the second day of production it was making salable tile."

Bob Stewart recalls another especially gratifying success story from his experience as a project engineer. "The closest collaboration between R and D and engineering that I was involved with occurred at the plant in Jackson when we were putting in a new line for making Stylistik Tile. Fred [W.] Joost [Jr.] was plant manager at this time. We had designed every piece of equipment to permit changeovers between patterns in the shortest possible time. And this is the only time I know of when a new line started up and produced salable goods the first day of production. We all took great pride in that."

Ronald C. "Ron" Carpenter, during his long years as an Armstrong engineer, was involved in several pivotal developments in the company's post-World War II flooring history. The plant at Fulton, New York, to which Carpenter was assigned early in his career, had been acquired years before, in 1926, to provide rag felt backings for linoleum and the Quaker line of printed rugs and floor coverings. Then in the mid-1950s came Hydrocord backing, also made at Fulton. Because it was unaffected by alkaline moisture, Hydrocord permitted the vinyl flooring with which it was used to be installed on grade-level concrete and even in basement areas.

This development lit up the flooring industry like a tiki torch. In 1962 the plant shipped 38 carloads of Hydrocord backing to Lancaster and also a much smaller quantity to the plant at Montreal. That amounted to some 400,000 square yards a year. Ron Carpenter, by now the plant engineer, found that suddenly more capacity was needed—enough for 20 million square yards of Hydrocord, in fact, to keep pace with the rapidly growing market for Vinyl Corlon flooring. Consumer demand for rotogravure floor covering was on the rise also, and that put further pressures on the Fulton plant.

"It was a scramble," says Ron Carpenter, "but we managed to meet the demands. Eventually we put in a line dedicated to making 12-foot-wide Hydrocord backing, and that allowed the people in Lancaster to take full advantage of the growing rotogravure business. Later they were able to apply a thicker wearing surface to the backing, and that meant they could make 12-foot rotogravure flooring, not just floor covering."

The plant at Lancaster had to have a backing material suitable for printing, in sufficient quantities to meet its needs. It relied on Fulton to meet these needs, and the staff there didn't fail.

Prior to joining Armstrong in 1960 Ron Carpenter had been an engineer with a printing-grade paper company, so he had a good idea as to what printers wanted and needed as a surface on which to print. That knowledge served him well in his work at Fulton, and it proved even more valuable in a subsequent assignment.

"In the mid-1980s," he says, "we were making a flooring tile with a production cost of 24 cents apiece. The Taiwanese were making a similar tile for 19 cents. How could Armstrong compete with that? But we were determined to try."

Richard A. "Dick" Graff, general manager of production for Floor Products Operations, undertook to analyze every cost involved in making the tile. His analysis was painstaking, meticulous, and entirely thorough. Once he completed it, he recognized that the company needed to take a new approach, to find a new way to make tile.

At research and development, John C. "Jack" Kaufmann came up with a breakthrough on a product that would eventually be known as Stylistik Tile. In essence, here's how he worked it out. The Lancaster Floor Plant was to produce a base sheet of neutral-color vinyl. To this was to be applied a decorative image, printed on the reverse side of a transparent sheet of vinyl. This arrangement protected the image between the base sheet and the clear wear layer. It was an ingenious idea. Everybody thought it could succeed in reducing production costs, if only it could be made to work successfully.

One of the first steps was to determine how to create the printed images. The company had been working with a contract printer who could deliver a finished sheet 26 inches wide. For Armstrong's purposes, though, something wider was preferable. This suggested that Armstrong needed to purchase its own printing equipment. But where was it to be placed? In the early months of 1985 the decision was made. Like almost everything else about this project, it was a clean break from the past. In Beech Creek, Pennsylvania, the company owned a facility that it had used for making carpet yarns. Armstrong, however, had found only limited success in the carpet business, with its thin margins, and the plant at Beech Creek had stood idle and vacant since Carpet Operations closed it in 1982. The closure had been a blow to the economic health of this small community. Now things were going to change again, this time for the better.

Beech Creek was to be the site of the new printing operation. The aim was massive cost reduction, and yesterday's methods wouldn't do. It was time to cut for a new deal, and Ron Carpenter and his fellow engineers examined every square foot of the vacant plant to figure out how to lay it out most productively. That was only the start. G. Wayne Bonsell, who had been plant manager at Beech Creek during the carpet yarn-making days, returned as plant manager, but this time for Floor Products Operations. He placed great attention on employee selection and training, for this was to be an all-salaried employee force. He sought out key employees from the former plant and rehired them—13 of them in all. Some of the employees traveled to Italy

The "Armstrong" sign that identified the outside of the plant at Beech Creek had been removed when the carpet yarn plant closed. The sign was shipped to Greenville, South Carolina, where another of the company's facilities was situated. It was never used at Greenville. When the Beech Creek plant was preparing to reopen to produce printed images for Floor Products Operations, the people there had the sign shipped back up north again. The first of the former employees who had been rehired at Beech Creek climbed a ladder and replaced the "Armstrong" on the building, screwing it right back into the same holes. It was a triumphal moment for the plant—and the entire Beech Creek community.

to become familiar with the new Cerutti press that Armstrong had ordered, with its capability of delivering a printed image 44 inches wide.

"The Beech Creek experience proved so successful," says Ron Carpenter. "Things that people said wouldn't work did work. At Beech Creek we first used Applied Color Systems in flooring, to achieve perfect, reproducible matching of colors. So many innovations. Automatic roll changing without accumulators. That worked at Beech Creek. So did automatic, electronically controlled cylinder compensation. Later we found ways to use this method of press registration at other plants, such as Stillwater and the Lancaster Floor Plant.

"I call Beech Creek 'Project Resurrection.' What a team effort it was! And what a great boon to that community! I remember that we started the production wheels turning in June 1986, on a Tuesday. We would have started on Monday except for a burnt-out incinerator motor. We replaced that right away. On Wednesday, one day after the start of production, we were making shippable product."

Armstrong had found a way to compete successfully against the cost-squeezing Taiwanese, but the story doesn't end there. Consumer acceptance of Stylistik Tile proved to be so strong that it went almost immediately on allocation. Soon Armstrong produced Stylistik Tile not only at Lancaster but at other tile plants across the United States. As for the groundbreaking production techniques that Beech Creek introduced, the company was later able to apply them to other products, including the Vernay, Glazecraft, and Royal Solarian families of tile flooring.

A good engineer's work is never done, and Ron Carpenter had other projects to handle. One of the most important of these, the one he calls the "grand finale" to his Armstrong career, arose when the company decided to establish a new plant for sheet flooring materials in the western part of the United States. In early 1986 Carpenter, along with David W. Laubach of the corporate real estate department and Donald Byron, senior staff engineer, received a secret assignment: Find and nail down the most suitable site for an integrated rotogravure sheet goods plant. Dave Laubach, through his confidential contacts with industrial developers in the western states, narrowed the search to several promising choices.

The trio visited five sites in four states. They maintained strict silence on which company they represented and what they intended to do. Carpenter smiles as he remembers a minister, at a luncheon in Mississippi, saying grace and including these words: "Dear Lord, we thank you for these new friends, whoever they are and wherever they're from."

In March 1986 the three searchers visited a possible plant location at Stillwater, Oklahoma. Almost at first sight, Carpenter knew that this was the place. A 300,000-square-foot building already stood on the 100-acre property, it was served by major highways, the area had a good work force, and community officials were well organized and helpful. Of great importance also, the area had strong support from the local vocational-technical school and Oklahoma State University. Other members of the trio agreed, and they gave their strong recommendations for Stillwater to Dick Graff, general production manager. On the third visit there, they finally told Chamber of Commerce officials which company they represented, but they asked these officials to maintain the confidentiality. Not until August, at a luncheon attended by Alfred B. Strickler, Armstrong vice-president and general manager of Floor Products Operations, and Donald H. Betty, vice-president and director of engineering, did the general population of Stillwater find out.

Then the hive began buzzing. Armstrong brought staff from the vo-tech school to Lancaster to tour the rotogravure operations, so they would have a clearer understanding of the technical skills that would be needed in the new factory at Stillwater. A state grant helped in the educational process. In October 1986 Ron Carpenter hired the first employee. The employee force was intended from the start to be all-salaried—that is, with no hourly paid employees. In this Stillwater was similar to Beech Creek, although the plant in Oklahoma would be much larger and more complicated than the one in Pennsylvania. Most past Armstrong projects had been engineered almost entirely "in house." Because of schedule constraints and a desire to think outside the established Armstrong way, the Stillwater project was mostly engineered and its construction supervised by an outside firm, Sanders and Thomas, of Pottstown, Pennsylvania.

Plenty remained for Armstrong's own engineers to do. Carpenter had one of the company's speedy jet planes reserved for every Tuesday. He arranged for rental of a house near the new plant for his engineering team members to live in while they were in town. The on-site project supervisor was the same man from Sanders and Thomas who had handled similar responsibilities during the reopening of the Beech Creek plant, and his experience helped. Still, readying the Stillwater facility for production was a major effort.

Production of rotogravure sheet flooring began in the fall of 1988. "It was not as smooth a launch as Beech Creek had experienced," Ron Carpenter says, "because it was a more complex process utilizing a number of untried innovations." In time the wrinkles were smoothed, and the plant at Stillwater took its place among the several outstanding manufacturing facilities that produced Armstrong flooring in the United States and elsewhere around the globe.

As the Stillwater history exemplifies, Armstrong engineers often had to travel to meet their commitments. At one point in his career Bob Stewart spent much of his time commuting between plants at Kankakee, Illinois, and Jackson, Mississippi, during a critical period when both facilities were preparing to make Stylistik Tile. Bob's wife was about to give birth to the couple's second child, and Bob asked whether he might have some time at home in Lancaster while awaiting this event. The director of engineering draped a kindly arm around his shoulders. "Son," he said, "you're responsible for the laying of the keel, but not for the launching. We need you to keep things moving at those plants."

Production: People making products, making records

Floor Products Operations was a line organization, as contrasted with a staff organization, such as the centralized engineering, human resources, or advertising departments. Moreover, Floor Products Operations was considered a "profit center" for Armstrong. It included both production and marketing functions, and both directly contributed to the company's profit.

Basically, the men and women of production made the goods that the men and women of marketing sold. Well, yes, this is true, but that oversimplifies it.

"The responsibilities of production?" asks Lawrence E. "Mike" Bish, who spent years in Armstrong's manufacturing organization, then moved to Thomasville Furniture Industries to head production there before returning to the parent company in 1982 as executive vice-president and a member of the Board of Directors. He answers his own question: "Production is responsible for making a quality, salable product at a competitive price and to be in a service position to meet the needs of customers."

That summary pretty well ties up the package, but it can be dressed up with a ribbon or two, and at Armstrong it usually was. Bish says, "In our work at the Lancaster Floor Plant, new product development was almost a religion. So were cost reduction and profit improvement. These were always on the minds of our production teams."

He credits Edward P. "Ed" Davidson, who served as the plant manager at Lancaster and later as general production manager for Floor Products Operations, with starting a process known as the "new product production acceptance procedure." Bish says, "This worked well, and it eliminated finger-pointing." Here's the way it went. When production people were ready to take on the responsibility for

*W*hen Mike Bish first arrived in Lancaster to go to work for Armstrong, he was struck by an odor that pervaded the area. "I soon learned to think of it as an aroma rather than as an odor," he says. "It was the smell of linseed oil. Oxidized linseed oil was one of the main ingredients in linoleum, and to us it smelled like success. That was true of people out in town, also. When they could smell the linseed oil boiling, they knew that things were going well for Armstrong, and that was good for the community."

making a new product, they had to sign off on the project. So did those from research and development, engineering, product styling and design, and general management. This sign-off meant that the production people in the plant felt that they were ready and able to begin making salable products, and all costs were established for manufacturing the goods at an acceptable quality.

"As soon as that acceptance letter was signed, as soon as production took over, the plant immediately would begin undertaking cost tasks," says G. Wayne Bonsell, who served as a production manager at Lancaster and later became plant manager at Beech Creek. "The idea was to bring down costs in every phase of the manufacturing process."

Sometimes the tasks had a special bite. Bonsell adds, "The day after a 3 percent wage increase was granted to hourly employees, we all knew what we had to do. We wanted to get at least 3 percent out of our manufacturing costs. We were always working to become and remain the low-cost producer." Of course that attitude helped Armstrong maintain competitive pricing, which helped it stay at the No. 1 position in the flooring industry. The consumer ultimately benefited from the lowered manufacturing costs.

Joseph L. "Joe" Jones, who later became president of the company and a member of the Board of Directors, served in the flooring production organization through the years following World War II when massive changes occurred. He looks back on the period with admiration for what was accomplished: "Every member of the team was there, at the time needed, with his or her own special contribution."

One person may have had an influence for decades. Another may have touched the flooring story for perhaps just one significant event for which he is remembered. "After the heyday of the rotary machine in the Lancaster Floor Plant," says Joe Jones, "the molded press line, or stencil line as we called it, came on strong, contributing to profits for years. The man who developed improvements in this stencil process worked out the details for them while he was laid off during the Depression. When he was recalled to work, he built them into the production line, and it made an exclusive, proprietary Armstrong product. This line is what financially supported the beginnings of Armstrong plastic flooring after the Second World War ended."

Financial support was critical in those early days of making the transition from linoleum and asphalt tile, based on natural raw materials, to vinyl flooring, which relied on manmade materials. With the vinyl goods, the company's production people faced frustrating problems in achieving the proper balance of hardness, flexibility, indentation resistance, fade resistance, abrasion resistance, stain resistance, and other features.

The balance was eventually achieved. But think about this: Every time the production teams knocked down a problem, another challenge rose to take its place, thanks to Armstrong's product development activities. Tessera Vinyl Corlon sheet flooring, for example, was not easy to make, and, in 1958, during the first three months of its production the company lost a lot of money. Once Tessera was rolling smoothly, along came Montina Vinyl Corlon flooring in 1961, with its own set of demands. Tessera featured designs made with small, square-edged cubes of vinyl; Montina incorporated unevenly shaped chips with variegated colors. "It was much more difficult to make Montina than Tessera, because of the overlay of chips in Montina," says Donald J. "Don" Wain, who played a key role in the manufacture of both.

In time the problems were worked out, though, and along the way the people in production developed new techniques they could use elsewhere in their plants. "The No. 7 line in the floor plant," says Don Wain, "became the first concept of a rolling press line, with its greatly increased line speeds. Then, when the No. 8 line was put in, specifically to make Montina, we found that we could enhance its operation through electronic controls. It was the first line of its type. It was engineered by Armstrong for this proprietary product. And it worked so well that it stayed in existence for 40 years at the plant. Later the same concept was used at the plant in Montreal." Such development meant profitable success for the corporation—success of sumo wrestler proportions.

Product lines changed quickly. To keep up, production methods had to change, too. Mike Bish thinks back to the 1950s and 1960s, when some old-timers still were thinking of linoleum as king in the Lancaster plant. He says, "Linoleum was produced by using one of three different technologies—a rotary process, a calender process, and a stencil or molding process. All of the linoleum production lines were multistory operations and made products that required extensive curing cycles in large vertical stoves. The production cycle—that is, the length of time to produce a given product—was measured in months, depending on the type of linoleum we were making. This could result in inventory problems for the plant or product service problems for its customers.

"All of these linoleum operations were managed by general foremen who were long-term employees. They had worked their way up through the ranks and were considered the heroes of that time since they were the ones who knew how to make the various products and how to keep the ship afloat. I'm speaking of people like John Rampulla of the molded department, Jesse Shenk of the rotary department, and Mike Phelan of the calender department.

"Each of these men had a soft spot for his particular product specialty, and apparently they were not the only ones with that inclination. Each year we held formal planning meetings at which the individual divisions of the company were expected to present their plans for the five-year period ahead. At one of those meetings,

George Johnston, who at the time was responsible for sheet goods sales, intended to tell the group about plans to discontinue using the rotary product line. I was to follow him and tell how we were going to use the space in the plant freed up by the removal of the rotary machine. [Maurice J.] Moose Warnock was sitting in the front row. He was chairman of the board. As George finished his presentation, Moose spoke up. All right, he said, we could shut down the rotary machine. Then he added, 'But be sure to keep it in mothballs, because those rotary products are coming back.' That left me with nothing to say when I stood up except, 'If we were going to dismantle the rotary machine, this is what we would do with the space.' Moose Warnock died several years ago, at the age of 100. And we're still waiting for that rotary machine to make a comeback!" (Actually, the machine was dismantled about a year after the planning meeting that Bish describes.)

The rotary machine, which had been installed in the mid-1920s with much pride and an investment of $2 million, was out. Linoleum itself was on its way out, and by the end of 1974 Armstrong ended its production. Despite the "linoleum plant" legend borne by city transit buses, which for years to come would refuse to change, the plant at Lancaster was no longer the linoleum plant. It was now known as the Lancaster Floor Plant. The company's move into vinyls mirrored what was occurring in society generally. To some it seemed that the whole world was switching to polymers.

At Armstrong's plant, the old guard was still old-guarding what was left of linoleum production, but the new techniques necessary to work with vinyls demanded a new kind of workforce and a better-educated management team, especially in engineering. The transition to plastic flooring had tremendous implications for inventory requirements, both for the company and for its wholesaler and retailer customers. Also, it changed the way consumers thought of flooring. So much more could be done with vinyls and other synthetic polymers. They offered advantages that never would have been possible with linoleum,

*F*ew people outside the Lancaster Floor Plant knew of this, but the plant was a large user of lumber. Why? Employees in what was known as "the crate shop" assembled a protective wooden framework around every roll of goods 12 feet wide. (Goods in the 6- and 9-foot widths were simply wrapped in heavy kraft paper for shipping.) It was a cumbersome system, especially because the retail dealer had to uncrate his 12-foot roll when he received it, but it went on for many years.

including installation on grade-level, greater durability, improved maintenance characteristics, and lighter, brighter colors. Almost before anyone realized it, the flooring business became a fashion business.

In the mid-1950s, Fred A. Spracher had spent a lot of time in the Lancaster Floor Plant as a project engineer. Then he moved over to production full-time, and for the next 30 years he was deeply imbedded in the manufacture of sheet flooring, tile, and adhesives. He was there during the development of the rolling press line to make Tessera Vinyl Corlon, then Montina and other products. He remembers how difficult this work was—and how important it became. Because the company could produce a succession of proprietary products on the rolling press line, Armstrong moved to the top spot in the industry and stayed there for decades.

"The company had the assets and the willingness to invest them, and that enabled us to undertake new ideas and to bring them to fruition in the shortest period of time," Fred Spracher says. "We were working with a group of brilliant people, and it was an exciting time in the plant."

He mentions the production of Montina Vinyl Corlon flooring as an example of the near-miracles achieved on the production floor. "By the time we were done perfecting that line," Spracher explains, "we had a 40-foot heating table, then a cooler, then another 40-foot table, with vibrators to distribute the vinyl chips on the moving belt. Along the way we had built in the capacity for three belt feeders in line. We had never done anything quite like this before. At that time, I believe, Armstrong knew more about 'feeding chips for a purpose' than anybody else in the United States. And just about all of it was developed in-house."

The importance of the in-house development of processes and the designing of machinery to make them work can hardly be overstated. The flooring industry was sometimes characterized as an oligopoly. That is, it had relatively few participating companies. Any of these could influence the market, but no one company controlled it. In such conditions, if Armstrong needed a new machine to make vinyl flooring, let's say, it couldn't simply go to American Machine and Foundry and order one from stock. There was no such stock. So Armstrong had no choice but to develop its own.

Francis X. Schaller, Jr., was involved in such development activities for a remarkable career that spanned 40½ years. He joined Armstrong's flooring plant in mid-1948 and soon found himself as a machinist apprentice in an "8,000-hour program" registered with the Commonwealth of Pennsylvania. He moved from weld shop to sheet metal shop to tool room, working where needed to complete the 8,000 hours that would lead to full certification as a machinist. "When 6,800 hours were completed," he remembers, "at the end of 1951 I came home from a shopping spree, having purchased my first suit and a typewriter, only to find a

In mid-1956, Francis Schaller and the engineer with whom he was working made dozens of sketches while designing a system of conveyors for the Rotary Department, intended to transport the linoleum mix from the sixth floor down to the milling machines on the second floor. "These sketches were on calendar pages, on torn sheets of scrap paper, on everything but pieces of toilet tissue," he says. "Lots of the notes were on the backs of the pieces of paper. It was on that assignment that I decided to use only yellow quadrille sketch pads, and only on the front sides. This system worked very well, and from then on I followed it all the time I worked in the plant."

letter directing me to report to New Cumberland Army Depot on the 5th of December. After training I went to Germany for 17½ months, returning to Armstrong in the middle of December 1953. I ended my apprenticeship and somehow got selected to join the newly formed plant engineering group."

Quick to learn, and with an inventive mind, Schaller showed an unusal proclivity for his work. Having begun his career as an hourly paid employee, he eventually moved into salaried status. All the while, he spun out sketches of new ideas that could be put into use on the production line.

Sometimes his work was done almost on the run. One lunchtime, for example, he was corralled in the tunnel of the Lancaster Floor Plant by one of the engineers, who wanted him to take measurements for a temporary water bath for the advent of Montina Vinyl Corlon flooring. Schaller went to work quickly. "With the cooperation of the carpenter shop, we built a tank lined with a plastic sheet. We ran the test the following day." He adds, "The reason I got things done rapidly was because I didn't waste time redrawing my layouts. My layouts were my finished drawings. Maybe not the prettiest, but they got the job done."

The plant engineering group of which Schaller was a part became involved mainly in three types of projects: First, solving a problem. "The plant was making a cushioned flooring product whose edges didn't quite match up because of slightly different thicknesses," says Schaller. "We found a simple solution by reversing the screens." That simple solution reduced complaints and call-backs on the product. It saved Armstrong about $10,000 the first month it went into effect.

Second, replacing one or more human beings with mechanical devices, for reasons of safety or economics or efficiency. For example, making marbleized linoleum patterns on the old rotary machine was fairly labor intensive. A piece of the linoleum blanket 72 inches long would fall by gravity to two men who would insert it into the nip of a calender. Meanwhile, another employee, stationed on the top of the calender, would flip another 72-inch piece of the material so the finished product would resemble marble. Schaller worked out a way to eliminate the top man's job by using a mechanical conveyor to reverse the direction of the material while transporting it to the target point of the machine.

Third, designing and constructing new machines. When the flooring plant was getting into the production of materials using small chips for their designs, a granulated "dry blend" was often added to fill in the gaps between chips. The granules could cause a problem, however, if they ended up on the surface of the chips. Schaller perfected a vacuum system for sucking away the excess bits of dry blend.

Schaller and his fellow employees in plant engineering were known as "Dunie's boys." The nickname came from a Lancaster scrap metal dealer, and the implication was that they made their machines from junk they had picked up at Dunie's. That was certainly not the case. About three-quarters of the machines they designed and built used metal from the plant's own salvage yard.

Like Schaller, David H. Byrne began his employment with the company in an hourly paid position. But unlike Schaller, Byrne remained an hourly employee all through his career. And what a career it was! When he retired in May 2006, he could look back on 33½ years with the flooring plant.

The Byrne story goes far beyond mere statistics. At the time of his retirement, he commented, "For the first time in 80 years, there will be no one from the Robert B. Barton family working in Lancaster for Armstrong World Industries." Byrne's maternal grandfather, the Barton with whom this family story begins, didn't work at the Armstrong plant. He was a Posey Iron Works employee. "But his children did their share to help build Armstrong Cork Company into Armstrong World Industries," Byrne says.

Barton's oldest child, Byrne's Aunt Anna, worked in the company's Lancaster offices in the mid-1920s. (That was before Armstrong moved its headquarters to Lancaster from Pittsburgh.) There she met Nathan Y. Newcomer, a millright with a fine head of wavy red hair. When they married, Anna, as was the usual practice at the time, left her employment with the company. Her husband stayed on. "By the time my Uncle Red retired in 1973, the wavy hair had long since retreated," Byrne says, "but his devotion to the company never wavered as he advanced through the ranks to become a maintenance supervisor."

The Newcomers had three children, Elizabethanne, Carrielee, and Nathan, Jr. All three worked for Armstrong. The eldest, Elizabethanne, met her husband, Jim Hammel, at the plant. She left to raise their children, but Hammel stayed on till the mid-1990s, when he retired as a maintenance supervisor with more than 30 years of service. Carrielee worked at research and development on the Columbia Pike. So did her husband, Marty Fidler. Both retired from Armstrong after years-long careers. Nathan, Jr., like his father, followed the mechanical trades in the Lancaster Floor Plant. He retired in late 2005 with more than 44 years of service.

In addition to his daughter, Anna, Robert B. Barton had a son, Robert B. Barton, Jr. He joined Armstrong just as the Great Depression tightened its talons around the national economy. Still, he managed to hold on, building a long career in production before retiring in 1973.

Robert B. Barton had another daughter, Rita, who married John Byrne, an attorney. They became the parents of David H. Byrne, who says, "None of my brothers was inclined toward factory work. Neither was I, or so I thought."

In 1972 the young David worked in the Pennsylvania State Library. He felt that he could earn more in the private sector, so he applied to two prospective employers, Armstrong and Hildy's Tavern. Byrne laughs with relief as he recalls that Armstrong called first.

When he started at the plant, he found that he made about as much money in

*I*n Lancaster's Buchanan Park one may find a monument in memory of famed local boxer Leo F. Hauck. He was known as the "uncrowned middleweight champion of the world." He beat the champion in the ring, but it was a non-title bout, so he never received full recognition for his accomplishment. His brother, John Hauck, was employed for years by the Yard Department in the flooring plant. He also had been a promising boxer in his youth. "But Johnny lacked the killer instinct," the story went. "He was too nice a guy to make a real success in the boxing ring."

During John's formative years, Lancaster had a number of neighborhood breweries, especially in the Cabbage Hill area of the city. Some of these breweries regularly sponsored boxing matches. When he was a teenager, as Johnny Hauck related it, he was boxing a much older, much heavier man at Rieker's Brewery. The match was held on the second floor, with an open window overlooking the alley below. With a few spectators crowded in, the room was too small to be adequate. Two sides of the ring were formed by ropes, and the other two were brick walls, including the wall overlooking the alley. Young Johnny Hauck took a knee-crumpling right to the chin and went reeling backward. "He knocked me right through the window," he said years later, in recalling the episode. "I managed to throw both my elbows out, away from my body, just before I went all the way through. And that's all that saved me from falling to the bricks in the alley beneath me."

three days of training as he had in working five days for the state. Armstrong, as he discovered, was one place you could work without a lot of education and still make a good living. "I thought I would work at the floor plant for a year or so and sock some money away while I figured out what I wanted to do with the rest of my life," Byrne says. He stayed—stayed for more than 33 years before retiring, his future supported by the monthly pension check deposited in his bank.

The people who worked in the Lancaster Floor Plant, not surprisingly, developed special interests in their off-the-job lives. Robert B. Barton, Jr., who had joined the plant during the Depression, was an amateur boxer. "My grandmother disapproved of this," Byrne says. "So whenever he was mentioned in the newspaper, they would hide the sports section from her." He remembers another employee who had a talent for hand-carving fishing lures, which he sometimes sold to others. As for David Byrne himself, he developed his skills as a writer. Following his retirement from Armstrong, he continued working, as a sportswriter for the *Sunday News* and the *Lancaster New Era.*

"It was a great ride," he says, speaking of the years he spent in the plant. "Armstrong provided a comfortable living for my peers. We married, raised families, bought homes, and became responsible members of the community, and along the way contributed to the economic well-being of the county."

David Byrne represented the third generation of his family to be employed by Armstrong. Such legacies were not unusual. "In fact," he says, "family connections were what made the Armstrong family strong."

Look at the family story through the other end of the telescope and you might come across Evan H. Phillips. He spent his adult life as an hourly employee in the Lancaster Floor Plant, working in inspection, tile production, and plastic mixing operations. Just one generation, but what came out of his work is worth noting.

His story is told with pride by one of his sons, Dr. Spencer D. Phillips, a family-practice physician in Lancaster. "My father grew up at Quakake, in the coal region," he says. "When his mother died, he came to Lancaster, where his sister lived, to look for work. He was 16. He found employment at the Armstrong flooring plant, and he stayed on the job there for 43 years."

In time Evan Phillips married, and in further time four sons were born. The eldest died in infancy. The surviving brothers were Evan Gilbert, born in 1954; Spencer D., in 1957; and Jason Keith, in 1965. All of the sons were tightly stitched into their father's Armstrong employment. All of them, one way or another, felt a part of it. And all of them shared his pride in his work.

Dr. Spencer Phillips says, "I remember the family picnics and the occasional family tour days at the plant. And we would go every year to the Christmas party that Armstrong would put on for the young children of employees. It was held at McCaskey High's auditorium, which seemed huge to me at the time. When I was older, perhaps 14 or 15, I remember seeing plaques at the hospital: 'Armstrong donated this space.' That gave me a feeling for what the company was doing in the community. I became a member of the Medical Explorers group, sponsored by Armstrong's research and development department, and we could use the lab facilities to dissect things or to do chemistry experiments. When my dad would bring home a copy of the *Floor Plant Journal*, we'd race to look through it to see if his name was in there. We wanted to see if he had won an award in the 'Suggestions for Progress' program, and sometimes he had."

Mrs. Evan Phillips was involved, too. When her husband worked an early shift, she rose before daybreak to pack his lunch. "I'll never forget that gray lunch bucket," Dr. Phillips says. "My mom would put in a sandwich, and something for dessert, with a Thermos of coffee in the lid."

While he was in college, Spencer himself worked at the plant for a couple of summers. "It paid well, but it was hard work," he says. "This gave me an incentive to stay in school. Of course the main incentive came from my father. He had never had the opportunity to complete high school because he had to earn a living at a young age, and he continually instilled in us the need to get a good education."

And get a good education they did. While maintaining a reasonable standard of living through his 43 years as an hourly employee, Evan Phillips managed to send all three of his sons to The Pennsylvania State University. Evan Gilbert, a computer specialist, now does highly classified work with the National Security Agency. Jason Keith went for further study at Texas A&M University, then came back to Penn State for his doctorate. He now teaches business at West Chester University. Spencer D., who moved on to Temple University Medical School, has practiced family medicine in Lancaster since 1985.

*I*n the early days of Evan Phillips' employment, soon after World War II, the Lancaster Floor Plant wasn't equipped with all the labor-saving devices that came along later. Boxcars, for example, were loaded by hand. Working side by side with others in such labor-intensive tasks tended to foster good fellowship among the plant employees. Dr. Spencer Phillips recalls his father telling of those days: "When a job was done, the men might relax a bit with contests they staged on their own. For example, while someone held a stopwatch, they would climb to the top of the warehouse, then crawl across one of the girders to the other side, then come back down to floor level, to see who could do that the fastest. Or they would sometimes hold wrestling matches between jobs."

Evan Phillips is proud of his sons for what they have accomplished through higher education. His sons are proud of what their father was able to do for their careers through his work at Armstrong.

During their extended careers in the plant, Frank Schaller, David Byrne, and Evan Phillips were a part of many a change in methods and machinery. That statement gets an understanding nod from Fredric E. Bulleit. "Technology changes are what made Armstrong grow," says this former vice-president for manufacturing services. Such changes affected much more than the production equipment, he explains. They affected attitudes of people, also.

"Take quality," Bulleit comments. "All along we were interested in making sure the quality of the product was right. Then that evolved into something much broader, something we called quality management."

By the time the quality management program was fully implemented at Armstrong, every employee was involved. In the beginning, though, one person had found himself, through circumstances of time, place, and responsibilities, in a position to introduce quality management to the organization. That person was John H. Moore, and when the opportunity arose he seized it.

Working in the early days of his Armstrong career as plant industrial engineer at the flooring plant in Lancaster, Moore was establishing incentives for production employees, doing time and motion studies, and refining job classification and evaluation standards. In this and subsequent positions, he was concerned with product quality. When he became manager of quality control for Floor Products Operations, he was primed and ready for his venture into full-scale quality management.

"We came to realize," Moore says, "that we were not making comparisons as we should, particularly in the tile plants." Tiles made in one of the four U.S. plants would not always match those of the same pattern made in the other three plants. They might be slightly off in color, design, and physical dimensions. Even within the same plant, tiles from one production run might not precisely match those from other runs. The company faced a quality problem, and a serious one. If Armstrong tiles were being installed in a large school building in St. Louis, and one could see where the Kankakee-made tiles ended and the Jackson-made tiles began, that would lead to complaints—and sometimes to redos.

"We increased the intensity of our quarterly quality meetings," Moore says. "We'd have 36-square-foot layups of tile from each production run, then runs of tile from other plants. For any given product, you'd have a formula covering every raw material, every step in mixing, calendering, and finishing. A 'master sample' set the standard we tried to follow. We'd do similar comparisons for sheet flooring."

All of these measures helped to improve quality, but the emphasis remained on the finished product. John Moore had a growing feeling that more could be done, especially in the early stages of the production process.

Then in the mid-1970s came a going-over-the-waterfall moment. He had an opportunity to visit the Harley-Davidson motorcycle plant in York County, Pennsylvania, and he was immediately impressed with what he saw. The Harley people, he found, had procedures set up to make sure that every motorcycle coming off the assembly line was perfect. Not just close, but perfect. Any of a number of people could shut down the line in an instant if he sensed that something was not going quite right with a part or a procedure. "There was more to it than that," Moore says. "The York operation had in place a set of evaluative parameters that could measure just about every important event taking place in the plant. They told me, 'If you can measure it, you can improve it.' It was statistical quality control like nothing I had seen. And for Harley-Davidson, it was working."

How did you find out about this? he asked. Philip Crosby, they said, down in Florida. He had a lot of innovative ideas to improve quality for any company. They said, You should read his book, *Quality Is Free: The Art of Making Quality Certain.*

John Moore traveled to Winter Park to talk with Crosby and to take the course he offered. "When I was talking with Phil Crosby," he remembers, "I said to him, 'You don't advertise the Quality College much, do you?' He said, 'We don't have to. Other people advertise it for us, through word of mouth.'"

After Moore returned to Lancaster, he asked Armstrong's controller's department to help him determine how much it cost the company to correct mistakes it had been making. They began measuring the costs of scrap, of redos, of the labor to produce products that were less than perfect, of claims from the field because products had been shipped incorrectly. The results were attention-grabbing. "We had been thinking of ourselves as a quality-oriented company," he says. "Yet here were the figures, and we couldn't ignore them. A lack of total quality was costing us millions of dollars."

Armed with the statistics he had sought, Moore met with the Armstrong executive committee, urging that the company buy into Crosby's program. Two of the marketing divisions wanted to sign on right away, but some of the others held back. Then Harry A. Jensen, the president, and Joseph L. Jones, executive vice-president, made a decision. They said that Armstrong should embrace this quality management program corporately, not just piece by piece.

Now the ball was rolling. "We kept the company's two Convairs busy," Moore says. "Each one could carry 44 passengers. It took a little longer than a year, but by the end of that time we had flown more than 400 managers to Winter Park to attend the Quality College. And more than 4,000 salaried employees took a 30-hour course taught by Armstrong people who had been given special training as instructors. Our feeling was that you had to have everybody involved. Secretaries, everybody. Even suppliers."

And everybody was. Production people in the plants learned about quality. So did the field marketing people across the United States. In time the program spread to Armstrong operations outside the United States.

William A. Mehler had been appointed as the company's first director of corporate quality management. In his book *Let the Buyer Have Faith*, Mehler describes the experience this way: "Quality management preached the need for a massive cultural change. Its implementation…was actually the fulfillment of over 120 years of Armstrong principles and aspirations. It was summed up in a new policy statement that prominently took its place alongside the four Corporate Principles: 'We are committed to quality performance. As an organization—and as individuals—we will continually seek out the specific needs of those who depend upon us. We will then consistently satisfy those needs by doing everything right the first time.'

"Quality management emphasized that everyone is both a customer and a supplier. Pledging to 'seek out the specific needs of those who depend upon us' was simply an extension of Thomas Armstrong's original promise, 'Let the buyer have faith.'"

Fred Bulleit, who at the time was vice-president for materials management, comments, "Quality management had to do with process improvement in every area in which we worked. It meant trying to improve everything we did, at every level. Color matching was always important in our flooring products, and sometimes it was a big problem. Quality management taught us to correct the problem at the outset, rather than attempting to do so in finished products. We learned, for example, to order titanium dioxide [a pigment that Armstrong used in great quantities] from just one supplier rather than from several sources. A simple step like that did wonders for our color consistency." Armstrong's Central Purchasing people came through admirably in augmenting the quality management process with suppliers, many of whom found this quite a departure from their normal way of meeting their customers' requirements.

Bulleit adds, "Any process can be improved. Any process. We learned to correct mistakes, simplify, reduce costs. 'If it ain't broke, don't fix it' doesn't apply to quality management. We trained ourselves never to stop looking for ways to do things better."

Fred Bulleit retired as vice-president and director of manufacturing services, but much of his Armstrong career centered around production planning. A central staff department, production planning was in the vital position of managing material and labor. Which flooring products are to be run? When? In what quantities? To be shipped out to customers at what rate (as contrasted with simply moving finished products to company warehouses)? What level of crew staffing will be needed? What quantities of raw materials (limestone, linseed oil, polymers, solvents, pigments, backing materials) will be required? These were the questions the production planners faced every working day. On top of that, they often had to plan the production, assembly, and distribution of thousands of sample sets over the course of a three-month selling season.

"At regularly scheduled production planning meetings, we would bring our own people together with those representing production and marketing. From these meetings would come the operating schedules and levels for each product line made at each plant," Bulleit says. "This was a critical function at Armstrong. We had to supply our wholesalers on a short-term basis, but without building up too much inventory in the warehouse. The wholesaler, in turn, faced a similar situation because he had to supply the retailers who were his customers. It paid us, and paid our wholesale distributors, to churn our inventories with frequent turnover."

An important link between wholesalers, who were ordering every week, and

*T*he production people in the Lancaster Floor Plant devoted most of their effort to making products for sale through the Floor Division. At times, however, they were called on to produce specialty products for mobile and manufactured homes, sold through Armstrong's Corporate Markets Sales Operations (CMSO). One such product was a flooring that was unusually tough and durable. Eric Berman in advertising came up with the name "Rhino." Then the decision was made to promote the new product with the use of an actual rhinoceros, perhaps by installing the flooring in its cage. Officials at the Philadelphia Zoo were willing to consider the idea, but first they wanted to make sure that if their rhinoceros, Billy, were to ingest some of the new flooring he wouldn't be harmed. Somebody in Armstrong's R and D organization commented, "This is the first time anybody ever asked us, 'What happens if a rhinoceros eats your floor?'" They were able to assure the zoo officials that, yes, the animal would be okay if he swallowed some of the flooring. Billy was moved out of his cage, the flooring was moved in, Billy was returned, and the cage was photographed with Billy standing on the tough-as-hide Rhino flooring. Then another doubt arose. John B. "Jack" Helmer, the vice-president in charge of CMSO, asked, "What would happen if the zoo's rhinoceros were to slip on our flooring and fall down? We might be sued." Don't worry about it, he was told. As soon as the photography was completed, the Rhino flooring had been removed from the cage. Billy's time in the advertising spotlight was over, and his life had been restored to normal.

Armstrong plants, which were shipping every week, was an organization known as the Floor Division Sales and Order Department. The men and women in this group served as the petri dish from which came the road-level reality to meet the needs of the company's customers, and to meet them on time.

"For years Carl M. Fickes was manager of the Sales and Order Department," says George F. Johnston, "and he did a fabulous job of getting [rail] cars and trucks loaded and shipped out. Carl published a weekly stock sheet that went to our wholesalers and to our district offices and marketing representatives in the field. Wholesalers ordered against futures, and this way everybody knew what was going to be available and when. It meant that we could have better turnover and the wholesalers could have better turnover. And that was a money-maker, when you could turn your inventory from four to six and a half times."

Bulleit amplifies the point: "Production people liked to start their machine and let it run for three days. But through production planning we were able to introduce shorter runs, so we could provide better service to our customers."

The shorter production cycle for vinyl flooring, compared with that for linoleum, helped in this move toward better service. Oddly enough, another influence was the development of the interstate highway system. As it spread, Armstrong diverted more shipments to trucks rather than rail cars, which usually meant faster delivery times for customers.

Mike Bish looks back on his lengthy experience with production operations at Armstrong and the transition from natural raw materials to manmade materials. He comes up with an interesting observation: "Unfortunately, it appears that the flooring market is going through this transition again, only in reverse, with flooring made from natural raw materials such as clay, ceramics, and wood apparently commanding a greater share of the overall flooring market."

Advertising: Tell the old story, make a new friend

For years *Advertising Age* magazine ran an annual feature that listed the top 100 advertisers in the United States. For years Armstrong ranked among those 100 elite.

The Advertising and Marketing Services Department created advertisements in magazines, on television, and in other media, and that was only the start of its responsibilities. The department was centralized, reporting to the President's Office rather than to any single division. It represented all marketing arms of the company, but without question the bull's-eye of its work, the organization that called on the largest portion of the department's time and manpower, was the Floor Division.

A flooring product, linoleum, had been the subject of the first national consumer ad back in 1917, when the *Saturday Evening Post* carried a page showing an attractive home interior. "Armstrong's Linoleum: For Every Room in the

House" was the message.

Henning W. Prentis, Jr., who left his distinguished thumbprint on so many worthwhile innovations, started it all. In that same year, he persuaded the company's management to go along with a courageous commitment of $50,000 for consumer advertising. The campaign ran through a three-year period because, as Prentis insisted, if Armstrong was to advertise effectively it must advertise importantly.

Through most of the next 80 years the company took on a battery of different media, including radio, television, slide films and motion pictures, product labels, showroom displays, premiums, even matchbook covers (though never, to anyone's recollection, skywriting). Magazine advertising always led the procession. In America's magazines Mrs. Consumer could count on Armstrong to keep her informed about what was new in flooring, what was new in interior design, what was new in ideas to make her home more beautiful, more comfortable, and easier to care for. It was an old story, but Armstrong somehow kept finding novel ways to tell it.

The company kept in mind Prentis's admonition to advertise importantly. "This is what led in time to our 'owning' inside cover positions," says Donald G. Goldstrom, who retired as vice-president and director of advertising and marketing services. "We earned these valuable inside covers through consistency and longevity, going back to the linoleum days. In a given year we might have 13 covers in the *Saturday Evening Post,* perhaps 10 in *Better Homes and Gardens,* others in other magazines. The schedule was expanded when we began advertising vinyl flooring. At first publishers didn't charge extra for these inside cover positions. They charged the same page rate as for any inside page of the magazine. Later they recognized that they could charge more for the covers, and they did."

It was like the drip, drip, drip of water torture. Only in this instance it wasn't torture, it was a happy experience that readers had when they encountered one of Armstrong's beautiful rooms in a magazine ad. And it wasn't so much a drip, drip, drip as a splash, splash, splash. What the torrent of messages meant, over the years, was that Armstrong managed to take a rather prosaic product like linoleum and build it into brand awareness and brand favoritism that few companies could match.

Goldstrom tells of an interesting way in which this was tested. "We had Allen Funt do a 'Candid Camera' thing," he recalls. "He was in a flooring store, acting as a retail salesman. A woman came into the showroom and said she was interested in buying tile. 'Armstrong tile,' she said, 'that's what I want.' Funt had two stacks of tile on the counter. They were not labeled, and the customer didn't know this, but they were identical. Both were Armstrong tile. He held up a tile from the stack on the right. 'Here's your Armstrong tile,' he said. 'But take a look at the tile in this other stack. It's just as good, and I can sell it to you for a lot less.' 'No,' the woman said. 'I don't think so. I want Armstrong.' And Allen Funt could never sway her off of that position."

He laughs, remembering, "We liked to believe that we had a lot of customers like that. The brand loyalty that that woman showed was what we were trying to achieve through our advertising. And through the quality of the product, too, of course."

Glen P. Dalrymple served as manager of advertising for flooring products, and magazine advertising was at the core of his group's work. "We showed rooms," he says, "because people weren't really interested in buying floors. They wanted to buy what those floors could do for them. The rooms featured in Armstrong magazine ads were beautiful and stylish, but there was more to them than that. We always wanted to fill those rooms with ideas that people could adapt for use in their own homes."

Coming up with such ideas was the job of the people in a special group within the advertising department. They made up the company's Bureau of Interior Design. The artistic wonders this group produced formed the face that millions of consumers recognized as Armstrong.

The designers would start with marketing. Which product should be featured in an upcoming ad? Then the ideas would start to flow. Let's say they felt that this particular flooring could be attractively shown in a family room. What about a nautical theme? someone might suggest. Good idea. Now the room was assigned to one interior designer on the staff. She might do dozens of thumbnail sketches before arriving at the one she wanted to develop. She would then rough out a large sketch of the room. When that was approved, she'd do a color schematic, to scale. It would prominently show the chosen flooring, of course, and also would incorporate ideas that consumers could relate to—all tying into the nautical theme that would attract the reader's attention in the first place.

The marketing people would have their opportunity to okay the room illustration the designer had completed. Then other groups of specialists would jump in to work their magic. Within spaces similar to Hollywood sound stages, cabinetmakers would construct the room. Some of the nation's top photographers, who had developed skills as lighting experts, would work with the designer to transfer the three-dimensional room to two-dimensional color film. These room photographers included Frank S. Errigo, Richard A. Garland, John G. Gates, Charles W. Groff, Allan K. Holm, Carl K. Shuman, Carl B. Vernlund, Forrest E. Wagner, and, for a time, Gary W. Bradt. From the work of the photographer arose another in the series of attractive Armstrong magazine ads.

When in 1976 the Bureau of Interior Design occupied its own studios in downtown Lancaster, every day thousands of people passed the site in the second block of North Queen Street. Few had any idea of the miracles being accomplished just a few dozen feet to the west of them.

That year, 1976, the Bureau of Interior Design could look back on 55 years of existence. Soon after its first magazine ad ran in 1917, Armstrong issued a booklet on decorating for the home. Frank Parsons, a well-known authority on home decoration, prepared it. The favorable response to this booklet led Henning Prentis (again, Prentis!) to wonder whether it might be possible to provide more direct personal assistance to consumers. He made inquiries, and those led him to Hazel Dell Brown, a Pratt Institute graduate who was supervisor of art education in the Indianapolis school district.

Brown demurred. Why would a company that made a basic, almost commodity product like linoleum need someone like her? It made no sense. But it did to Prentis. He talked with her again—persuasively. She was a widow in her late 20s, and she was just adventurous enough to consider the new experience being offered to her. At last she assented. In the fall of 1921 she became the company's first interior decorator.

From that time until she retired in 1957, probably no one had a greater impact than Hazel Dell Brown on establishing Armstrong as a name tied to good design. Soon after she arrived in Lancaster, the company's advertisements began featuring the Bureau of Interior Decoration, as it was first called. Brown reached thousands, eventually millions, through personal counseling, clinics, and booklets. For years this tiny figure, barely 5 feet tall, was the driving force behind the illustrations in Armstrong flooring ads. Always with a black velvet bow in her hair, she hovered like a hummingbird over every room her staff designed as it was readied for photography. The room had to offer more than just visual attractiveness, she insisted. It had to offer practicality, with innovative suggestions that the homemaker and home owner could pick up and make their own. Until she was satisfied, the room was never complete.

Upon her retirement, Hazel Dell Brown was followed as head of the Bureau of Interior Design by other talented designers. They included Margaret Gordon Dana Lestz, Frank J. Vargish, Jr., Louisa Cowan, and Thomas Hills Cook. Each left a rich legacy of beautiful rooms that helped to establish Armstrong as one of the truly important decorating voices in America.

Armstrong's first experience with broadcast advertising came in 1928, when "The Armstrong Quakers" went on the air over 17 radio stations east of the Rockies. Radio was still a new medium, with the first station, Pittsburgh's KDKA, having been licensed less than 10 years earlier. Armstrong used its broadcasts to introduce listeners to Quaker Rugs, the commercials featuring a different pattern on each program. "The Armstrong Quakers" came to a close on New Year's Eve, just as the year 1931 died away.

In 1938, after the worst of the Depression years, the company tried again. Quaker Rugs and Floor Coverings were still being headlined in the commercials, but this time the vehicle was "The Heart of Julia Blake," a 15-minute serialized drama aired three times a week.

Three years later, as war clouds grew darker in Europe and it appeared almost certain that the United States would be drawn into the conflict, came "Armstrong Theatre of Today." Unlike anything else on radio, it was a weekly half-hour show that featured a five-minute news broadcast, followed by a three-act drama that starred well-known Hollywood actors and focused on some item in the news. If the news portion mentioned submarine warfare, for example, the dramatic fictional portion might begin in a submarine factory.

"It's high noon on Broadway, and time for 'Armstrong Theatre of Today.'" These words opened every show, and listeners were intrigued.

Cameron Hawley was director of advertising at this time. "His genius was to put on 'Theatre of Today' at noon on Saturday, when supposedly people weren't listening to the radio," says Don Goldstrom. "He was intent on keeping the Armstrong name in front of people even if their world was being torn by war." Hawley succeeded even beyond his own self-confident expectations. It wasn't long before more Americans were listening to "Theatre of Today" than to any other daytime half-hour show in the country.

About this time, especially during the five years just after World War II, massive cultural changes were taking place in the United States. GI Joes were returning home from the armed forces, marrying their Janes, buying their first homes and starting their families, pursuing college educations under the GI Bill, gravitating from farms to towns, then to cities, then to the suburbs that became the center of gravity for the housing boom that was taking place.

Then there was network television, which began serious development during 1948. "In 1948 TV was still a novelty," recalls Glen Dalrymple. "People bruised

*C*ameron Hawley, director of advertising at this time, was a talented but unconventional and demanding boss. A prolific writer, he penned the script for the first episode of "Armstrong Circle Theatre" and wrote a number of others. William A. Mehler, who worked with him in the advertising organization, repeats a story concerning a meeting that Hawley and representatives of ad agency BBDO, including its president, Charles Brower, had with NBC executives as they planned for the inaugural show. During the meeting Hawley told the network executives, rather grandly, "You'll find that I'm very easy to work with." Charlie Brower immediately spoke up: "The first guy from BBDO who laughs is out of a job!"

their noses against dealer windows, watching television. Its flickering blue light became the lightbulb for the masses, and TV antennas grew out of rooftops like the weeds of summer."

By 1950 six and a half million homes in the United States had TV sets, and it was clear to just about everybody that television was the medium to, um, watch. Clearly, it was destined to dominate. Armstrong acted quickly when the NBC network, which had 35 affiliated stations, offered it a Tuesday night slot at 9 o'clock, right after the popular Milton Berle show. On June 6, 1950, "The Armstrong Circle Theatre" made its debut, and a new era in the company's advertising had begun.

The initial "Circle Theatre" programs did not draw audiences as large as radio's "Armstrong Theatre of Today," which would continue on the air until June 26, 1959. At first "Circle Theatre" followed a format similar to that of the radio show, but with no pretense of being tied to a news item. The format changed September 27, 1955, when Armstrong introduced the "documentary drama," a format based on dramatizing stories (with some fictional license) that "actually happened," according to William F. "Bill" Early, who for years played a pivotal role in the company's broadcasting and audiovisual activities.

"Circle Theatre" shows dealt with such subjects as war orphans, narcotics, medical quackery, and the finding of the Dead Sea Scrolls. Serious subjects, designed to appeal to serious members of the audience. Armstrong was willing to leave the frothy comedies and variety shows to the companies that made impulse-purchase items, such as soaps, soups, and cigarettes. Flooring was a "considered-purchase" item, like a refrigerator. The consumer had to think about the purchase before investing his money in it. Considered-purchase marketers tended to aim for selective audiences. Such audiences may be smaller than those who watch Milton Berle, the thinking went, but they include a greater number of people who are likely to buy the advertised goods.

Max Banzhaf, who followed Cameron Hawley as advertising director, was quoted as saying, "We built the show with one basic idea. We wanted something that offered more than mere escapism, something that would stick to the ribs— point a moral—educate and entertain." It's worth noting that at least two doctoral candidates, at different universities, based their dissertations on "Circle Theatre," its writing, and its production. It was adult programing, and Armstrong wanted it to be regarded that way by its managers and employees as well as prospective customers.

At first the room sets shown in "Circle Theatre" commercials were created and constructed by the Bureau of Interior Design right in Lancaster. Each set was torn down and shipped to New York City, where it was reassembled at the television network's studio in time for the live broadcast. Because of various union rules and other regulations, it was a cumbersome and expensive practice. Armstrong wanted

*A*bout 15 minutes before this live colorcast went on the air, Craig Moodie, who was heading the production of commercials for the show, told me that we still had not decided on an opening shot," says Glen Dalrymple. "There wasn't much time to produce anything elaborate, so in desperation I came up with something. Here's the way the show opened. A black screen, with background music. Then a drop of yellow appeared, then a drop of red. Gray, more yellow, more red, small splotches of color splashing onto the screen. This picture dissolved into a floor of Spatter Linoleum, our newest best-selling product. It all worked. It was just one of those things that happen when you get lucky sometimes."

to make sure that its sets showed off its products as attractively as possible, and this process assured that goal.

In these pioneering days of television, part of what NBC was attempting to do was to get into more use of color broadcasting. Each of its major advertisers was offered a colorcast for one program a year. When Armstrong's time approached, the company's advertising managers, working with people at the ad agency, BBDO, decided to do something that had not been done before. They elected to do the color broadcast on closed-circuit television, linking major-city locations to which wholesalers and selected retailers were invited to attend. (In Lancaster, the Brunswick Hotel was the site for the audience.)

During commercial breaks, the stars of the show were two Armstrong employees, James E. Hazeltine and Hazel Dell Brown. Jim Hazeltine represented research and development. He explained in an authoritative but understandable way how the complex chemistry used in making vinyl flooring provided better products for the consumer. Hazel Dell Brown spoke for the company's interior designers. She described how Armstrong flooring products were adaptable to any color scheme. Helping the television audience to visualize this, the commercials used two attractive young women, identical twins, in two different sets. As Brown told how a certain scheme could be changed, the camera dissolved from one set to another. In today's television, effects like this can be easily accomplished through electronic dissolves. This broadcast occurred before such technical advancements were available, and the innovation made for a lot of word-of-mouth buzz after the show.

"Incidentally," says Bill Early, "this was not the only time we used identical twins in TV advertising. One time we wanted to do a commercial around an infant playing on an Armstrong floor. Because of child labor laws, we could not use the infant for more than two hours. That wasn't quite time enough to complete filming for the commercial, so we used two infants, identical twins dressed exactly alike, and worked it that way."

In October 1957, "Armstrong Circle Theatre" moved from NBC to a different network, CBS. The company maintained its efforts to provide American viewers with programing that made them think, and it was generally pleased with the quality of its audiences, especially those who were considering the purchase of flooring.

When "Circle Theatre" left the air on June 5, 1963, it was being called "the oldest continuous live dramatic show on television." The June 1–7 issue of *TV Guide* featured a cover story on its passing. Commenting that Armstrong "has doubled in size on the average of once every eight years in this century," the magazine added, "As befits such a solid, enlightened company, it has sponsored for these past 13 years one of the most solid, enlightened programs ever to grace this sometimes superficial medium of television."

When television was young, many of the major national advertisers owned their own shows. "Kraft Theatre." "The U.S. Steel Hour." "Armstrong Circle Theatre." Programs like these were under the control of their sponsors, who arranged for writing, producing, and other details. During the early 1960s, though, Newton Minnow of the Federal Communications Commission famously called television a "vast wasteland," and subsequent discussions led the FCC to pressure the networks into taking over control of their broadcasts. This move was intended to improve the quality of television. (Whether it did so must be the subject of another monograph.)

The demise of "Circle Theatre" came suddenly, without warning. Max Banzhaf, director of advertising, learned of it when he read a story in *Variety*. It said that Armstrong's long-running program was to be axed. CBS wanted to make room for a new show to star comedian Danny Kaye, a show that the network believed could draw a larger audience—and a show that, in response to the FCC demands, CBS would control.

"Once the networks took over, the rates went sky high," says Don Goldstrom. "Armstrong wanted to remain in television, and we did so. But we could no longer afford to be a big player on television, as we were in magazines."

With its choices attenuated, Armstrong agreed to be a sponsor of "The Danny Kaye Show." Following this came a caravan of shows for which the company served as partial sponsor. The list included "The Jimmy Dean Show," a live country music offering; "Gidget," starring Sally Field as the teenaged heroine; "Blue Light," a spy drama featuring Robert Goulet; "Big Valley," a western with Barbara Stanwyck; Lucille Ball's popular "I Love Lucy;" and televised adaptations of such Broadway musicals as *Brigadoon* and *Kiss Me, Kate*. What all of these shows had in common was an appeal for women, who were believed to be the important influence in flooring purchases.

In the 1970s the Armstrong Video Network came into being, in response to the need for enhanced internal communications as the company grew. Now flooring plants and district offices could receive regular management reports, launchings of sales promotions, and other information exchanges, each on its own videocassette recorder. The next step was to build and equip a video editing room in the advertising group's Lancaster Square location. This addition made it possible to complete complex productions for duplication and transmittal to Floor Products Operations facilities across the United States.

The size of the Advertising and Marketing Services Department peaked in 1972, as Goldstrom remembers it, when 148 men and women came under its sheltering mantle. These were talented people, and they were involved in a variety of activities that may have been almost unequaled in American business.

Gilbert D. Benson augmented the work of the Bureau of Interior Design, which concentrated on home interiors, with his designs for commercial and public buildings. It's important to note that by this time Armstrong offered the broadest line of commercial flooring, such as Imperial Excelon Tile and commercial-grade sheet flooring, as well as residential flooring. It could afford to employ specialists in both areas, within various disciplines.

As an example, Benson might visualize an interior for a modern airport waiting room, then oversee the construction of the full-size room, indoors. Photographs of the airport setting, which of course would show off commercial flooring and other Armstrong products, would then be featured in ads appearing in *Architectural Record* and other magazines aimed at architects and specifiers. The company also undertook sizable advertising efforts in trade magazines read by discrete audiences, such as administrators for schools and hospitals.

Another aspect of Benson's commercial design activities was the preparation of exhibits for national trade shows, such as those held each year by the National Association of Home Builders and the American Institute of Architects. "This could be challenging," he says. "We always had to be able to come up with something innovative. At the show it might take somebody only a few seconds to pass your booth. Those few seconds might be all the time you had to attract an architect's attention, then intrigue him enough to have him stop for a talk."

Certain Floor Division district offices had spacious showrooms in which to display the newest flooring patterns. The most important was at Chicago's Merchandise Mart, site of a winter home furnishings market, but other showrooms were at district offices in New York City, Atlanta, San Francisco, and, for a time, High Point, North Carolina. Gil Benson and his staff played a continuing role in designing these showrooms and keeping them refreshed in appearance and effectiveness.

*I*n the window of this Rockefeller Center facility," says Gil Benson, who helped design its furnishings, "we had a large revolving platform, large enough to show several different room interiors as it turned." In each room was a mannequin, fitted out with a stylish dress. Anita Welch was the one in charge of the Product Design Center. As it happened, she wore the same size dress as the mannequins. "Anita has a good sense of humor," Benson says. "Occasionally she would put on one of the dresses, take the place of a mannequin on the platform, and freeze while the room set revolved. Sometimes it took our visitors awhile to catch on to this."

Materials specifiers for architects and major builders were of major importance to Armstrong, of course, in the area of commercial and institutional construction. But a number of the company's wholesale distributors, accustomed to calling on retail dealers, were not as experienced in working with specifiers. To serve this market more effectively, the Floor Division selected some of its most seasoned field sales representatives, gave them special training, and designated them as architect-builder consultants.

In 1980, to tie in with the New York World's Fair, came the opening of the Armstrong Product Center in Rockefeller Center. Noted architect William Pahlman was called on to design it. The Product Center was a core-of-the-Big Apple location, intended to make selecting Armstrong flooring products easier for the major specifying influences, notably architects and interior designers. Here, in an attractive, relaxing setting, they could take the time to look over the full range of flooring products, hold the samples in their hands, and obtain authoritative technical and decorating advice. It became a stirring example of how far Armstrong would go to meet the distinct needs of certain customer groups.

Advertising worked with marketing to develop a model homes program that had great importance in placing Armstrong flooring in the millions of tract homes being built across America. The company would offer a builder incentives to offer its products as standard in his homes. In the builder's selection center he could show, on attractive displays designed by the advertising people, other choices the home buyer could opt for, at a higher price. In this way the selection center became a trade-up center. It provided home buyers the opportunity to choose just the floor they wished and also added somewhat to the profit for the builder and for Armstrong. Originally the company offered its selection-center design service to builders at no cost but later charged for it.

Each year advertising people were in the thick of the production of the flooring pattern book, which showed a reproduction of every pattern in the line. It was a beautiful, impressive book, but getting it off the press was almost always a struggle. It was to be shipped to retail dealers right after January 1, and there were always a few new-product patterns that proved difficult to reproduce, in approved form, in time for the book's distribution.

The work with the pattern book reminds Gil Benson of a similar problem he had. "Our group was responsible for putting together the displays of new products for the wholesalers' convention held in December," he says. "But often the products we wanted to show were being made for the first time by the production people in our plants. Understandably, they needed time to get everything just right. I would always try to get a 6-foot by 6-foot sample of each pattern. But sometimes I had to settle for something as small as an 18-inch by 18-inch sample, and that one may have been made in the pilot plant at R and D."

"The annual convention was a major concern of ours," says Don Goldstrom. "The strength of our flooring business at Armstrong would not have been achievable were it not for our distribution system. And it was a tribute to this system that the managers of our wholesale distributors were willing to travel to Lancaster in midwinter each year to attend the convention. It was important to us, and we tried to make sure it was important to them."

The two-day convention was all business, though its sessions included plenty of lighthearted humor, also. Skits and musical numbers, often with live orchestra accompaniment, were included, though these too were pointed at sending a message to those attending. Along with reports on the state of the business came introductions of new products, descriptions of new marketing incentives, and new programs to help the wholesalers market Armstrong products effectively.

What's new? The convention placed plenty of emphasis on that. Goldstrom says, "In June of each year we would begin discussing this. 'What are we going to do at the convention in December?' That was the question. And out of the answers would come the marketing plan for the year."

The introduction of new sales promotions always played a prominent role in the conventions. Typically, the wholesaler guests were told that if their retail accounts ordered a certain minimum quantity of Armstrong products, they would be rewarded with something worthwhile to help them sell the goods—a display rack, for example, or a selling kit to use in the customer's home, or dealers' listings included in direct-mail advertising to be sent out by Armstrong, or special literature, or decorating aids.

In the Armstrong marketing program, such sales promotions played a part that may not have been fully recognized outside the business, but it was a potent pill for pulling in positive sales results. William W. Adams, who took part in the development of many such promotions during his early career days in the company's advertising department, says, "Sales promotion for Armstrong flooring was a juggernaut whose intensity and scope were seldom matched in American non-food marketing. It was a system in the sense that the basic mode of promotion was repeated over and over, year after year, with the creation and execution of the promotions carried out by a changing cast of characters in Armstrong's Lancaster management, the Armstrong advertising and promotion group, and Armstrong field sales personnel and flooring wholesaler personnel."

He continues, "One could hold that this ongoing promotion juggernaut, coupled with weak and inconsistent competitor marketing, was the single most important factor in maintaining Armstrong's share of market, in increasing its sales revenues, and in generating profit margins that not only supported more investment in the business but also made possible the excellent staff departments that served the whole company."

The people in advertising helped the Floor Division launch promotions throughout the year, on a schedule of about one every three to five weeks. The rhythm started in January, slowed in July and August, then picked up again through November.

A sales promotion, Bill Adams says, was intended to accomplish one or more of the following six goals:

First, to lauch a brand-new product line (most frequently in sheets goods and residential tile, less frequently in commercial tile, and occasionally in "luxury tile" or adhesives and accessories).

Second, to refresh an existing product line, usually with new pattern colors.

Third, to defend store space (corresponding to "shelf facings" in grocery-store terms).

Fourth, to spur wholesaler salesmen to higher-energy sales calls.

Fifth, to fill dealers' "open to buy" options, based on their cash flow, and to close such options to competitors.

Sixth, to increase Armstrong's "share of mind" with dealers—an important consideration, given the varying quality and frequency of Armstrong and wholesaler representation.

Product launches could be aimed at retail dealers, to commercial contractors, to home builders, and to specifiers who included architects, interior designers, and in-house building departments of such firms as Walgreen's and J. C. Penney's. Launches to dealers usually covered a four-week period from the time when goods or samples were introduced into the retail showroom. The promotion launches to specifiers had a much longer time frame. The process was to make sales calls with product samples and predrafted Armstrong specifications, which could be inserted verbatim into materials specifications. These sales calls were followed in ensuing months with suggestions as to how new or existing items in the Armstrong flooring line could be used for the specifier's particular projects.

Even though they may have been highly successful, some of the sales promotions aimed at dealers were, well, transitory. Early in Don Goldstrom's career he was involved in a promotion involving wastebaskets made of Quaker Floor Coverings. He remembers a jingle sung at that year's convention. It began, "A new cancan, the wastecancan, was brought here by the wholesale man." Goldstrom, who wrote the jingle more than half a century ago, may be the only person on earth who still can sing it.

Other promotional programs announced at the convention had lasting significance. At the 1953 meeting, for example, wholesalers learned of plans for the Merchandising Motorcade of 1954. It comprised two huge semi-trailer trucks, specially designed and outfitted. They would be parked parallel to one another. Then, when the inboard walls were opened, the trucks became an auditorium on wheels for an audience of more than a hundred. Traveling most of the year, the twin trucks visited 150 cities and all but 2 of the 48 contiguous states. In all, some 22,000 retailers and their sales personnel heard the message of the Motorcade, which was aimed at helping them sell Armstrong floors more successfully.

Enthusiasm for the Merchandising Motorcade led to another highway adventure in 1960. This time Armstrong introduced 22 mobile showcases that wholesalers could take right to the doors of their important retail accounts. The following year the same trailers, redesigned, crossed the country with a show on flooring fashions and interior design. The trucks went right into shopping center parking lots for consumers to view.

The people in advertising were those most directly involved in creating and carrying out such promotional programs, whether large or small. In the mid-1960s, wholesalers attending one of the December conventions learned of the new Floor Fashion Center concept. One of the main departures here was, instead of having consumers look at linoleum or vinyl sheet flooring in rolls standing on end, to have 6-foot-wide materials displayed horizontally. Now it was easier for customers to visualize the flooring in place in their homes, and it was easier for the retailer to sell from samples instead of from the limited number of patterns he might have in stock. Raymond Loewy, the biggest name in the design field, laid out the first Floor Fashion Center showroom, which was presented to the wholesalers at their convention. Floor Fashion Centers developed many refinements in subsequent years, making them even more effective.

Not every effort won laurel leaves. Occasionally one was draped with poison ivy. Take cooperative advertising, a program to encourage retailers to advertise in their hometown markets. In general, the Floor Division pledged to match dealers' expenditures. "The major appliance dealers did a lot of this," says a Floor Division marketing manager of the time, "and we were sort of forced into it. It was a tough one for the salesmen in the field, as it took a lot of their time to administer."

Don Goldstrom recalls it well: "Coop advertising had a lot of rules to play by, and that was by design. But it was hard to control, and an unethical dealer could take advantage of you. I remember going into the office of [executive vice-president James V.] Vic Jones one morning and telling him that we were a million dollars over budget on coop advertising. A million dollars! That afternoon I went to the doctor and had my blood pressure checked. Some manufacturers could make it work satisfactorily. I don't think we ever did."

More successful was another program that sprang from the advertising department. The Retail Development Center, as it was called, was a "test kitchen" the size of a large store. It enabled Armstrong and any of its customers who sold products to consumers to experiment with innovative merchandising concepts. For example, if representatives from Kmart were coming in, a portion of the Retail Development Center could be fitted out like the flooring department of a Kmart store, with colorful displays of merchandising, new types of overhead signage, even special packaging

O*ne time several Armstrong representatives from the Chicago District were showing a training film to a sales meeting at Glabman Brothers, one of the company's wholesalers. "Sitting in on the meeting was Izzy Glabman, president of the company," one of them recalls. Glabman Brothers was an extremely loyal wholesaler, going back to the time when Izzy Glabman had telephoned Henning W. Prentis, Armstrong's president. "Mr. Prentis," he said, "we've had a terrible fire, and we're out of business. We want to get started again, but we have no money to buy inventory." Prentis told him, "Send us a list of what you need, and we'll ship it to you. Pay us back when you can afford to." Izzy Glabman never forgot that kindness, and he paid back every penny that Armstrong had advanced him.*

Now, years later, he was watching the training film as it was being presented to his salesmen. The Armstrong representative picks up the story: "Suddenly Mr. Glabman was waving his arms and shouting, 'Stop! Stop! What are we doing here?' [David A.] Dave Whinfrey, one of the Armstrong men, said, 'We're talking about how to sell Linogloss Wax.' 'No, I'll tell you how to sell Linogloss Wax.' Izzy Glabman pointed to each of his salesmen in turn, saying, 'You! Go sell Linogloss Wax! You! Go sell Linogloss Wax! You! Go sell....'"

when appropriate. Gerard M. Schouten oversaw this activity. It was first housed in a rented building at Greenfield Industrial Park, then moved to quarters specifically designed for it at the Armstrong Technical Center on Columbia Pike.

Early on, the Advertising and Marketing Services Department became the source of training films for the company's customers as well as its employees. Some still talk about a filmstrip that was issued in the 1950s for retail salesmen. Titled "The ACC Sale," it cleverly played on the abbreviation for Armstrong Cork Company, as the corporation was then known. It featured a brash cartoon character named Aloysius Chumbley Chipwhistle, who in the film suggested to the salesman an effective way to sell flooring: Ask—choose—concentrate. In other words, the salesman was advised, when a customer comes into your store, first ask her questions to determine her real needs. Then choose which type of flooring would be best for her. Finally, concentrate on selling that particular item. It was a basic technique, perhaps, but it was sensible selling, effectively demonstrated in the film, and it helped many a retail salesman to approach his job more confidently.

Despite all the activity going on, the people in advertising never allowed themselves to be distracted from the focus on magazine ads. At one time, during the 1960s, they were running three campaigns at once. "Mass, class, and innovator" were what they called them. Some ads, intended to reach mass audiences, ran in such magazines as *Reader's Digest.* Others, aimed at a somewhat higher average income, ran in *House Beautiful* and similar publications. The third campaign, appearing in *The New Yorker, Holiday,* and other special-audience magazines, showed Armstrong floors in esoteric settings. For example, one of these "innovator" ads depicted Sherlock Holmes examining the chips of Tessera Vinyl Corlon flooring under his magnifying glass.

During the 1960s Armstrong broke away from its long-established reliance on inside covers to run a series of "blockbuster" ads in magazines. These were usually multipage ads featuring vinyl flooring. "The Indoor World of Armstrong" and Armstrong Idea Houses provided other opportunities for the multipage approach.

Adding a certain patina to the work of the people in advertising were those who handled product publicity for the Floor Division. One of the more successful efforts in this field originated during the 1960s when the author, who did flooring publicity, was talking with Robert K. Marker, his counterpart for the company's ceiling materials. "What if we tried combining our efforts into a single project?" one of them must have suggested.

"I think that that could be interesting," the other concurred. The final idea sprang from their joint minds: "Let's show people how they can gain an extra room in their home by converting an unused basement area into a family room. If the home owner does all the work himself, it might prove quite inexpensive to do this."

The two sought help from the young women in the Bureau of Interior Design, who enthusiastically began spilling over with ideas. You know those high windows in a basement? Disguise them to look like full-length windows, they said, with striped draperies that hang from the bottom edge of the window and reach all the way to the floor. Flank the windows with panels of fiberboard, painted dull black to look like shutters. Add color with posters of foreign lands. You can obtain the posters from travel agencies, so they don't cost anything. Move in the furniture that's outside, on the patio. And of course the labor is free. The home owner can do the work himself, including the installation of Armstrong Excelon Tile flooring and Cushiontone ceiling materials.

They kept precise records of the expenditures for the project. It added up to astoundingly little: less than $300. That covered the retail costs of all the materials for this room conversion, including flooring tile, ceiling material, lighting fixtures, and drapery material.

The finished room took shape in the basement of an actual home. It was quite livable and attractive, and of course the well-documented price tag was hard to ignore. Who could resist the idea of adding a room to the home for just $300? The company sent the story of this do-it-yourself project, with accompanying photographs, to newspapers all around the United States. Scores of them ran it, with full attribution to Armstrong and the Armstrong products used in the project.

Henning W. Prentis, who more than half a century earlier had shown that he knew a bit about the subject, would have been pleased to see the output from the advertising and publicity activities of the late twentieth century. He had started it all.

Marketing: All artillery aimed at meeting customers' needs

Describing what it was like to play football in the Southeastern Conference, Joe Kines, defensive coordinator for the University of Alabama, once said, "Either you have speed, or you're chasing it." During the years following World War II, the resilient flooring business was like that, too. Developments were moving so fast in the industry that every competitor had to scramble to keep up. The people in Armstrong's Floor Products Operations were determined to do more than keep up. They wanted to be in the lead, in the pace car ahead of the field. Sometimes it was a scramble at first, but almost always, they were able to stay in front.

Headed by a corporate vice-president, Floor Products Operations was a line organization. It was a "profit center" with two arms, each able to directly affect the company's profit, if any. Reporting to the vice-president were a general production manager, who headed the manufacturing arm, and a general sales manager, who was in charge of a marketing team in Lancaster and in the field.

The marketing team for resilient flooring was known as the Floor Division.

Reporting to its general sales manager were three groups of people devoted to specific marketing activities. First were the Lancaster-based product marketing managers (generally five of these in the 1960s and 1970s, one each responsible for Corlon products, Coronelle and linoleum products, resilient tile, rotogravure products, and sundries) and two or three managers responsible for selling to discrete markets, such as the residential builder, mass merchandiser, and contract markets. Second was the organization headed by the field sales manager, who also was an assistant general sales manager. The field sales manager was responsible for district offices and the sales representatives within them, relationships with wholesale distributors, the hiring and training of Armstrong field sales representatives, and the Installation School. The third group, known as operations, was led by another assistant general sales manager. Included in this group were organizations known as sales and order services, sales administration, and consumer relations, as well as a team of sales service assistants.

This marketing group that called itself the Floor Division at Armstrong—was there ever another organization that could match it? Another sales division, in another company, in another industry?

Maybe. American business could offer up lots of success stories from those days, it's true. But Armstrong's Floor Division, by almost any standard, was special. General Motors. IBM. General Electric. All fine companies. But compare their records against those posted by Armstrong flooring during the period from the end of World War II into the early 1990s, and you'll find that Armstrong, though much smaller in corporate size, holds up well against them.

Research and development, product styling and design, engineering, production, advertising, distribution—they all played major roles in this endeavor. In fact,

---

*S*ometimes *Armstrong employees were called on for unusual services. William A. Mehler provides this example. When the Floor Division was expecting a visit from an important Japanese architect from the Midwest, O. William Fenn, one of the division's marketing managers, was expected to be one of the key men in the greeting party. Fenn, who was fluent in the Japanese language and in fact had served during World War II as an interpreter for the armed forces, brushed up on his language skills. The guest arrived, and Bill Fenn greeted him warmly in Japanese. "Oh, Armstrong is always so well prepared," replied the visitor in perfect English. "I apologize. I speak no Japanese."*

---

*O*nce *during Bill VanPelt's early days in recruiting, Henning Prentis commented to him, "I just don't understand why you bother going west of the Mississippi on your college visits." VanPelt's explanation lasted about 20 minutes. Then Prentis, who had listened patiently, took a deep breath and said, "That's why I'm president. I can change my mind." VanPelt says, "He never questioned it again, and we continued to get a lot of fine people from the West Coast."*

every one of these activities was vital to the effort. So were a number of other activities that had at least a dotted-line relationship with the Floor Division, such as economic research; marketing research; the services of legal, financial, and control organizations; human resources; and salaried compensation. But it was marketing that drew everyone together into one giant shoulder against the wheel. The overriding thrust was to determine what customers wanted and needed, then to meet those market demands. Everything else was secondary to that.

Sometimes, as has been several times noted, nosebleeds occurred. But such were the thews of Armstrong's marketing organization, and so accomplished did its members become as the years went on that any failure was soon swallowed up by the storming successes. Those in the Floor Division learned from their mistakes as well as from their triumphs.

Hiring the right people was a Floor Division priority. Armstrong was one of the pioneers in corporate college recruiting. Henning Prentis had begun that in the early 1920s. After World War II the practice was expanded and refined, with other companies often copying Armstrong's example.

For years the college recruiting activity was headed by William J. VanPelt, who introduced many an innovation into the system. "Training classes would traditionally start the first Monday in February and the last Monday in June," he says. "The Floor Division had as many spots to fill as anybody, and we'd generally have our recruiting schedule made up a year in advance."

Understandably, VanPelt and his team of recruiters concentrated their campus visits to the colleges and universities that had proven most fertile in the past. The number of such institutions was limited, but the others weren't neglected. "Through a monthly recruiting newsletter, we were able to keep in touch with the colleges we didn't visit," he points out. The list of colleges on the recruiting schedule changed from time to time to reflect experience. For example, Iowa State University was added to the list when it proved an unusually good source for interior designers.

Armstrong's business was growing, which created a new demand for marketing trainees, especially for the Floor Division. To make its position known, the company began holding conferences for marketing professors in San Francisco, New Orleans, and elsewhere. Typically, about 20 Armstrong marketing executives would speak before a group of 30 to 50 educators at each conference. Also, the college recruiting function set up a speakers' bureau, through which company spokesmen went out to address college marketing clubs on their own campuses. Such programs helped the company become more widely recognized. A professor at the University of Illinois was quoted as telling his business classes, "An MBA is a coming thing, but you should take a look at Armstrong. They have their own MBA program: Master's of Business at Armstrong."

To assure that it was paying its people properly and in balance with the pay scales of other American companies, Armstrong's flooring people counted on the guidance of the company's salaried compensation team. This group of specialists was headed for years by C. Richard Farmer. Another of Armstrong's attractions for young marketing representatives was that the business was strong, and the company could offer plenty of room for promotion for the right person.

Under VanPelt, the recruiting of a new employee didn't end when that employee was hired. The recruiters also kept an eye on him during his training and his assignment to a position afterward. Even then they were ready to step in if necessary, with counseling or some other means of follow-up.

"We were so fortunate to be with a company that had a feeling for people," he says. He cites the case of a Texas A&M student who appeared a promising prospect for flooring research. When he was offered the job, he said no. His father, a small grocer in Massachusetts, was dying, he said, and he couldn't accept a position in Lancaster, so far away from home. VanPelt talked with the management people in research and development. "Our plant at Braintree [Massachusetts] is nearby. Can't we work out a project he could undertake there? He can come to Lancaster later." That's what was done. For nine months, while his father lived, the young man was on a special assignment at Braintree. Eventually he transferred to the company's corporate research and development facility in Lancaster, and in a long career he earned numerous patents for his work. "We liked to think of ourselves as hard-headed business people," Bill VanPelt says. "But we never wanted to be hard-hearted business people."

During the 1960s, while VanPelt was in charge of college recruiting, he had the pleasure of seeing a major upgrade at the Armstrong Manor on the Lititz Pike. Armstrong had purchased this restored farmhouse, which housed unmarried marketing representatives during their initial training in Lancaster, in the 1920s. Mrs. Charles D. Armstrong, wife of the company's president at that time, reportedly was appalled at the living conditions of some of the trainees, including those of her son, Dwight, who was working for Armstrong in Lancaster and sharing an apartment with another young man. "It was Mrs. Armstrong, really, who bought the Manor," says VanPelt. "And she helped to furnish it with antiques from their own home." Now, 45 years later, the Manor underwent a complete remodeling, adding a new wing that was three times the size of the original farmhouse.

The Manor was, of course, a showplace for Armstrong interior furnishings, and it continued to house marketing trainees. Most of the company's presidents spent the early days of their careers in this beautiful setting.

According to legend, Mrs. Charles D. Armstrong, though she lived in Pittsburgh, was the impetus behind another Armstrong development, also. She encouraged employees to gather in the company's office building each holiday season for the singing of Christmas carols. Unusual as this may be in American industry, it's a tradition that continues today, more than three-quarters of a century after it was begun.

Training was important, and Armstrong never neglected that. The training was well planned, intense, and at times grueling. John R. Baldwin joined a Floor Division sales training class in the summer of 1948. Back then, all the sales representatives were men—unmarried men. Baldwin, who invested $41\frac{1}{2}$ years in his career with the company, picks up the story: "There were 10 of us in that Floor Division class of '48. I was paid $250 a month to start. That was a little more than some in my class. I was paid a small extra amount because I had had Navy service. We all lived in the Armstrong Manor, and in those days it was eight to a room, bathroom down the hall.

"Our workdays were spent learning and gaining experience. That was for six months. Classroom periods were spent in learning the product line. Then we spent day after day in the floor plant, finding out how flooring is made. We were in the Installation School for two weeks, learning how to install every kind of flooring the company made, cutting in around toilets—fortunately for us, they were not really hooked up—and learning how to make perfect seams. We worked with wholesalers and retailers, even serving as retail salesmen for a time. Then, toward the end of our half-year's training, we were sent out on our own for a month. My assignment included the New York metropolitan area and parts of Connecticut and New Jersey. And we had to get around on public transportation, as none of us had a company car as yet."

Baldwin says, "The training was designed to help you understand the business and how to sell Armstrong flooring. But also, I think, it was intended to see whether you could survive on your own. For those who did so, the training developed great loyalty. And we ended up with 'Circle A' imprinted on our consciousness."

Gordon T. Levering adds, "Armstrong's sales training was nationally recognized and was considered on a par with IBM's." In addition to practicing selling skills over and over, the young salesmen learned how to read financial statements and even went over the basics of how to conduct themselves as businessmen—how to dictate letters, how to respond to telephone calls, all sorts of things they needed to know when they were working in the field.

"By the time all these young college graduates, from diverse backgrounds, were finished with their training, they were imbued with a special feeling about Armstrong," Levering says. "It was a cultural indoctrination. That's what it was, in a positive way. And it helps to explain why people of our age feel the way we do about Armstrong, with a special loyalty to the organization."

Typically, not until the week of the wholesalers' convention in December did each sales trainee learn to which district office he was to be assigned. The young Armstrong salesmen found early that they were expected to wear conservative business attire on the job. Out with the argyle socks and the saddle shoes. "And when we traveled," says John Baldwin, "we always wore hats. That was a given."

Hats. It's remarkable that when Armstrong sales representatives of that post-war time get together, almost always the subject comes up. S. Todd Lewis, who came in with the winter training class of 1965, says, "By the time I was hired, the training period was down from six months to five and a half months. And when you went out on your own, you were now allowed to rent a car if you needed it. As for hats, they became optional for the summer class of 1965, the class after ours."

"Yes," agrees M. William "Bill" Jones, who joined the Floor Division in 1950, "but before that time, hats were always required." He remembers a story that became almost legendary among his peers. "[Curtis N.] Curt Painter [general sales manager of the Floor Division] was making a visit to the Minneapolis District Office. He was going to make sales calls with a young salesman. The salesman, impressed with the importance of this visit from Lancaster headquarters, told him, 'Now the first call we're going to make is on a dealer on the north side of town.' 'No,' said Curt Painter, 'the first call we're going to make is at a clothing store, where you're going to buy yourself a hat.'"

Levering says, "Our training class went as a group to Filling's Men's Wear on Lemon Street so we could all be fitted for hats."

Todd Lewis laughs, "When the requirement for hats was done away with, it really hurt the Filling's business. They've probably never recovered!"

When he completed his training in Lancaster, and just before he went out to his assigned district, each proud new field marketing representative was presented a valise with his name on it. This valise and what it contained would become as important to him as a medical bag was to a country doctor making his rounds.

First, the salesman's kit held several items put together by the Floor Division sales administration group (headed by Leroy E. Michener, then Clarence E. Trego), which did sales analyses and handled printing of flooring price lists. These items included general sales notices, covering just about anything to do with Armstrong flooring, including news of personnel promotions within the division. Also included was a price and policy book. Unlike the general sales notices, copies of this book went to wholesale distributors as well as Armstrong district managers and field salesmen. The price and policy book was revised as necessary to reflect changes in flooring prices and terms of sale.

In his valise the young salesman would find a pattern book, a brochure on advertising aids and samples, and of course a pad of order forms. When he made a sale, the order form was filled out in quadruplicate: white copy to the wholesaler, pink to the retailer, green to the district manager, and yellow kept by the salesman himself.

The sales administration group, in particular, had a vital responsibility in assuring that everything worked smoothly and efficiently for the Floor Division organization. It provided the official communications that linked the company's people with those of wholesale distributors. The brand-new marketing representative could move out to his first field assignment with confidence that this sales administration group back in Lancaster would remain a steady force to keep him informed with what he needed to know on the job.

The information carried in his valise by the Floor Division field sales representative was an example of the continuing communications flow that moved up and down through the holes in the four doughnut shapes described earlier (see p. 24) as representing the marketing concept as it was envisioned at Armstrong. But this was just the start of the parade of communications that marched out of Armstrong's headquarters. One can find another example in the communications from a marketing manager as he prepared to introduce a new product. Six weeks before the scheduled introduction at retail, the marketing manager wrote a preliminary letter to each Floor Division district manager. In this letter he spelled out necessary details about the introduction: the name of the new product, how it was made and what was special about it, the market niche it was designed to fill, the selling kit that would accompany it, advertising plans for the product, and the allocation of promotional items to be provided to each district. Most important, the letter told the district manager what had to be done right then. Timing was essential.

Closer to the introduction of the new product, the district manager would hold a meeting with the marketing representatives within his district to plan for the kickoff. Meanwhile, about two weeks before the official introduction date, all the wholesalers received an addition to their price and policy books that provided what they and their salesmen needed to know about the new product. The aim was to have all the wholesaler salesmen, all across the United States, beginning their calls

R ecounting the Merchandising Motorcade experience, John Baldwin says, "One time, when we were attempting to back one of the trucks in a tight spot, we bumped into a farmer's shack and moved it off its foundation a little bit. He said, 'What are you going to do about this?' I asked the farmer, 'How much will it cost to put it back into position?' 'I reckon about $35,' he said. So I gave him his $35, and that took care of that. I put it on the expense account under 'moving expenses.'"

on retailers the same day. Introducing an important new flooring product called for an all-out blitz, and Armstrong tried to overlook nothing in its planning and execution.

Among John Baldwin's most vivid memories of his years as a field marketing representative is the Merchandising Motorcade. This show on wheels was introduced to wholesale distributors at their convention in December 1953. It involved two huge trucks that could be parked next to one another in a wholesaler's parking lot to form a sizable auditorium. "These trucks toured the country through most of 1954," Baldwin says. "I was brought in from the Cleveland office, and H. C. Long came in from Nashville. We alternated in touring with the Motorcade. Our basic purpose was to train retail salespeople how to sell more effectively. The auditorium could hold from 125 to 135 people. We had 140 meetings through that year, sometimes as often as three meetings a day." Baldwin recalls, "We took along a stick that was the height of the trucks so we could check whether we had clearance enough to make it through underpasses."

Each district office was responsible for making up the schedule for the Merchandising Motorcade while it was in that sales district. By the time they were through traveling in the United States, before being passed along to Armstrong's subsidiary in Canada, the trucks had visited 150 cities in 46 states. Bill Jones says, "The Motorcade was very professionally done. In the field, we were proud of it."

As mentioned previously, every Floor Division sales trainee spent two weeks at the Armstrong Installation School, in a learning-by-doing experience of installing both sheet flooring and tile. "Bloody fingers among all the trainees," says Bill Jones. The Installation School was established under its original name, the Armstrong Laying School, in 1923, basically to teach retailers' installation people how to install linoleum properly. In later years the school was overseen by three acknowledged experts, H. V. "Jake" Neiss, Guy Edmiston, and Carroll W. "Pappy" Stokes.

"The Installation School provided the obvious, which was to train installation mechanics, and that was always a need," says Todd Lewis. "Less obvious, but just as important, is that without this resource it would have been difficult or impossible to introduce many of our new products. For example, with a product called Cambrian we were offering a way to seal the seams. But it was the Installation School that perfected that method of seam-sealing. Time after time, the school enabled us to introduce new products with confidence."

Jones adds a comment about the Perimiflor method of installation. This new technique permitted a new sheet vinyl flooring to be installed right over existing resilient flooring. That meant reduced cost, time, and cleanup for the customer. "One of the biggest jobs we ever sold in Manhattan was for replacement of resilient flooring in a large apartment complex," Jones says. "This called for 120,000 square yards of material to be installed. That is a large order by any standard. We recommended that the old flooring not be removed but simply covered over with this new technique. Actually, the Perimiflor method wasn't even on the market yet, but the people from the Installation School came to New York and showed how it would work. That was probably the instrumental difference that led to our getting the job. At times they became an important part of our selling team.

"But the installation experts not only helped in selling. They also solved problems and helped settle complaints."

Todd Lewis says, "When you were in the field, they were a wonderful resource to be able to call on when you had a problem. It gave us a huge advantage, and Armstrong's competitors couldn't match it."

The Installation School in Lancaster existed to serve the needs of retail dealers. For many of these retailers, having an adequate number of qualified installation mechanics was a recurring problem, intensified by the parade of new products marching out of Armstrong's plants. A dealer in Boston, say, or Winston–Salem or Sacramento could send his people to Lancaster to learn all the newest techniques. The dealer paid for their travel and expenses, but Armstrong supplied the training for free.

Over the years the Lancaster school trained thousands and thousands of installation mechanics. With such success in hand, the school began sending out its instructors to remote locations. Sometimes a wholesale distributor would open

*I*n early 1969 the Installation School presented a plaque to Morris Roselli of Associated Floor and Wall Supply Company of Lakewood, New Jersey. Roselli was recognized as being the 30,000th graduate of the school. Many more graduates followed him.

part of his warehouse for one of the training sessions, inviting his retail accounts to take part. In the late 1970s, Armstrong opened regional installation schools—one at Chicago, another at San Francisco—so more mechanics could be trained without their retailer sponsors encountering excessive travel costs.

"Installation was vitally important to the success of a flooring job," says Lewis. "Armstrong had the best adhesives and the best maintenance products, and most people who specified flooring knew that. They also knew that we wouldn't guarantee a job unless Armstrong adhesives were used. That helped us sell flooring for a lot of major construction projects."

Bill Jones adds, "We were able to sell the World Trade Center job on the use of Armstrong adhesives with the Armstrong tile that was specified. They could have bought another brand cheaper, but we showed them that using our adhesives would be worth the extra price because of the peace of mind this would give them."

Jones remembers with pleasure the introduction of Tessera Vinyl Corlon flooring in the 1950s. "Tessera had been developed as a commercial flooring, and it was introduced with eight pattern colors," he says. "I showed it to a dealer on Long Island, who immediately said, 'It's monochromatic. It's what my customers want in their homes. I'll take eight rolls, one of each color.' That was a big order for me, and I was delighted to write it up. When I told my district manager, though, he said, 'Well, yes, it's a big order. But are you sure that this is right for the dealer?'" Jones laughs. "It was right for him. He knew his market, and that was a smart buy on his part."

In the late 1950s, recognizing the importance of the commercial and institutional construction market for its growing line of flooring products, the Floor Division selected certain of its more experienced veteran field salesmen and designated them "ABC representatives." The ABC stood for "architect-builder consultants." These specialists no longer called on retail dealers. Now they called on architects, designers, tract builders, and specifiers.

Bill Jones, who was one of the first ABC reps selected, says, "We were learning as we went, and our effectiveness was increasing. We soon came to realize that flooring contractors were the key to our success, and now the ABC came to stand for 'architect-builder-contractor' representatives."

Jones was assistant district manager in the New York office, in charge of contract sales, and he was involved in another watershed moment for the Floor Division: the appointment of its first sales representative who happened to be a woman. "Anita Welch had been in charge of the Armstrong Product Center in Rockefeller Center," he says, "and she had done a fine job. But the novelty of that facility was no longer there. So she was named an ABC representative for the New York metropolitan market. She knew color and design, as that was her background. She had never gone through the same degree of training in such things as product specifications and installation techniques as our other marketing representatives. But Anita was smart, and she was relentless about catching up. She learned on the job and added her own flair. The architects and designers loved it because she could speak their language, and the contractors soon learned that she could hold her own with them on technical details."

Todd Lewis comments, "Boy, did she open a lot of doors for us! Do you know how hard it is to get into an architect's office? Every company wanted to get in. We had a group of specialists in commercial work, specifying, installation, and design that could go where our competitors often couldn't tread.

"The career concept played a big part in this. When you had a problem in the field, an architect knew that when he was talking with Armstrong he was dealing with someone who for maybe 20 or 30 years had been proving himself as reliable."

Jones agrees. "The important thing was to talk with the right person at the right time about the right product. When the job captain was writing the specifications for a building, that's when you wanted to be there. And what got you in to see him was experience.

"When you could, you would fight for a closed spec. That way your competitors would be virtually locked out of the bidding. And often we could achieve this with vinyl sheet flooring—for a hospital job, for example—because Armstrong had proprietary products for that market that nobody else made."

Competitors fought back as best they could. This generally meant setting their products' prices lower, sometimes artificially lower, as they bid on contract jobs. When a contract was awarded on a lowest-cost basis, with no other consideration, Armstrong tile often lost out. "We tried to sell on the basis of everything our goods offered, including square corners, design consistency, accurate count in the carton, availability of palletizing, everything," says Jones, "but it was hard to sell against price. We would receive documentation from our wholesaler: 'This contractor, we have found, can buy competitors' tile at such-and-such a price. I can't match that with Armstrong tile. How can I compete?'"

The flooring contractor, it must be understood, was under considerable pressure. He was submitting his bid to a general contractor who was trying to cut costs at every step of the construction project. Even when he didn't want to use competitors' goods, the Armstrong price often stood in the way. Armstrong made a superior product, and it cost a little more. That little more was enough to lose the contract award on some jobs.

This situation led to a departure from the old everybody-pays-the-same practice the company had been following. The departure, worked out under careful legal guidelines, was known as the contract basis of sale. It enabled Armstrong to match competitors' prices on a given job, or almost match them. It was what enabled the company to sell tile within the extremely competitive environment in which it was operating.

Initially Armstrong tried out the contract basis of sale in a few selected district offices. Then, with refinements, the practice was expanded to others. Eventually it was in place throughout the United States. Now a wholesale distributor could approach the flooring contractor and say, "All right, we can almost meet the price you've been offered by our competitors, and look what else we can offer."

Jones says, "We could quantify our product features, actually quantify them in cents per square foot, in order to compete. We would say to the contractor, 'You're interested in the price, and you should be, but you need to keep other factors in mind, too. On the job what's it worth to you to know that you have an accurate count within each carton of tile? What's it worth to you to have precisely square corners to reduce installation problems? What's it worth to you to offer top styling?'" With its products, Armstrong could assure the contractor of all these advantages.

Jones believes that Armstrong's success under the contract basis of sale traces back to the establishment of the ABC group. When the World Trade Center was being planned, he called on a contractor named Circle Floors, which later became Circle Industries. Jones told the contractor, "This is going to be a huge job, extending over four years. Armstrong and only Armstrong can handle it. You don't want to get tied to a manufacturer who may let you down in the middle of the contract." It was a huge job, with something like 12 million square feet of tile to be installed. The contractor won it bidding Armstrong tile, which Armstrong had offered to ship in bulk-palletized deliveries rather than in thousands upon thousands of cartons.

Bill Jones remembers that sale with pride. "We were shipping two truckloads of tile a week to the job site in Manhattan," he says. "One floor of a World Trade Center tower would typically use 32,000 square feet of tile. It would be installed around a central core containing elevators, plumbing and electrical systems, and other mechanical features. And the installation people would tell me, 'When we go all the way around that core and come back to the beginning, you know what? The joints in your tile match up!' That was important, and that's what Armstrong tile had come to stand for."

In 1970 the no-wax urethane finish called Mirabond made its appearance on Solarian Corlon flooring. Within a couple of years, Solarian was king. The company's flooring ads featured the word "Solarian" larger than "Corlon," even larger than "Armstrong."

During this same period the Floor Fashion Center (FFC) concept received renewed emphasis. In 1969 Gordon Levering, who had been serving as the Floor Division's New Orleans district manager, was called to Lancaster to serve as manager of the Bureau of Marketing Services (formerly the Bureau of Merchandising).

The Bureau, in addition to maintaining its traditional roles in hiring and training of field salesmen and in providing product displays and other merchandising help to retail dealers, was just preparing to launch the Floor Fashion Center program.

"The majority of retailers were mom-and-pop operations whose skill set was in installing floors," says Levering. "But Armstrong felt that there was an opportunity to have retailers operate in a more structured environment, one that would offer greater benefit to their customers. The Floor Fashion Center concept was built around new showroom displays and intense training at the retail level, training that incorporated design and decorating portions that most of the dealers had never been exposed to."

He adds, "We used to have a saying, 'A loaded dealer is a loyal dealer.' The ideal was to sell dealers lots of inventory, so they'd have all these rolls of sheet flooring standing around their showrooms and in their back rooms. The FFC program changed that. By this time there were so many types and patterns of sheet flooring that it wasn't practicable for most dealers to stock them all, anyhow. So the good FFC dealer began carrying a more selective inventory and displaying it better."

The dealer began to rely more on cut-order business from his wholesale distributor. After one of his customers purchased sheet flooring, the dealer would ask the wholesaler to cut off just enough of that specific pattern from the wholesaler's inventory to meet the consumer's needs. The wholesaler generally liked this sort of business and so did the retailer, as they could charge a premium for such service. Furthermore it meant that the retailer could rely on his wholesaler to maintain inventory that he now didn't have to stock.

When the Floor Fashion Center program was just getting started, each district manager identified a limited number of retailers as potential FFC dealers. Such a dealer would be invited to see a typical FFC showroom that had been set up in the wholesaler's warehouse. He was told, "This is what the retailer of the future will look like," and he was invited to take part.

If he accepted, he was making a major commitment. He paid a fee of $1,500 to participate, and with that he implicitly agreed that he was going to make a significant change in the way he did business. Armstrong was making a major commitment also. The company would be providing product displays, local advertising with FFC dealers listed, and, above all, training for the dealer's staff.

Some of it was trial and error, in the sense that Armstrong refined the program as it spread across the United States. In the end, it worked remarkably well. George Johnston says, "The Floor Fashion Center idea brought up flooring industry standards. It improved merchandising and marketing with everything it touched. The key was that it was what the retailer's customers needed. It was a great boon to consumers, because it helped them understand what was available to them and led them to concentrate on the purchases that were right for them."

In the early 1970s Todd Lewis, as assistant district manager in Los Angeles, was in charge of implementing the Floor Fashion Center program in his district. "We'd send a team of people into a retail store that qualified as an FFC dealer," he recalls. The team included the wholesaler salesman for that retail account, the wholesaler manager, the Armstrong sales representative, and Lewis as assistant district manager. "We would say to the dealer, 'Step aside and let us go to work for you. In fact, why don't you go out and have a cup of coffee? When you come back you're going to see something new that'll be the most attractive part of your store.' We would look for the best place in the showroom to put in our FFC displays. Then we would drill holes right into the brick or concrete walls and put them into place. We didn't want those displays to be moved once they were in. And they weren't moved. They were as attractive as we had said, and the dealers liked them."

As Floor Fashion Center participation grew, dealers involved in the program began to seek improvements. Armstrong willingly complied. The company began offering exclusive products to them, products not offered through non-FFC dealers. It set new standards for FFC dealers, came out with new product displays, and issued the industry's first manufacturer-sponsored credit cards, intended for consumers who were purchasing resilient flooring at retail. The Floor Fashion Center program continued to prove what a successful idea it had become.

Always occupying key spots in the Floor Division organization were its marketing managers. Generally there were five of these, each heading up sales of a specific line of products. John P. "Jake" Hill, who began his 35½-year Armstrong career in 1954, is especially well qualified to discuss the work of the marketing manager. After serving in field sales assignments in several districts and serving as district manager at Buffalo, he successively held marketing manager posts for various product lines, including Coronelle Vinyl Corlon flooring and linoleum, sheet rotovinyl flooring, all Vinyl Corlon sheet flooring, and installation, maintenance, and accessory products combined with sales to the builder market.

"The first responsibility of the marketing manager," he says, "was to be the 'product champion' of his particular products. You would do everything possible to assure their success in the marketplace." The marketing manager established linkages among various groups within the Armstrong organization, including research and development, production, product styling and design, advertising, and the senior management of Floor Products Operations. The marketing manager also maintained close ties to the wholesale distributors through Armstrong district offices, and sometimes to corporate senior management through the Floor Products Operations management. "Note that none of these reported to the marketing manager. He worked through dotted-line relationships with all of them," Hill says, "but he had to be the one who brought them together on a task."

Critically important to the marketing manager was the success of the high-gross margin items in his line of products—those that earned the highest return—as they helped to carry other products. He gave high-margin products special attention, and he continually prodded his dotted-line associates to find new examples to add to the line. The manager was heading a team effort, and sometimes the path to success was tortuous.

Jake Hill describes the intricacies encountered in the development of Sundial Solarian flooring when he was marketing manager for sheet rotovinyl flooring products. One of the top products in his stable was Castilian flooring, a rotogravure-printed product that was offered in 6- and 12-foot widths and was designed to be permanently installed. "Castilian was a fine product, but it was not a true no-wax flooring," he says. "We had Designer Solarian, which had a urethane wear surface, but it was made only in the 6-foot width. We were desperately trying to develop a urethane-surface product, a true no-wax, that was 12 feet wide."

A mini–task force came together to work on the project: Robert Desch at R and D, Abram Rudisill at product styling, Charles Anderson in production. Later, John M. "Jack" Hughlett from advertising joined the group. Jake Hill quarterbacked the team.

"It was Charlie Anderson who came up with the idea of how to put a urethane finish on roto goods 12 feet wide," he recalls. "That was a start." But a problem bobbed up. A urethane finish tends to get sticky in high-humidity areas, and in this instance the problem was exacerbated by the foam content of the substrate—that is, of the underlying base to which the urethane coating was being applied. The research people went to work, and through reformulations they found a way to minimize the stickiness.

Still, Jake Hill was reluctant to sign off on the new product. He remembered a couple of earlier products, Easy Street and Cambrian flooring, that had been introduced perhaps too hastily, without adequate field testing. Both had encountered problems initially, with complaints coming in and adjustments necessary in the products themselves. He felt that this time, with a truly important product in the works, he wanted no mistakes, no missteps. "Let's test this one in the field," he said.

There were howls of disagreement. The new 12-foot no-wax product had been scheduled for announcement at the wholesalers' convention that year, and field tests would mean a delay in its introduction into the following year. Jake Hill stood firm. Armstrong arranged with about a hundred homeowners, primarily in the Philadelphia area, to allow 12 x 12-foot pieces of the new product to be taped down in their homes. "Give us your opinion after 90 days," they were told.

The marketing test proved the product worked, and in due course Sundial Solarian flooring was successfully introduced. All the work of the task force had paid off. "The thing is," Hill says, "that because of Armstrong's product leadership and the general strength the company had in the flooring industry, wholesalers and retailers probably would have bought the product on faith, anyhow. But I felt that we had to be certain that we had solved the stickiness problem before we announced it, to make sure that it wouldn't lead to complaints once it was out there. We did the right thing to test it first." Sundial Solarian turned out to be a huge seller, because it met the desires of consumers.

As the Sundial Solarian experience illustrates, it served the marketing manager well to have the compound eyes of a housefly, as he had to keep a number of variables within sight at the same time. Jake Hill lists several of the concerns the marketing manager had. First, he had to be aware of competitive threats and opportunities. "You would ask yourself, What products are out there that could infringe on ours? Are competitors missing anything that offers us an opportunity?" Second, it was important to offer a styling and color assortment that would appeal to end users. Consumer focus groups were begun during Hill's time as a marketing manager. Third, he would study distribution strengths and weaknesses in various markets, then help district managers organize to reach their full potential. Fourth, he had to work with research and development to find out what was required to eliminate potential problems, such as staining, before a product was introduced. And fifth, he had to be sure how a new product was to be installed, and here the specialist instructors at the company's Installation School were the key. Managing a product line was a chain with a lot of links, but at Armstrong the Floor Division marketing managers generally found a way to forge it into a whole.

Gordon Levering, after serving as manager of the Bureau of Marketing Services, became field sales manager for the Floor Division. He assumed oversight not only of the Bureau and the Installation School but also for the management of the division's field sales organization and, directly or indirectly, of the relationship with wholesale distributors.

George Johnston, who was general sales manager of the Floor Division, explains, "Wholesaling was a low-value-added business, in contrast with Armstrong, which was a high-value-added business. The wholesaler's opportunity to increase his profitability rested on his ability to increase his sales, to improve his turnover, to balance his mix of products sold, and to control his costs. And the genius of the system was that, in our relationship with our wholesalers, we made sure that each one of them could make money. In fact, we wouldn't allow a wholesaler not to make money." To assure the success of its distributors, Armstrong provided them salvo after salvo of training programs aimed at polishing their business methods. Seminars on selling. On financial management. On general management.

"If you were in the wholesaling business," says Levering, "you considered it a plum to be associated with Armstrong. And we became a lot better as business-people ourselves, as we continued to work with our wholesalers to improve their businesses."

Playing key roles in the work to help customers' businesses succeed was a group of financial specialists in the Treasurer's Office. Galen D. Robbins worked closely with the wholesalers, while Dennis J. Craig served in a similar way in his work with contractors. At first the Credit Department, as it was known, concentrated on the "accounts receivable" line in the company's balance sheet. Wholesale distributors and other customers were encouraged to pay their bills promptly, and they were rewarded with discounts if they did so. These discounts were significant. At one time in the sheet-goods part of the business, for example, a wholesaler could earn a 5 percent discount if he paid his Armstrong bill within 15 days and 4 percent if within 45 days, with the net amount due within 60 days. (These terms of sale changed from time to time, especially as bank borrowing rates changed.) "That was a real incentive, and a wholesaler who paid his bills on time found that this would add a lot to his profit," Robbins says.

On one occasion Robbins went to Seattle to work with a wholesale distributor who needed extra help. The Armstrong man found that he was advising the wholesaler on a whole range of subjects. "We were consulting, not telling," Robbins says. "But he seemed to be listening, and we got into things that we didn't usually talk about. Your personnel numbers are too high, your turnover is too low, subjects like that."

From this Seattle experience grew a greatly expanded function for Armstrong in working with customers. "We moved from our emphasis on collecting bills to the front line of financial management," says Robbins. The Credit Department changed its name to Customer Financial Services to better reflect its new role. Robbins developed something known as the "Armstrong Floor Division Wholesalers Operating Study," which was published every two to three years, and more often when the basis of sale changed. Based on a survey of the company's wholesalers, it covered in extensive detail what the averages were in such areas as gross sales, net sales, inventories, receivables, general and administrative expense, and cost of goods sold. "In 1970 we had 52 wholesaling companies that participated in the study, representing more than 100 branch locations," Robbins remembers. Every wholesaler could compare his operations against those of other Armstrong wholesalers. It provided the distributor with a tool unlike anything he previously had had access to, at least in such detail, and it helped him pinpoint areas in his own business that might be out of alignment. To help him, the wholesalers who took part were grouped with others of similar size. The information in the study was coded, so no individual wholesaler's figures could be identified by name.

Armstrong and its herd of wholesale distributors were grazing in happy, golden meadows. Then, in 1980, something happened that changed that peaceful picture in a neck-snapping instant.

Harry A. Jensen, as president of the company, took a phone call from his counterpart at William Volker & Company, a wholesale distributor headquartered in Burlingame, California. Volker had been one of Armstrong's original flooring distributors. By 1980 it was the Floor Division's largest wholesaler account, with its 28 branches in the western United States representing about 20 percent of the division's total sales. But Mohasco, a carpet manufacturer, had acquired Volker a few years earlier. Now Mohasco was dropping the hammer, and it fell squarely on Armstrong's head. What the president of Volker told Jensen was that Mohasco had decided to get out of the distribution business. Immediately.

To his credit, Jensen did not panic. The first wave of reality to wash over him must have been one of despondency, and he considered calling a special meeting of the Board of Directors. The undertow was more positive. Armstrong still had some assets on which it could draw. Jensen called to his office Alfred Strickler, vice-president in charge of Floor Products Operations; Dennis Draeger, general sales manager of the Floor Division; and Gordon Levering, field sales manager of the division. He told them that he recognized the serious situation facing their business, but he expressed confidence that they could come through it if they attacked the problem correctly. Jensen had informed Volker that Armstrong would protect its investment in warehouse stock and in fact was willing to purchase its inventory at 100 percent of its value. "This way, you won't lose any money, and it'll give us some time to deal with the situation," he told Volker's president.

The flooring team in Lancaster had no time to lose, and they didn't lose any. Within days they formed a task force to deal with the problem. Having substantial talent and experience to call on helped considerably. "Look," the members of the task force were told, "we know what's needed to succeed in wholesale distribution. Let's start with a list of what we're looking for in a replacement for Volker. What

*A*s Armstrong *attempted to fill out its roster of wholesalers with replacements for William Volker & Company branches, the head of each prospective distributor was invited to Lancaster to look over Armstrong's facilities. One of these, a man from Seattle, was fond of a particular brand of gin, not always found in the East. During his Lancaster visit his Armstrong hosts took him to dinner at the Hamilton Club, and he asked the bartender there, "I don't suppose you have Boodle's Gin, do you?" "Oh, yes sir," the barman replied, pulling up a bottle to show him. The guest was impressed. The Armstrong people, always attentive to details, had previously alerted the club to be sure to have Boodle's on hand for this special guest.*

does it take to make an Armstrong distributor?"

With those requirements in mind, a Floor Division official visited every district office in the West. Each district manager was told that his biggest (and sometimes his only) customer was about to go out of business. It was up to him to seek out and suggest a replacement for the Volker location he was losing. Distributors of competitive flooring were to be left alone. Except for that, any substantial wholesaler could be considered.

The recommendations came in from the field, and the traveling part of the task force began its grind-'em-out work. Its members included not only Gordon Levering but also Galen Robbins, who provided financial management skills; Clarence Trego, with his wide experience in sales administration; Gordon P. Walker, an expert in information technology; and William S. Ziegfeld, a logistical specialist who could help with any phase of warehousing and inventory management.

Singly and together, these five leapfrogged through the states west of the Mississippi, calling on distributors whose names had been suggested by the district managers. Typically, Levering and Robbins made the first contact from Lancaster. Robbins was there to carry out the all-important financial review of the prospective distributor. "In some cases," Levering says, "the prospect knew a lot about Armstrong already. In some cases, they knew almost nothing about us." If the initial interview was promising, the other task force members would make their calls. They helped evaluate the potential for success of each prospect, and also aided him in understanding Armstrong's relationship with its wholesalers. "We'd say to them, 'Have a question or a doubt? You don't have to take our word for it. Call one of our existing distributors. Feel free to talk over anything with them,'" says Levering.

Members of the traveling team totted up a frenzy of frequent-flier miles, with one member flying 116,000 miles to get his part of the job done. In about nine months they completed the job. New distributors replaced the 28 Volker branches that had been closed down. Armstrong purchased the flooring inventory from each branch, as promised, then resold it to the replacement wholesaler. Every one of the Volker sales managers stayed on the job, only two of the Volker salesmen left, and virtually all of the Volker "inside people" stayed. Of the new distributors, only two did not succeed in the long run, and they too were replaced. Armstrong was working with a new group of wholesalers in the West, and they proved eager to succeed in the flooring business.

It all worked out better than anyone could have imagined. Armstrong had turned what could have been a bases-loaded strikeout into a stadium-rattling grand slam. It was a signal triumph for the members of the task force, who had put so much of themselves into meeting the challenge. Ask them and they will tell you that the relationship of mutual trust that Armstrong and its wholesalers had built over the previous seven decades played a major part in the victory.

As the wholesalers who replaced the Volker branches soon learned, when they teamed with Armstrong they added a lot of new players to their side, players they could call on for help at any time. "We were always there to help our wholesalers get up to date and stay up to date," says Levering. "If, for example, your inventory levels were out of line in comparison with others, somebody from Armstrong could help you look at the situation and decide what to do about it." One might criticize this as paternalistic. In fact, it backed all the wholesalers with a group of unpaid consultants, and most were happy to call on these specialists from Armstrong as frequently as they needed to.

Dennis Draeger, as the Floor Division's general sales manager, was a key member of the team that found replacement distributors for the Volker branches. He would later be elected a vice-president in charge of Armstrong's U.S. flooring business, but he had come to the business in an unusual way. He was one of the first to enter it from another marketing area (in his instance, from industry products) in a studied attempt at cross-fertilization within the company. When in the mid-1960s he was assigned to the Market Research Department, he was first officially exposed to the Floor Division. Then, after another move or two, he was invited to become that division's manager of mass merchandiser sales, responsible for marketing to such accounts as Color Tile, Western Auto, and the company's biggest customer at the time, Montgomery Ward.

Other mass merchandiser accounts were simmering, some of them offstage, as Draeger recalls. "At one point," he says, "we were dealing with an account in Atlanta, represented by a couple of guys who had been let go by Wickes Lumber. They asked us, 'Is Armstrong with us for the long pull?' 'Yes,' we said, 'we're with you.' This account became Home Depot."

In the mid-1970s Draeger became marketing manager for resilient tile. Then came an unusual step in his career, when Armstrong asked him to go to Canada to integrate the company's U.S. flooring business with that of its Canadian subsidiary. He began gaining experience with manufacturing as well as marketing. The Canadian company had its own profit-and-loss statement to maintain, and running that company proved valuable in his later career.

After a couple of years up north, Draeger returned to Lancaster to serve as field sales manager for the U.S. company's Floor Division. Within months he succeeded Alfred Strickler as general sales manager, then as group vice-president. "When I became group v-p, we had an awfully good business going," he says. "The challenge was to make sure this great machine was kept oiled and moving forward."

In his new position Draeger found that he was involved with new sets of people who were important to Armstrong's business—Wall Street representatives, for example. He began spending more time with Armstrong production people, who now reported to him, than had been the case when he was responsible only for marketing the company's products. "We made twice-a-year visits to Armstrong flooring plants," he says. "And we formalized the quality process, which was an evolutionary development involving continuous improvement."

Malcolm Baldrige, who served as U.S. secretary of commerce under President Ronald Reagan, instituted an award for quality performance in American industry. Its criteria were penetrating and demanding. These requirements caught the attention of the people at Armstrong, who felt that by now they knew a little something about the quality improvement process. "Floor Products Operations was the first group at Armstrong to embrace those criteria and to seek the Baldrige Award," says Draeger. "We were finalists the first year we entered, and what we had learned we passed on to the company's Building Products Operations. They won the award two years later." One of the lessons learned through involvement in the quality management process, he adds, was to put a person in charge of it who had experience and clout, so he could work toward goals without wheel-spinning along the way.

Denny Draeger's earlier experience with sales to mass merchandisers proved a rich source to draw on, as the importance of these chains continued to grow. Lowe's, for example, was by this time a major account. Says Robert H. "Rocky" Caldwell, "We had the president of Lowe's speak at one of our conventions. He told our wholesalers, 'When I want to buy nails, I call U.S. Steel. When I want to buy Armstrong flooring, I call my wholesaler.'" It wasn't long, however, before a problem developed. The problem, from Lowe's standpoint, was that they had to call multiple Armstrong wholesalers to serve their many branches across the country. Draeger says, "They came to us and said that they wanted a centralized contact with Armstrong. A single price for all their stores. Single billing."

Meeting that demand was complicated by the company's traditional relationship with wholesale distributors. How could Armstrong sell to Lowe's, on the terms set by Lowe's, and still assure that its distributors were not cut out of the picture?

A dilemma. Armstrong's marketing team tried to think it through in a way that would be fair to everyone involved. Out of this process grew a new "national account basis of sale." Essentially, here's how it worked. The company had about 20 mass merchandiser accounts—Lowe's, Home Depot, Color Tile, Kmart, and others. Armstrong went to them and said, You define for us what kind of services you want. We'll decide how best to get them to you.

It was an ingenious approach. It found a way to provide each of the major accounts what they themselves said that they needed, while taking advantage of the services, such as local inventories and local deliveries, that the wholesalers could provide. Armstrong itself took care of credit services, and each wholesaler was paid on the basis of the services it provided. "The national account basis of sale worked," says Caldwell, "and it worked because the wholesalers trusted Armstrong not to cheat them." Once again the years of good relationships between Armstrong

W*e were receiving lots of information from our distributors, and we saw that it was necessary to automate the system to a greater extent," says Denny Draeger. "We told our wholesalers that we wanted them to send in their data on tape [that is, so the data could be read electronically]. One of them told us, 'Tape? Yes, I've got tape.' But he didn't understand what we were talking about, and his firm sent in the numbers enterered on mechanical tape, not electronic. It took a little while to get that straightened out!"*

and its distributors proved invaluable.

Another challenge arose. This time it involved a spectacularly successful product, Solarian no-wax sheet flooring. "When I came into the job," says Draeger, "I inherited this fabulous brand name, Solarian. How could we continue to capitalize on it by expanding the line?" "Solarian" and "Armstrong" were both important names, with both showing good recognition from consumers. He adds, "We wanted to position the Solarian line of products in a way that did not confuse customers. One of the first steps was to develop an easier installation method. This we called the Interflex system for the installation of residential flooring, and when we applied that to Solarian we called the result Designer Solarian II.

"We had a no-wax rotogravure product, and Sundial was the name we had for that. We didn't at first use 'Solarian' with roto materials, but eventually we developed a product that we thought deserved the Solarian name. We called it Sundial Solarian, and we put a total merchandising effort behind it. It sold more units in the 12-foot width, for do-it-yourself installation as well as professional installation, than in the narrower sizes."

During Draeger's tenure as vice-president, Armstrong's flooring business continued to move forward and to modernize. Consumers were offered a toll-free 800 number to call when they had questions about flooring or wished to locate retailers in their vicinity. The 800 number began appearing in the company's national ads. Floor Fashion Center dealers were given more responsibilities and more freedom to operate when Armstrong allowed them to settle any consumer claim of $500 or less.

The Wholesaler Advisory Committee, whose roots extended back to the 1930s, had continued to be an important link between the company and its distributors. "The Advisory Committee served a huge purpose," Draeger says, "as an ongoing feedback mechanism." Wholesalers within each of four regions of the United States (the number later increased to five) voted to select one distributor to represent them. These representatives regularly met with Armstrong's flooring management to discuss areas of interest. "Basically, we had wholesaler sales managers coming in," Draeger explains. "But we took it a notch further when we began financial seminars. Then we began holding 'presidents' meetings' once a year, with every wholesaler firm represented." A top wholesaler might be doing $50 million a year in business, so such meetings were rightly regarded as high-level conclaves.

With the longstanding success of the Wholesaler Advisory Committee to rely on, Armstrong formed a Floor Fashion Center Advisory Committee with similar aims among these top retailers of its line. As was the case with the wholesalers, the committee representatives were chosen regionally by their fellow FFC dealers.

For the last several years before his retirement in 1996, Denny Draeger says, significant changes began to emerge in Armstrong's flooring business. "We were continuing to look for ways to make our products more appealing through design and styling. But our fixed costs were going up because of the information technology required to manage the business as well as the increased costs of deliveries and facilities and other aspects of our operations."

By the late 1980s the company's worldwide business in flooring and related products had topped $1 billion. The annual report for 1987 recorded net trade sales of $1,116.9 million in "floor coverings." (For financial reporting purposes this industry segment included not only resilient flooring but also carpet and ceramic tiles.)

In the early 1990s, Armstrong globalized its flooring business, seeking to strengthen its stake in markets worldwide. Draeger, who at the time was group vice-president for Floor Products Operations, says, "We needed to consolidate and to manage the consolidation. During this period we were pleased to be able to say that we never lost one of our U.S. wholesalers for a competitor to pick off. Later this picture changed, as the number of wholesalers was shrunk."

Rocky Caldwell, who was later elected an executive vice-president of the company, began his career in Floor Division field sales. After gaining experience as a district manager and a marketing manager, he served from 1966 to 1971 as marketing manager for resilient tile sales. He recalls, "In the early days, the market leader was Kentile, not Armstrong. But then in 1960, to commemorate our company's hundredth anniversary, Armstrong came out with a tile that had an especially attractive design. We called it Centennial Excelon Tile. Consumers liked it right away. Within a week or so, Kentile's salesmen were out on the street, saying, 'We have the same thing in our line.' We came to find out that the samples they were showing were actually our Centennial Excelon." (The competitor had evidently taken Armstrong's 12" x 12" tiles and cut them down into 3" x 3" size for samples.) "Within a few weeks, they had their own product, copied from ours. But anyone could see the difference between their product and Armstrong's, and ours looked better. That was the first time we really took the lead in styling for tile products. And from then on the competition was on the defensive."

Another landmark in marketing tile occurred when Armstrong became the first manufacturer to bulk-palletize its tile for use by contractors on major construction jobs. This shipping option was a convenience for the contractors and their installers, but it also was an economic efficiency for Armstrong, as it was a less expensive way for the company to package and ship its tile. Rocky Caldwell suggested that the savings be passed along to contractors who had their shipments delivered in this way, and that helped popularize the method. One problem developed, though, when some contractors asked, "How do we get the pallets off the truck?" Armstrong began leasing its customers fork-lift trucks and other materials-handling equipment for use at the job site.

Sometimes Armstrong used its two Convair airplanes to take groups of flooring contractors to visit one of the company's tile plants, situated at Kankakee, Illinois; South Gate, California; Jackson, Mississippi; and Lancaster. "That was really effective," says Caldwell. "They had never seen tile made before."

Stephen E. "Steve" Stockwell adds, "While at the plant we would run a quality control meeting, with the contractors allowed to choose cartons of tile right off the warehouse shelves. They would check the number of tiles in an Armstrong carton to make sure the count was accurate, then do a similar count with a competitor's carton. We'd say to them, 'Think about this. If you use a competitor's tile and it's one tile short per carton, you've lost 2.2 percent of your margin.' As soon as the plane landed at the airport, we'd take a photograph of the group of contractors, then a few days later would send a print to each. Almost always, we found, the contractor would put that photograph on the wall right behind his desk. He was proud of that."

In the early 1970s Caldwell was elected a vice-president of the company, in charge of Corporate Markets Sales Operations (CMSO). The CMSO organization had been established in recognition that certain customers bought several different types of Armstrong products and that they could be served more efficiently with one sales representative. CMSO sold products from the Floor Division and the Carpet

---

*D*uring the Indoor World Invitational, golfing legend Sam Snead was approached by a teenager. "Mr. Snead, may I have your autograph?" Snead brushed him off. One of his fellow pros saw what happened and said, "Sam, I'll bet you'd give him your autograph if I gave you a dollar." Snead nodded, and the other golfer handed over a dollar bill. The boy got his autograph.

Division, as well as ceiling materials from the Building Products Division. It had responsibility for the company's architect-builder-contractor representatives and for sales to home builders, national accounts such as Home Depot and Lowe's, and makers of mobile homes and other manufactured homes.

"We needed a way to get to know the principals of homebuilding companies better," says Caldwell. "So in 1972 we did something that was a first for us. We sponsored a golf match, the Armstrong Indoor World Invitational, at the Lancaster Country Club." The event enabled leaders of the builder firms to play with and against some of the nation's top professional golfers, such as Johnny Miller and Chi Chi Rodriguez, and other celebrities, including Joe DiMaggio and Mickey Mantle. Participants were happy when Gene Littler, a popular pro who was playing in his first tournament since undergoing surgery, shot even par and won the event. Armstrong was happy, too, because the Indoor World Invitational unlatched doors to new accounts. Several days after the tournament, the president of Redman Homes in Texas telephoned to say, "I want to do business with you."

Golf played another part in Armstrong's marketing. In 1973 the company invited selected managers of do-it-yourself mass merchandisers for "A Day with Arnold Palmer." They assembled in Lancaster in time for dinner with their hosts. The next morning two of the company's airplanes flew the group to Palmer's home course, the Latrobe Country Club in western Pennsylvania, where the famed golf professional greeted them. He took them out on the 18-hole course, where he conducted a clinic for them, with tips on driving, putting, and golf strategy. Then he joined the Armstrong guests for a round of golf, switching foursomes regularly to make sure that every one of the visitors had an opportunity to play a hole or two with him. Each of the guests joined the pro for a photograph, which Palmer autographed. Then, after a visit to his golf museum and workshop and a banquet at the country club, it was back to Lancaster aboard the Armstrong plane for the happy, golf-sated guests.

Armstrong at this time owned two Convair 580s, named *Indoor World One* and *Indoor World Two*, and a smaller North American Rockwell Sabreliner. Some companies are accused, with justification, of using their aircraft as "executive taxicabs." Armstrong's airplanes were used mostly for marketing purposes, carrying customer groups to visit the company's facilities and other destinations considered important from a sales standpoint.

In 1980 Todd Lewis was the pivot man in an innovative approach Armstrong undertook when he became the first manager of new business for the Floor Division. "This was an attempt to grow beyond the assortment of products we had," he explains. Over the next few months he looked at several possibilities, including solar floors, which incorporated voltaic cells to gather and store heat.

A more practicable idea grew from an Italian company that had experimented with marble scrap combined with polymers. This might be a way, Lewis thought, to use inexpensive marble rubble to form a product that resembled expensive granite. If so, it could represent a new business opportunity for Armstrong, enabling it to compete more forcefully against the ceramic tile and stone products finding favor for use in entryways of commercial buildings. "Our vision was to make a cast product, perhaps 3/8 of an inch thick, that was combined with just enough polymers to make it flexible."

By 1983 Armstrong had entered a joint venture with Lone Star Industries, soon to be joined by Shell Chemical, in a company named ArmStar, with Lewis as president. The partners built a 76,000-square-foot plant at Lenoir City, Tennessee, brought in machinery from the Italian company, and began to turn out two kinds of products. Two-thirds of the plant was devoted to Pavimar cast marble tile, which was distributed through Floor Division wholesalers. The remaining one-third produced Armstone, a thicker, less flexible product that was sold through distributors of ceramic tile.

Lewis says, "With Pavimar we did open some new markets, such as bank lobbies, that in the past we had not made important inroads into. But we never did completely solve the problem of making a flexible product that would perform well on the job. So we discontinued Pavimar and concentrated on making Armstone. Eventually we sold the business to another manufacturer, who is still making Armstone even today.

"It was a good effort. Prior to that time, we had stayed within our 'comfort zone,' and this was a dramatic departure from that. It was the first joint venture we had ever undertaken in flooring, and it showed that the company was willing to invest a substantial sum to move in new directions."

Change, of course, is the only constant in business, as in society. Through the many transitions that Armstrong weathered, some of which Armstrong people themselves brought about, it was important to maintain stability within the organization. For the field sales representatives, nobody was more important as an anchor to windward than their respective district managers.

Armstrong had so many strong district managers, each anchoring an important territory across the United States, that it would be virtually impossible to identify them all. The names that come to mind among those who were especially effective during the 1960s through the 1980s certainly would include that of David A. Whinfrey, who for the final years of his career was district manager at Philadelphia.

After his training, Whinfrey was assigned to Chicago. Then he went to Baltimore, then to New Orleans as district manager, before moving to Philadelphia in 1965. During his tenure there, the Philadelphia office several times served the company as an incubator territory. Here Armstrong tested new approaches, such as the assignment of the first marketing representative who happened to be an

African-American. One reason Philadelphia was selected for such innovations was that it was close to Armstrong headquarters in Lancaster. But another, undoubtedly, was that Dave Whinfrey, who'd been a Hall of Fame wrestler at Rutgers, had the quiet, intelligent composure to grapple with these new ideas and do what was necessary to see them through. In the early 1970s the first female sales representative who had been through the rigorous Floor Division training was assigned to his office. "That was Janet Ward, and she was very effective," Whinfrey says.

Whinfrey also became the mentor for the first customer service representative to become a sales representative. Harry Jensen, who was president at the time but had served as a Floor Division salesman, is credited with the idea. "You know," Whinfrey remembers Jensen as saying, "we have some fine people in our organization who never went to college. Maybe we've been overlooking something. Let's see if we can find some of them who might work out as full-fledged sales representatives."

Whinfrey had a likely candidate in his Philadelphia district. Nora Winimore was doing a fine job as a customer service representative, someone whose primary responsibility was to evaluate and settle customer complaints. She was offered a position as field sales representative, and she accepted. "She worked in field sales for about a year and a half," recalls Whinfrey, "but she had three small children, and she left this position to return to her original work as customer service representative, which involved less traveling."

The personnel in a typical district office included a district manager and sometimes an assistant district manager; an ABC representative, who made calls with sales representatives on architects, home builders, and contractors; senior marketing representatives, who had the main responsibility for the major wholesalers in that district; and perhaps five other marketing representatives. Within this last group might be some who were newly assigned after their training, and some who were maturing in their district office work.

With all of these people, the training continued. "You traveled with them at first, sat in on their meetings with wholesalers, helped them evaluate their sales territories and anticipate problems," Whinfrey says. "It may sound odd when I put it like this, but you wanted them out of there. You wanted all of your people to be good enough so they could be promoted out of their current jobs in the district and step up to the next rung in their careers."

The Armstrong Floor Division salesman at work wanted to do a good job, and he was encouraged by several incentives. Probably Number 1 was his salary, along with his ability to grow in the job and his ability to be promoted. Then there was the bonus system, which added another, directly tangible incentive. "It provided for awards based on an entire district's performance as well as on individual performance," Whinfrey points out. The various Armstrong districts vied for what

W hen Armstrong district managers came together for their regional meetings, they enjoyed swapping success stories. Once when Dave Whinfrey attended such a meeting, as recalled by one of his contemporaries, he broke up the meeting when he said, "I don't have any success stories. But, boy, do I have a failure story to tell you!"

were known as "commodity awards." Which district had made the greatest progress over the past year in selling each of five types of products? These types, at one time, were listed as Corlon, Coronelle and linoleum, tile, rotogravure-printed products, and sundries. The districts that won commodity awards each year had accomplished something enviable, and they were rewarded appropriately.

Occasionally the manager called a district meeting. Usually, the main purpose was to discuss how to maximize potential. *Sales Management* magazine regularly published the Buying Power Index (BPI) for every county in the United States. These figures could be translated into the resilient flooring sales opportunity for every field marketing representative and every wholesale distributor in the district.

Of course a major responsibility of any district was working with the wholesale distributors that had headquarters or branches within that district. There were a sizable number of these wholesalers, and they exhibited a patchwork quilt of diversity, so they sometimes needed a lot of handling. In his initial assignment at Chicago, Whinfrey had had responsibility for two wholesalers, one at Logansport, Indiana, the other at Fort Wayne. Then he moved into metropolitan Chicago, where he worked with just one, Glabman Brothers. "When I came to Philadelphia," he says, "I found that we were working with 13 wholesaler branches."

That soon changed. Demands on wholesalers to buy and stock the entire, growing Armstrong line and to provide specialized management and sales services became unattractive for those with limited marketing potential. This situation eventually resulted in a consolidation into about half a dozen distributor branches in the Philadelphia district. "That was more effective," says Whinfrey.

As always, Armstrong marketing people were intent on assuring that the wholesalers made money. They never forgot that goal, because wholesaler profitability was a key to the success of the entire distribution system. In this, Armstrong had a quiver full of arrows it could pull out. If a wholesaler was planning to open a new warehouse, Armstrong could send out William Ziegfeld, a materials handling specialist, to help him design it. If he was having trouble because the product mix he was selling was out of balance, Galen Robbins's financial analyses could point out where he needed to devote his attention. The wholesaler knew that he could call on this sort of specialized counseling at any time. Occasionally there was some resistance if an individual distributor felt that Armstrong was trying to run his business for him. "We weren't geniuses," says Whinfrey. "We didn't know everything, and we never claimed to, but the smart wholesaler knew that Armstrong could bring along a world of experience to assist him. If he listened and went along, he knew that we would help him make money." And often, a lot of money.

How did a marketing representative work within an area that had overlapping wholesaler coverage? Whinfrey says, "You had to be fair without showing favoritism. When you made a sale to a retailer, you would ask him, 'From which wholesaler do you want to buy your goods?' You would never, never recommend one wholesaler over another in a situation like this."

He adds, "It was the wholesaler's responsibility to deliver the market for Armstrong. We'd define the market from our standpoint, using BPI figures and other measures. Then the wholesaler would try to sell up to at least the potential within his market area. Economics ruled, especially the freight aspects of shipping to dealers."

Armstrong would "equalize freight" with shipments from competitors. An example will illustrate how this worked. New York City was considered to be in Zone 1 for tile shipments. That is, retailers and contractors in New York were charged at the lowest level of freight rates, even though their area was farther away than Zone 1 from the company's nearest tile plant. Why did Armstrong do this, even though it cost the company money? To remain competitive with pricing from Kentile, a competitive tile manufacturer who had a manufacturing plant in the New York City vicinity.

In working with wholesalers, Armstrong marketing people had to be aware of regional differences across the country. Jake Hill, who served as a Floor Division district manager before becoming a marketing manager, draws on a contrast to explain this. "We had to consider products and markets. Knodel-Tygrett was a wholesaler in Dayton whose whole show, practically, was Coronelle and linoleum. But we had another wholesaler in the Cincinnati district, Ades Lexington Dry Goods, that concentrated its sales on furniture stores and coal-mining company stores in eastern Kentucky. There the emphasis was not on flooring but on floor covering—felt-base goods at first, later Vinyl Accolon floor covering—and Ades bought almost none of the higher-end Coronelle and linoleum products." The two wholesalers were not that many miles apart, but they encountered a huge difference in what consumers wanted to buy.

District managers helped their field sales representatives develop submarkets through personal relationships with dealers, architects, and builders—and, when possible, even with end users. Jake Hill says, "These end users were especially important when they had continuing projects. For example, NCR in Dayton had a complex of buildings like a college campus, and we sold a lot of flooring for those. In Kansas City, Hallmark did a lot of construction. And in the Boston area, every parish in the Catholic archdiocese was putting up a high school. We tried to make sure that our Excelon Tile was specified for every one of them."

Marketing research had been in place for a number of years, serving Armstrong's various marketing divisions with advice on what consumers wanted in the marketplace. But in 1980, when David J. Feight became general manager of marketing research 15 years after joining the company, he inherited a department that lacked depth because of the recent loss of two experienced people. "I felt from the start that it was important to build relationships with our marketing organizations. They needed to take a more sophisticated approach to marketing research, and we tried to build on that," he says.

Since 1969 Armstrong had conducted home furnishings purchasing studies among consumers. For these studies, which came to include interviews with 120,000 people, the data were collected by outside firms, but the analysis was done by people at Armstrong. The aim was to find out what really was happening in the "bottom doughnut" of the company's marketing scheme, the level represented by the consumer as Armstrong's ultimate customer.

As the consumer studies were expanded and refined, the company also began "pattern testing." Consumers, primarily women, were intercepted in shopping malls, perhaps 100 to 150 of them in each mall. These test subjects were asked to select their favorite flooring patterns, from among the 40 to 50 offered them, for kitchens, bathrooms, entryways, and family rooms. "No other company was doing this at the time," says Feight, who later served as Armstrong's vice-president and director of business development. His marketing research department also began "package goods testing," using techniques that had been developed by companies

*F*or one focus group, Armstrong had assembled a group of women to express their opinions about a selection of its flooring patterns. The women were gathered around a table in a conference room. On the other side of a one-way mirror, so the women couldn't see them, were a handful of the company's product styling and design people. One woman in the focus group didn't care for what she was seeing. "These patterns," she blurted out, "look as if they were designed by a bunch of old men!" The Armstrong designers, mostly men, could only look at one another and shake their heads.

such as Procter and Gamble, to test how effectively Armstrong products were being presented to consumers.

One of the challenges he faced was to restaff the marketing research department. "We began bringing in smart young people from the various marketing divisions," he says. "We'd keep them a couple of years, then they would return to another position within the same division they had come from, perhaps, but now with a new awareness of marketing research."

This tactic was part of the program to get the divisions to understand marketing research and to buy into it. "We were not always successful in this," Feight says. "But the Floor Division was ahead of the others. They doubled their marketing research budget over a couple of years."

As changes occurred in other parts of the Armstrong organization, a window opened to do marketing research for staff departments as well as the line marketing divisions. The marketing researchers increased their work with product styling and design, for example. By the mid-1980s advertising and marketing services organization was showing that it could benefit from more extensive attention.

That need provided a groundbreaking opportunity for Joann Davis Brayman, who had begun her career as a marketing representative for the Building Products Division, selling ceiling materials. She had joined marketing research in 1980, when Dave Feight came in as general manager. In 1986 Brayman, who eventually became vice-president for marketing in Building Materials Operations, moved into center-city Lancaster to concentrate on advertising research. In addition to advertising itself, she cast a spotlight on such areas as packaging and retail displays, especially Floor Fashion Center displays.

In 1989 she returned to marketing research, succeeding Feight as general manager of the department. "The budget was growing, and the Floor Division was the driving force in this," she says. "By now about half of our department's work was devoted to flooring."

Armstrong had begun using a technique developed at Harvard called Profit Impact of Marketing Strategies (PIMS). "The PIMS studies led us into correlation and regression analyses," Brayman says, "and taught us where our strengths and weaknesses lay in every marketing unit of the company." One of the points emphasized by PIMS was that increasing your position in the market could lead to greater profitability. The Floor Division had already achieved enviable goals in its business. "But the PIMS studies put up a warning flag," Brayman adds. "If you're highly profitable, they said, you'll find it difficult to maintain this position. Other good companies are going to be attracted to this business and its level of profitability."

Marketing research attempted to help the Floor Division enlarge its successes. After one series of studies, the researchers told the people in marketing, "For do-it-yourselfers, you're going to be selling only tile. Realistically, you cannot expect to sell significant quantities of sheet flooring to this market segment unless you find a simpler way for the homeowner to install it." The Floor Division listened. "Out of this," says Brayman, "came a system for installing sheet flooring by first cutting a pattern out of paper templates. The company was so confident that do-it-yourselfers could handle it that it guaranteed the method. The customer was assured, 'If you mess up the job while using this paper template method of installing, we'll pay you back for the flooring.'" It was one of many innovations that grew out of marketing research over the years.

Steve Stockwell, after several years in Floor Division district office assignments, came to Lancaster as manager of the Bureau of Marketing Services. "We changed the name soon after that," he says. His organization became the Bureau of Training and Development, and that name better described what the Bureau had evolved into. The focus now was on the hiring and training of field sales people for Armstrong—also, on the training of wholesaler salesmen, with beginning, intermediate, and advanced sessions throughout the year. "These were self-funded programs, which means that the wholesaler paid for them," Stockwell says. "The Bureau hosted them, but our marketing managers did a lot of the actual training." Later, training programs were added for Floor Fashion Center dealers and other specialty retailers.

The Bureau of Training and Development also oversaw the hands-on training offered by the Installation School. "In 1979, the Installation School took over a building in the Lancaster Floor Plant that had formerly been occupied by the Armstrong Building and Loan Association," says Stockwell. These were much better facilities than the school had been using, and they enabled the school to enhance its already fine service to the flooring industry.

From 1988 to 1994 Steve Stockwell served as field sales manager for the Floor Division. He remembers a significant Armstrong exclusive, developed in the search for simpler installation methods and thoroughly tested at the Installation School. The Interflex method, as it was called, took advantage of the "plastic memory" exhibited by vinyl sheet goods. That is, these vinyl products, if contorted, tended to return to their original size and shape. Armstrong developed a line of 12-foot-wide goods that could be gently stretched to cover a room, then stapled around its perimeter, without adhesive. Within a few hours, the vinyl material would "shrug its shoulders" and try to shrink to its original size. This caused it to draw taut over the subfloor, and the result was a floor that lay flat and smooth. It was much easier, faster, and less expensive to install than most traditional sheet flooring. Eventually the company produced a family of products that could be installed with the Interflex method. They included flooring with the names Four Score, Treadway, Designer Solarian II, and Solarian Supreme.

Reporting to the Floor Division general sales manager were usually two assistant general sales managers. One served as field sales manager. The other was in charge of divisional operations. Occupying this latter position for a number of years after World War II was Kenneth R. Stephenson.

Amid the turmoil and intensity of their activities, younger marketing people sometimes needed an experienced shoulder to lean on. Providing that support was Ken Stephenson. When things didn't seem to be going well for a rookie salesman, perhaps because he was making call after call without landing a sizable order, he might get a buck-up from one of Stephenson's favorite expressions. He would say to the young salesman, "Remember that not all your luck can be bad. Keep goin' after 'em."

Rocky Caldwell says, "Everybody loved Ken Stephenson. He was highly intelligent, a Phi Beta Kappa in fact. And he was the human side of our business, the father confessor."

Stephenson's strength was as an administrator, and he was succeeded as assistant general sales manager by another highly respected administrator, Robert D. Gates, Jr. Reporting to Gates as head of the operations branch of the Floor Division were several sections of specialists. The group known as sales and order services, led by Carl M. Fickes, among its other functions worked with shipments of products from current stocks and future deliveries to assure that wholesalers had the inventories to serve their retail customers. Sales administration, which gathered sales statistics and handled the publication of flooring price lists, was directed by Leroy Michener, later by Clarence Trego. Consumer relations, which had been created to handle complaints from the field, had evolved under Jane Deibler into a source of helpful information for consumers across the United States. Then there were the sales service assistants, a quiet-working, absolutely reliable team who backed up everybody else. Need a tough job done? Call on one of these sales service people, then stand back out of the way while he does it. That was the unspoken rule within the Floor Division.

Corporate control functions: Peripheral but vital

Through the years, Floor Products Operations received steady assistance from several corporate-level organizations. Among these were the secretary's office, the treasurer's office, and the controller's office.

Larry A. Pulkrabek had numerous occasions to work with Armstrong's flooring organization as an attorney, then as manager of the legal department, then as vice-president, secretary, and general counsel before his retirement in 1997 as a senior vice-president of the company. Working in accord with legal and Federal Trade Commission (FTC) order requirements, he developed the legal parameters for the contract basis of sale, the direct basis of sale, the national account basis of sale, and the Floor Fashion Center program. "You did your legal work," he says, "by not letting problems happen."

Avoiding problems often was a matter of not only being aware of applicable laws but also walking through them without stepping on any lines in the pavement. In a consent decree signed with the FTC in the 1960s, Armstrong didn't acknowledge any wrongdoing (and paid no fine), but it did agree to modify certain of its practices involving volume rebates and resale pricing. "The FTC said, 'Don't try to control your wholesalers. Once you have sold goods to the wholesalers, it's their business,'" Pulkrabek remarks. "That became a part of how we attempted to run our activities. Basically, we couldn't tell the wholesalers how to operate. We could suggest what they might do, and we could add, 'If you follow our suggestions, we believe you'll be successful.' But we didn't dictate to them. This troubled the marketing people at times, because they would point out, 'Our competitors are doing it.'" Even if this were so, though, Armstrong had developed its own approach. It restated its commitment to the wholesaler method of distribution and moved on, following the new agreement.

"Part of our responsibility was to keep Floor Products Operations advised of what its rights were," Pulkrabek says. "An important part of running a business is to have a basis of understanding with the parties you're working with, such as suppliers, distributors, and contractors." Armstrong established rules of the road that were designed to protect its own interests and those of the other parties. "These were not laws but rules," he says. "To our wholesalers, for example, we would say, 'These are the rules we've set up. If you want to work within these rules, with the possibility of making a lot of money in the flooring business, then sign the contract.'" Most of the wholesalers agreed. Most of them did make a lot of money.

The contracting business, which had begun as a local enterprise, went regional, then national. Armstrong's attorneys helped the Floor Division draw up a contract basis of sale that enabled it to operate competitively within this environment. Then the retail business moved the same direction, with the evolvement of the "big box" chain stores, such as Lowe's, Home Depot, and Hechinger's. That development called for further legal advice, which helped the Floor Division move to a means of selling direct to these mass merchandisers while still allowing wholesale distributors to participate in the business.

"To sell flooring direct to the retail customer was a big change for Armstrong," Pulkrabek says. But the company found a way to deal with the change. Eventually the pattern it had developed with the big box chains was applied also to Floor Fashion Center dealers, when Armstrong dealt directly with the FFCs on products sold exclusively to them. "This was all driven by changes in the marketplace," he says. "With the position we had with the retailer, who wanted to sell Armstrong products, and with the consumer, who wanted to buy Armstrong products, we found that we could accomplish a lot even within the restrictions we faced."

When lawsuits alleging asbestos-caused injury began to cascade onto Armstrong and other American companies, the legal advisors were of course in the thick of the action. "In 1990," says Pulkrabek, "we began to see positive results from insurance litigation. Even though the number of cases continued to increase, we found ways of jointly resolving the situation by working with insurance companies and other defendants." Eventually, though, the burden of lawsuits hanging over the company led it in late 2000 to seek relief through a filing of bankruptcy, as a number of other companies had done.

"When you're in the thick soup of a lawsuit," Pulkrabek points out, "part of legal counseling is to say, 'We're in a war. This suit is a battle within that war. We think we are in the right and should win. But what if we don't? How will it affect us? What will the next battle be?' It was our job to keep Floor Products Operations informed as to what to expect."

Included in the secretary's office at Armstrong was the responsibility not only for general legal matters but also for patents and trademarks, insurance, real estate, and, at one time, tax obligations. As to patents, Pulkrabek says, "Sometimes it's better not to patent a process. The first guy in gets the cookies, and he deserves them, if you keep the process secret." But if the production process doesn't remain secret, quite possibly competitors will find a way around a patent. "How do you protect a production process that is not patented?" he asks. "You keep people out."

The job of Armstrong's insurance department was to assure asset protection and security against damage and loss. Plant managers would meet with insurance specialists twice a year to make sure that assets were being properly protected. "Plant managers tended to like this arrangement," says Pulkrabek, "as a protected plant is a plant that's safe to work in."

Real estate department responsibilities included procuring and protecting real estate assets through purchase and lease. The object was to have the best holdings within an area at a reasonable cost. "These highly skilled professionals were an important part of our team in the secretary's office," Pulkrabek says.

The tax department, originally part of the secretary's office, eventually was transferred to the controller's office. No individual person is obligated to pay taxes greater than he owes. Neither is a corporation. "Through aggressive action, our tax people saved the company a lot of money," he says.

The treasurer's office, with a lot of fingers reaching into various organizations within the company, provided support at every level of Armstrong. Its activities included customer financial services (earlier known as the credit department), billing, accounts receivable, payroll, stationery stores, central stenographic services, pension fund management, claims and adjustments, and administrative services. It also boasted a group known as methods and procedures. The name may

W e had 10 or 11 trainees in our class," Chuck Walker remembers, "all of us right out of college and all pretty green." To welcome the group to Lancaster, Keith Powlison, who was vice-president and controller, had a party for them at his home on Ridge Road. "I don't remember too much about that party," Walker says, "but it must have been a rouser. One of our trainees managed to fall out of an upstairs window."

have been pedestrian, but not the work produced by this innovation-minded group. It was the forerunner of the sizable data systems organization ensconced within Armstrong today.

Charles A. "Chuck" Walker entered training for the controller's office in 1951. Years later he retired as vice-president and treasurer of the company, but along the way he served in two Armstrong plants and as the company's credit manager. During the early 1960s he went to Oshkosh, Wisconsin, to become the controller for Deltox Rug Company, a fiber rug manufacturer that Armstrong had acquired.

"Floor Products Operations learned a lesson when we bought Deltox," he says. "These fiber rugs were being distributed through a lot of the same wholesalers Armstrong used to distribute its flooring. But about a third of the Deltox business came from direct sales to Sears. Somebody in our flooring organization said, 'We're not making enough out of this business with Sears. Let's sell all the Deltox rugs through wholesalers from now on.' That didn't work at all with Deltox." This clumsy attempt at Armstrong-izing an acquisition probably was one of the factors that contributed to the less-than-satisfactory results Armstrong had with Deltox Rug Company. After a few years, it sold off the company.

Under Walker, then Dennis J. Craig, then Galen D. Robbins, the credit organization grew in importance. The name was changed to customer financial services to more accurately describe what it had become. "We would have wholesalers asking not only, 'How big should our warehouse be for the amount of goods we're selling?' but also, 'How many fork-lift trucks do we need?' We encouraged this, because we wanted to do what we could to help them succeed," Walker says.

He speaks of the wholesaler basis of sale, with its program of stepped discounts the distributor could earn by paying his bills within specified dates, as "the best guard of the big investment Armstrong was making in its relationship with wholesalers." He adds, "That's how the wholesaler could make money—by paying his bills promptly."

This basis of sale could add a lot to the profit pendulum of the wholesaler's

A few years into his Armstrong career, Bill Wimer was assigned to the Floor Division's order department to handle orders for luxury tiles. He says, "We were selling cork tiles in a 9" x 9" size and also in a 6" x 6" size, which was cut from 9" x 9" off-goods. This was good, because it reduced the scrap from these off-goods. But the 6" x 6" size was so popular that we found that perfectly good 9" x 9" tiles were being chopped up to make the smaller version. I went to [Richard A.] Dick Angle, who was the marketing manager for luxury tiles, and told him, 'Hey, we've got to stop this. We're not making any money this way.'"

operations, it's true. Collecting those receivables in quick order meant a lot to Armstrong, too. That's why the company was willing to extend such generous discounts for prompt payers.

Another important step the company took to speed cash flow was to set up a lockbox system. Across the United States, the treasurer's office arranged for regional banks to open lockboxes. Armstrong customers could pay their bills close to home, and the banks would electronically credit the money to Armstrong's account right away. It was a significantly faster method than could be achieved by sending checks coast to coast through the postal system.

When he retired in 1995 as senior vice-president for finance, William J. Wimer could look back on a 43-year Armstrong career that had begun unostentatiously. In 1952 Wimer, right out of high school, had joined the company as a clerk in the Lancaster Floor Plant. Seven years later, encouraged by the progress he was making through several promotions, he enrolled in night school. In 1968 he was graduated from Franklin & Marshall College as an accounting major.

Even before his graduation, Wimer had been assigned as a data processing manager to oversee the company's conversion from one computer system to another. He put in a year as data systems manager for Building and Industry Products Operations and International Operations, then went to Europe to help Armstrong affiliates in England, Germany, and Spain organize their data systems. In 1978 he was elected a corporate vice-president and named controller of the company, and in 1990 he became senior vice-president for finance.

Years earlier, when Clifford J. Backstrand was president of the company, Wimer had created "profit centers" by combining production activities and marketing activities within organizations that were known as operations. Floor Products Operations was one of these profit centers. Armstrong was unusual in the breadth of the involvement of its controller's office with all its operations.

"Assigned to each operation within the company was an operations controller, an operations accountant, and other personnel," Wimer says. "When planning was underway for a new product, and that happened often with Floor Products Operations, all of them were working with both production and marketing teams to establish the costs of that product. Our people would help determine what margin they'd earn."

It was important for the operations controller to make sure that costs were charged to the right area. "The end result," says Wimer, "was that the numbers were rolled up right into one set of books. For the flooring business, we produced a profit-and-loss statement every month. That was of great interest to everybody involved, whether in production or marketing."

Another vital function for the controller's office was to help the operations put together their annual budgets. "[Chief economist Albert G.] Al Matamoros would develop what were known as 'basic assumptions,'" Wimer says. "Floor Products Operations would come into the picture with estimates of how many units of its products would sell, at what price. This would lead to the establishment of the budget for the coming year."

In September or October, all budgets from various components of the company would be offered to the forecasting committee for review. Then, several weeks later, they would be presented to the planning committee.

In budgetary planning, there was some give and take between the Floor Division marketing managers and the controller's office. Wimer says, "There were times when we might point out, for example, 'Okay, sales of this unit are down somewhat. But look at the growth we're achieving from new products. We have to take that into consideration when we're budgeting for the months ahead.'" As this example illustrates, in a dynamic business like Armstrong flooring, the mix of products sold became an important consideration. Floor Products Operations could adjust its budget at midyear if circumstances had changed.

The budget was a plan. It also was a great motivator. Says George Johnston, "In the Floor Division we always tried to do better than the budget. There was a good personal reason for this. You had to hit the Floor Products Operations and corporate budgets before sales incentives kicked in."

When Bill Wimer retired in 1995, he had been with Armstrong long enough to observe the results when Home Depot and other mass merchandisers put pressure on the company to reduce the number of wholesaler stocking points. "They insisted that we have regional warehouse stocks, as they didn't want to have to go through so many wholesalers across the country," Wimer recalls. A study had suggested that Armstrong would risk losing up to 30 percent of its top-end sheet flooring business if it substantially reduced the number of its wholesalers, Wimer says. "But the decision was made to do it anyhow, cutting the number down to 13 regional wholesalers. Now some of the Armstrong wholesalers who had been cast adrift took on competitive lines. The dealers had closer relationships with the wholesalers than with Armstrong, so they too began selling competitors' products."

By 1988, when Steve Stockwell became field sales manager, electronics was leading to serious changes in the way marketing was handled. "We had 32 wholesalers, with about 65 stocking points, and by 1994 we were down to 13 distributors," he says. "And our Floor Division offices had decreased from 18 to four regional offices. During the 1990s, what had been known as district offices were closed down, replaced with the regional offices. Then the regional managers worked out of their homes. So did the field sales representatives. A lot of what they did at one time was consolidated into what is known as the Customer Service Center, here in Lancaster. Much of what is done there is handled through 800 numbers or fax."

The wholesalers were severely affected by the changes. To keep up, they had to invest in sophisticated new electronic systems. Many found they had to reduce the manpower involved in their warehousing activities. Some of them had to learn to get along with margins of little more than half of what they had been accustomed to over the years. Now they competed against more manufacturers who sold direct to retail dealers.

Armstrong attempted to help its surviving wholesalers succeed, but there was a downside to what was occurring in the industry. In the consolidation of wholesalers, as Bill Wimer had noted, some former Armstrong distributors decided to take on the flooring lines of Armstrong competitors. The competition became even more intense for those wholesalers who continued to distribute the Armstrong line.

Part of the difference is attributable to changes in the product line. Rocky Caldwell describes it this way: "At one time the flooring business was characterized by heavy products, at low prices, that had to be shipped long distances and that needed professional installation. Under such conditions, the wholesaler served a real function. Today that has changed."

The traditional wholesaler evolved into a materials handling center, Steve Stockwell explains. One major reason for this is the increasing dominance of the "big box" stores. When in 1994 Stockwell was named to head an Armstrong organization called Corporate Retail Accounts, he decided to concentrate this business around three huge accounts—Home Depot, Lowe's, and Menard's. Each was handled by its own team of Armstrong sales representatives. At the time these stores sold not only flooring products but also Armstrong ceiling materials, adhesives, pipe insulation, and ceramic tile.

These corporate retail accounts had subtly changed from being building materials yards to home stores to big box retailers, and Armstrong was reacting to their demand to be served by "one Armstrong face." They were too big to be ignored, and the ground was shifting beneath Armstrong's feet.

Meanwhile, consumer preferences had begun to turn away from resilient flooring toward hardwood floors and ceramic tile, so the company's flooring business suffered a double whammy. As 1995 dawned, those who had been closest to the business during the now-fading "glory years" could look back—with mixed fondness and regret—at what was being left behind. The resilient flooring business, though it still offered a lot of potential, was in a state of dégringolade—a tumbling decline from its previous levels of success.

The breadth of that success is difficult to measure in simple terms. Armstrong Cork Company's annual report for 1945 reported sales from its domestic operations of a bit under $109 million. That was for the entire corporation. Armstrong World Industries' annual report for 1995 reported net trade sales of floor coverings, worldwide, of about $1.054 billion. So by 1995 sales of floor coverings alone had grown to almost 10 times what the company's total sales had been half a century earlier.

Sales dollars alone don't tell the whole story. Production of the Floor Division's goods, particularly production of installed flooring materials, had grown many times in square yards of sheet material, square feet of tile, and gallons of floor finishing materials. Yet the dollar sales had grown at an even faster rate because, with the introduction of flooring innovations through the years, the company's product mix had improved. So the growth occurred in profits as well as sales. It was a dazzling record, one to be proud of.

The wholesalers' convention: From show business springs business

Any Armstrong employee involved with the Floor Division during the glorious half century from the end of World War II until the mid-1990s almost certainly was involved with the conventions attended by senior and sales management of the company's flooring wholesalers, held each year in December. The meetings were that important.

The wholesalers' convention. Was there anything like it? William W. Adams doesn't think so. He participated in 1956, at the convention held the first year he began his Armstrong career, as a unit manager backstage. Years later he addressed the convention guests as the company's president and chief executive officer.

"These meetings may not have had a parallel in any other industry," he says. "They represented decades of annual gatherings of distributors of a single brand at the product marketer's home office. These were the true believers in the Armstrong flooring line and in the company itself. The enthusiasm of the wholesalers was not the 'squealy glee' of Mary Kay Cosmetics agents. It was the quiet satisfaction that they were surrounded by other good businessmen in a relationship that worked well for Armstrong and for almost all distributors."

The conventions were free of the glitz of road-show productions in other industries. The stars of the show were the eight to ten company and Floor Products Operations executives who spoke and whose presentations were augmented by films, dramatic skits, and musical numbers. These sessions were often intended to be entertaining, and they were—bringing a smile to your face and a rhythm to your step. But never were they intended to be only entertaining. Each skit, each song-and-dance number had a purpose, and each helped to get across a serious message that Armstrong wanted to convey to its wholesaler audience.

Even the timing of the convention was chosen for a purpose. December was just the right season for wrapping up one year and preparing to charge into the next.

The same was true of the Floor Division's general sales meeting, which was held each year one day before the opening day of the convention. Floor Division executives and marketing managers, district managers, and the teams of field marketing representatives who reported to them all looked forward with great anticipation, even excitement, to the general sales meeting. Here a young marketing representative assigned to the San Francisco district could renew friendships and compare the past year's experiences with those who had gone with him through training and were now assigned to offices at Boston or Atlanta. Here the district manager from Dallas could swap success stories with his counterpart from Minneapolis, and perhaps each could learn new techniques he could adapt in his own territory. Here the field marketing representatives and the district managers would find out which districts had won the product commodity awards for the year. There were six of these awards to be presented, with the winning districts those that had achieved the greatest percentage sales increase for each of the various product categories. The competition was extremely intense, and the awards presentation ceremony was a significant part of the meeting.

Perhaps most important of all, the general sales meeting was the opportunity for everyone in the Floor Division organization to receive a preview of the upcoming wholesalers' convention and of the year ahead. What new products were to be unveiled? What sales promotions were on the horizon for the coming year, and what was the schedule for their introduction? To which district offices were the new field marketing representatives, with their formal training period now behind them, being assigned?

The general sales meeting intended to accomplish one thing more. "During this meeting," Adams remembers, "members of the marketing organization were reminded that enthusiasm is contagious. They were urged to lead the applause at every appropriate moment during the convention sessions and, at the breaks, to talk up the good things that had been presented."

"In its way, the general sales meeting served as big a purpose as the convention itself," says George Johnston, who as Floor Division general sales manager played a key role in both meetings. "Among the people in our sales force, it renewed the feeling that 'I'm in one terrific organization here.' As you looked around the meeting, you were freshly motivated, with a feeling of pride that you were in a group that stood apart as a leader in the industry. At the end of the day, each individual walked out of the door with a strong sense of being a part of a team."

Meanwhile, as members of the Floor Division marketing organization were together in their daylong general sales meeting, wholesale distributors arrived in Lancaster from all over the United States. Many flew in, some came by rail, a few drove from their homes if not far from Lancaster. Armstrong transportation people would help arrange their travel schedules, as it was important for all the wholesalers to be checked into their reserved hotel rooms (for many years these were at the Hotel Brunswick and the Stevens House) and settled in, well before the next day's activities began. The Floor Division people wanted their guests to be well rested and relaxed, ready for the important messages they'd receive at the convention.

If the general sales meeting was held on a Monday, as often was the case, the convention began the next morning, Tuesday. Buses picked up the wholesaler delegates at their hotels and brought them to Armstrong's general offices on West Liberty Street. In the lobby of the auditorium, they circulated among old friends, including fellow wholesale distributors and Armstrong people, whom they perhaps had not seen for the past year. Then, at 9:30, the doors to the auditorium opened and the wholesalers moved in.

The convention was about to begin.

The room darkened. On a giant screen appeared patriotic or regional scenes as "The Star-Spangled Banner" rang through the morning air. (In later years, when wholesalers from Canada were added to the audience, it was followed by the playing of "O Canada.")

When the audience again took its seat, the grand opening continued with a rousing musical number by the Armstrong chorus, intended to welcome the guests, to hype their enthusiasm, and to set them up for the business sessions that lay ahead.

A word about the Armstrong chorus. In the early days of the annual convention, chorus members were Lancaster residents, selected from the ranks of Armstrong employees. Beginning in 1971, professional singers and dancers brought in from New York augmented the local people. Either way, the results were admirable. Their musical numbers were well thought out and well rehearsed, and the audience always reacted with an enthusiasm that was richly warranted.

Commenting on the chorus, Jack Cox wrote in the December 10, 1971, issue of *Home Furnishings Daily*, "OK now—all those who think Armstrong Cork's in the business of manufacturing building products, raise your right hand.

"You lose.

"Armstrong's real business is Show Business—and its most recent production…was in the best tradition of Broadway." Cox went on to point out that, as a means of stimulating a distributor organization year after year, the convention program was "tremendously effective."

Back to our convention program. In these annual conventions, the program varied from year to year depending on circumstances. What follows is a description of the program for a typical convention as it might have been presented during the 1960s or 1970s.

After the grand opening, as the applause faded, the general sales manager of the Floor Division stepped to a lectern mounted at the side of the stage. This was the first of his recurring appearances, as he served as the master of ceremonies for the entire convention. His comments this time were brief, as he quickly reviewed the year just past and assured the audience that they would learn a great deal during the next two days.

The next speaker was the vice-president in charge of Floor Products Operations. His remarks were a bit higher in overview than those of the general sales manager. He reviewed the improved capabilities of his organization, including comments on production as well as marketing. In tone and content, his could usually be considered the keynote address of the convention's business sessions.

The vice-president then introduced the company's chief economist—in the earlier years Dr. Walter E. Hoadley, and from 1966 on Dr. Albert G. Matamoros. He described the state of the U.S. economy and commented on regional differences, such as comparing conditions in Southern California with those of the Midwest and the Northeast. He then discussed various market segments for which Armstrong flooring products were intended, talking about the residential replacement market, the new residential building market, the commercial and institutional construction market, and perhaps sub-segments of these.

Next the Floor Products Operations chief called on the general production manager for his report. He was in a position to discuss the Lancaster Floor Plant and all of the company's other flooring plants, coast to coast. His presentation covered what had been done to expand or modernize these plants or to prepare them to make new types of products. He could always be counted on to end his presentation with words along these lines: "We have worked with the Floor Division on all the plans you will hear about, and we will meet all of our requirements. I have told [the general sales manager], 'Don't worry. We'll be ready for you. You sell the products. We'll make 'em.'"

Following the chief economist and general production manager's talks, the vice-president in charge of Floor Products Operations came back to the microphone for a summing up, generally pointing out how the year ahead was going to provide plenty of opportunity for the wholesale distributors—if they pursued it aggressively.

It was time for a break. More mingling in the lobby—but for just 15 minutes, strictly observed.

After that the general sales manager, in his role as emcee, returned to the stage. He would set up what for the Floor Division was the real meat of the convention, the product-line presentations. He might do this by reviewing in greater detail the successes, and perhaps some problems, encountered during the current year. He then elaborated on the keynote theme, with a teasing preview of what was to come.

He would introduce the marketing manager for Corlon and linoleum products for the first of the product-line presentations. The talk would be enhanced, perhaps, by slides projected on one or more large screens or by motion picture segments produced just for the occasion. If the marketing manager was bringing forward an exciting new line of flooring, such as Montina Vinyl Corlon or Coronelle Vinyl Corlon, he would call up Richard Flanders Smith, as director of product styling and design, to describe the new line in detail and to show how it had been created to elicit the greatest favor among consumers.

For the marketing manager, his spot in the convention program was a chance to show that he had the chops for the weighty responsibility he had been given. It was the job of the Floor Division's general sales manager and of the vice-president in charge of Floor Products Operations to look ahead three to five years in medium- to long-range planning. The marketing manager, by contrast, was expected to keep his eyes on a more near-term future, extending one to two years, while running his part of the business. Now came his opportunity to shine, and to shine before an audience that could hardly be more important to him.

The prospect of a year-end convention of distributors, preceded by a general sales meeting of the Floor Division, had a wonderful effect on focusing the marketing manager's planning, Bill Adams points out. As December drew ever closer, he had to come up with something important for his product line. Perhaps that "something important" would involve a new product introduction, an update of the line with new pattern colors, the launch of a variation of the product (such as self-stick adhesive backing on residential tile), or a significant improvement in the way his product was presented at retail or to specifiers.

"There were two strong motivations for him to put his best efforts into this," Adams says. "First, he wanted to get his share of attention, or even more than his share, from the 'selling machine' represented by the convention audience. Second, and this too was an admirable motive, he wanted to show that he was really competent and worthy of promotion to more responsibility—and higher income."

The marketing manager recognized that in his day-to-day business activities he had to fight for time and attention. The annual convention cycle was the primary arena for that struggle among his friends and associates who were his fellow marketing managers. His was an individual effort. He knew that. He also knew that it was best done as part of a team. He had to keep the two goals in balance, for the good of the organization.

Following the first product-line presentation was another dramatic skit, reinforcing the points made by the marketing manager who had just spoken. Then it was time for lunch. The general sales manager directed the wholesaler guests to a door at the front of the auditorium, from which they would move on to the cafeteria in the Lancaster Floor Plant.

At about 1 o'clock, members of the audience returned to the auditorium. They entered to music provided by the orchestra that accompanied the Armstrong chorus throughout the convention. For years the group was Jack Morton's Orchestra, conducted by Fred Woolston. After everyone was seated, the chorus came on for a 15-minute segment intended to further the aims of the convention.

The general sales manager would introduce the marketing manager for resilient tile, who would present the second of the product-line stories. His talk would be followed by a skit that reviewed the tile presentation or set up the next part of the program—or both.

The marketing manager for rotogravure materials would come on to talk about the coming year's plans for his product line. Then would come another skit, lighthearted and humorous, for a change of pace. That part was welcomed by the active people in the audience, who by now had been sitting in a darkened auditorium for the better part of five or six hours. They needed a break, and the master of ceremonies gave them one—for perhaps 15 minutes.

Then it was back to the same intense pace. The fourth product-line presentation would be offered by the marketing manager for luxury tile products. They included homogenous vinyl tile and rubber tile. Most of these products at the higher end of the price scale were made at Armstrong's plant in Braintree, Massachusetts. They helped to round out the company's line of flooring products, known as the most complete line in the industry.

By the time the luxury tile presentation was over, members of the audience had been told of numerous new designs and patterns among various types of flooring. They had seen examples at a distance—on stage, maybe, or in slides projected

*T*he room in which the product displays were set up was known, unofficially, as Moose Hall. Why? Because it had been added to the general office building during the time when Maurice J. "Moose" Warnock served as president.

onto screens. Now they were invited to see the new flooring effects up close. The general sales manager asked them to move into a meeting room just off the auditorium lobby, where they could visit displays showing the full pattern assortments of the new flooring lines about which they had been hearing. As they did so, the Armstrong field marketing representatives hovered about to hear their wholesalers' comments, with an eye toward writing up sales orders during the weeks ahead.

Impressed by the new flooring effects they'd now be able to sell to their customers, the wholesaler guests reassembled in the auditorium at about 4 P.M. Now came an especially serious segment of the convention, one whose subject transcended the day-to-day concerns of the Floor Division. This was known as the president's address, when Armstrong's chief executive officer addressed the audience. He was spotlighted as he spoke from a center lectern, with closed curtains behind him. The subject of the president's address evolved somewhat over the years, at the choosing of the speaker. For example, Henning W. Prentis, Jr., might speak on national affairs, James H. Binns on personal motivation, and William W. Adams on the transformational possibilities in the quality management process. Always the talk was carefully thought through and provocative, delivered from a prepared script. If appropriate, it was later reproduced in booklet form and sent to all wholesalers as well as to Armstrong field personnel, plant managers and supervisors, and home office managers in all departments.

As soon as the first day's business sessions concluded, the wholesalers boarded their buses for a return to their hotels. They didn't have long, for they had to get ready for what many of them regarded as the most memorable single event of the convention: the evening's banquet and entertainment. In the years just after World War II, the banquet took place at the Hotel Brunswick in downtown Lancaster. Afterward, the guests would walk across Queen Street to the Boyd Theater, or to the Fulton Opera House a block or so away, for the entertainment. In later years, as the number of those attending the convention grew too large for the Brunswick, both the banquet and the entertainment were held at the Host Farm Resort on Lincoln Highway, east of the city.

"For years," Adams remembers, "the master of ceremonies for the entertainment was the genial and witty Kenneth O. Bates, one of Armstrong's executive vice-presidents. He would comment on the speeches of the day, one by one, chiding each speaker for some reach of reason or some odd phrasing he had used. It was yet another example of how this forceful, self-confident organization showed its humanity by presenting its foibles. Up to a point."

Then Bates invited all the wholesaler "rookies"—those who were attending their first convention—to come to the stage for the famous "beanie ceremony." For this initiation rite, carried out with great good humor but with no malice or discomfort for those being recognized, each of the newcomers was required to wear a little felt beanie hat with Armstrong's Circle A logo on the front. The initiates were asked to raise their hands and recite a pledge, repeating phrase by phrase the words given them by Bates. He would lead them gently along, then turn mock serious as each rookie vowed to do whatever an Armstrong district manager told him to do: "...no matter how impractical"—"no matter how impractical," the group would intone— "or expensive"—"or expensive"—"or just plain stupid." The newcomers would inevitably break up before they could complete this last phrase. And the rest of the audience, almost all of whom knew what was coming, laughed just as hard. It was always a great moment.

The professional entertainment for the evening would be a celebrity whose identity was revealed just as he or she walked on stage. Flown from New York to Lancaster for this single performance, over the years, were such big-name entertainers as Danny Kaye, Jonathan Winters, Gordon MacRae, Jane Morgan, Imogene Coca, and Robert Goulet. Occasionally the performer stayed overnight and was re-introduced for some role at one of the convention sessions the next morning.

The entertainment ended the evening on an upbeat note—but not too late. Armstrong saw to that. It wanted the wholesaler guests to be fresh for tomorrow. Another busy day lay ahead.

With all the wholesalers back in their seats in the Armstrong auditorium on Liberty Street, the morning's program would begin. A lively musical number from the chorus got everyone's pulse throbbing as it continued, in a humorous way, the themes introduced the previous day.

It should be noted that, in these presentations from the stage, the company held firm to one of its operating principles: "To respect the dignity and inherent rights of the individual human being in all dealings with people." While the convention might poke gentle fun at the foibles of Armstrong people, no speaker, no skit was allowed to get a laugh at the expense of any stereotypical group.

Armstrong also tried to follow the maxim "Under-promise and over-perform." That had begun as a basic tenet of the company's early consumer advertising, back around 1920, and it was absorbed as a principle in sales meetings and conventions. For example, if a new flooring product was likely to be ready to ship between January 15 and January 31, you always stated the later date. It was part of the foundation of wholesaler and retailer trust of Armstrong.

Following the opening, the general sales manager introduced the marketing manager for sundries to tell about flooring installation and maintenance products. He often concentrated his remarks on new installation methods, professional or do-it-yourself, that had been developed to make Armstrong products more salable to home owners. And for this he might call on one of the company's research scientists to explain the technical advancements that had made the new installation techniques feasible. Out of such discussions members of the audience were exposed to many a scientific term that was new to them. ("Thixotropic" comes to mind. It describes the property exhibited by certain gels that become fluid when shaken or otherwise disturbed.)

Next came a series of short but significant presentations by other managers on various submarkets served by Armstrong: the new residential housing market, for example, and the commercial-institutional construction market, the mass merchandiser market, and the residential renovation market. The speakers covered the potential offered by each segment, with tips on how to approach that segment more effectively.

Then it was time for the advertising story, and this one was always memorable. The marketing of Armstrong flooring products was backed by powerful and broad-reaching campaigns in various media, including network television, general consumer magazines, and, most extensively and consistently, women's and shelter magazines. The head of the Advertising and Promotion Department (later known as the Advertising and Marketing Services Department) would describe the reach and frequency of the print campaigns. He would explain the rationale behind the latest advertising efforts, which usually featured the company's well-recognized "beautiful room" ads on the inside front covers of consumer magazines. His job was once again to drive home for the wholesalers a reason for the power in their partnership with Armstrong.

One of the favorite methods of reinforcing this advertising message was to use a "stringer." Picture a pretty girl at stage right, holding the cover of *Good Housekeeping*. She is joined by another pretty girl. The first girl remains in place. The second begins unfurling an accordion-fold of magazine covers that have been hidden by the first *Good Housekeeping* cover. She walks slowly across to stage left, while magazine after magazine pops into view: *House Beautiful, Better Homes and Gardens, Reader's Digest, Ladies' Home Journal,* and on and on. By the time the entire stringer is in view, the audience sees dozens and dozens of magazine covers, each representing an advertisement for the company's flooring that will appear during the coming year. It was an often-used technique at conventions, and it never failed to impress. It was another message that no Armstrong competitor could match.

The general sales manager, as emcee, would introduce the Floor Division's field sales manager. His presentation almost always focused on some aspect of wholesaler management or sales effectiveness. As an illustration, he might show a motion picture in which film crews interviewed six or seven wholesaler executives across the country on inventory management methods or on how to achieve better cooperation between inside sales and outside sales personnel. It was not unusual for Armstrong to sell a new idea by trying it out with a select few wholesalers, then bringing them to the convention stage to discuss the results during a sit-down panel discussion. As part of his presentation the field sales manager might also invite the manager of the Bureau of Merchandising to talk about a new display program or a new Floor Fashion Center program.

But wait. What's this? As the field sales manager is speaking, he is interrupted by a voice from the audience. He recognizes the voice. Almost every member of the audience does. It's everybody's favorite wholesaler, Tom Mightby, of the fictional firm of Daffin & Mightby. For years, well into his 60s, the Mightby character was played by Howard York, who headed his own advertising firm in Lancaster. At the convention, his job was to shake up the routine.

"Just a minute, Bill," Mightby would say from his seat in the auditorium. "What you just said makes no sense to me." With the audience grinning at the repeat of this familiar ritual, the speaker would respond with something like, "Tom, if you'll just let me finish, I believe that we can put your fears to rest."

Indignantly, Mightby would rise from his seat: "Oh, no, Bill, you don't get off that easy. I think a lot of us sitting out here in the dark want you to give us some straight answers right now." With a shrug of exasperation, Bill would invite Tom Mightby to come to the stage. Then Mightby would bring up what could indeed be a sore point, such as, "You want us to drop everything in January and spend three solid weeks introducing a new product, which by the way is priced higher than almost anything we have ever sold. You guys in Lancaster may not realize this, but we wholesalers have complex businesses to run, just in taking care of our regular orders, sales, and shipments. We can't give 100 percent effort to just one of many lines—and a new one at that!"

Now beautifully set up, the field sales manager would acknowledge the concern as valid. Then he would explain why the extra effort was worth it. As the whole audience knew he would, Tom Mightby would concede that Bill had made a good point. He would return to his seat amid spirited applause, but not before firing a parting shot: "All right. But you and all of your people at Armstrong better keep this in mind. We wholesalers listen to every word you say. When you tell us something, you should be sure you can back it up."

Finally, the general sales manager returned to the stage for another eagerly awaited part of the program. He presented the product commodity awards to the wholesaler branches that had performed the best during the year just past. He presented attendance awards to those individual wholesalers who were marking special-service anniversaries of long-term attendance. He joined each group being honored as it had its photograph taken. And he announced the names of the new members of the Wholesaler Advisory Committee, which included one representative from each of five regions of the United States. They were selected earlier in the convention by a vote of their peers, from candidates proposed by the whole-

> *I*n one memorable sketch, an actor played a distributor who had just returned to his wholesaler firm from attending the Armstrong convention. When asked, "How was the convention?," he told of listening to presentations by James H. Binns, president of the company; Albert G. Matamoros, vice-president and chief economist, and George F. Johnston, general sales manager of the Floor Division. He reported, "Jim Binns was bullish on Armstrong. Al Matamoros was bullish on the economy. George Johnston was bullish on the flooring business. I never heard so much bullish in all my life!"

salers themselves. This group met twice a year to give counsel to Armstrong on its wholesaler policies, on the effectiveness of its sales force and marketing actions, and on the efficacy of its manufacturing and administration. During the year each distributor received questionnaires that he was to return to his regional representative, to be summarized at the committee meetings.

At last it was time for the general sales manager's bugle call to action. Meant to be both challenging and inspiring, his final talk of the convention laid out what Armstrong expected of its wholesale distributors during the year to come. It was hard-hitting and to the point, and it served as the lodestar for both the wholesalers and the Armstrong field marketing people who were in the audience.

The grand finale. Everyone who had previously attended a convention awaited this segment and expected it to be spectacular. It always was. It usually would be introduced with a skit that resolved a dramatic conflict that had been set up the morning before. Then the audience would be treated to a 20-minute musical closing that had its collective fingers snapping and toes tapping—though even here the business theme of the convention was maintained. The musical numbers always ended on a zinging emotional zenith, perhaps when an entire marching band entered and paraded through the auditorium.

The business sessions were over, but there was one final bit of nostalgic tradition to take place. Members of the chorus would come once again to center stage. In front of a beautifully decorated Christmas tree, they would sing "A Holiday Wish." Many in the audience simply referred to this as "the Armstrong Christmas song," and some had heard it so often through the years that they were able to sing along.

Truly this was Armstrong's own anthem. Two Tin Pan Alley songsmiths, Ira Avery (lyrics) and Harold Levy (music) wrote "A Holiday Wish" especially for the company. It was first performed at the wholesalers' convention in 1952. The words

> *D*uring *his address at the 50th convention, Neil Armstrong showed himself to be a student of Armstrong family genealogy. He explained that the name "Armstrong" grew from an event during a battle fought in* A.D. 1022. *When a wounded Scottish king fell from his horse, his armor bearer lifted him, armor and all, and placed him back in the saddle. For this the king rewarded him with the appelation "Arm-strong," which eventually became one word. The name has not always been associated with honors, the astronaut went on to say. He noted that in one year, 1528, some 32 Armstrongs went to the gallows simultaneously: "And that's got to be some sort of world's record." He added, "Since those days the clan has been continuously working to create a new image for itself based on honesty and hard work."*

summed up what was on everybody's mind at the climax of the convention: "Now is the time when parting is near; / We'll say goodbye until another year. / Farewells are sad, but we can't be blue, / Not with so much to look forward to. / This is not the usual parting, / No sadness, no tears, / For we're really only starting, / We'll have the best of years, / And now comes the wish the season imparts: / Goodwill to men, and peace in every heart; / All friends we know in fellowship sing, / Sharing the wish that the holidays bring: / Merry Christmas, Happy New Year, Merry Christmas and a Happy New Year!"

The convention was over for another year.

Among the constellation of conventions, certain ones stand out in particular. One of these, certainly, was the 50th convention, held in 1971, for which George Johnston served as master of ceremonies. For this one the Floor Division had the Franklin Mint produce a limited-run commemorative coin, strikingly beautiful with its gold plating, and each wholesaler attending received one. C. Richard Whitson, manager of advertising design for Armstrong, had designed the piece. It featured a star formation created by five "X" Roman numerals, representing the 50 years of conventions. After 1,500 of the coins were struck, the dies were destroyed to protect the numismatic value of the commemorative piece.

The 50th convention, as noted earlier, was also highlighted by a surprise appearance by Neil A. Armstrong, who on July 20, 1969, had been the first man to walk on the moon. He told the wholesalers of technical advancements that were resulting from the space program. As an example, he commented that one of the ways in which flights into space have proven their importance to mankind was in weather forecasting.

This 50th convention, held in December 1971, was actually the second convention to be held that year. The 49th had been scheduled for the previous December, but because of a labor dispute at the Lancaster Floor Plant and the uncertainties caused by this unsettling situation, the convention was delayed until February 1971 and moved to two remote locations, Atlanta and San Francisco. It thus became the first Floor Division convention to be held outside the company's headquarters city of Lancaster. Also, it was the first convention for which Armstrong invited the participation of not only wholesaler management but also wholesaler salesmen. The salespeople attended by the hundreds. These "people on the street" discovered for themselves the stirring experience of taking part in an Armstrong convention, then delivering the story to their retail accounts.

That alone would have been enough to make the 49th convention special. More important, it became a bellwether for what was to come. Through their experience at this meeting, Armstrong people learned that it was possible to take their show on the road. And they did so, under the direction of Fredric A. Stoner, who headed the Special Promotions group and later served as vice-president and director of advertising and marketing services. The 51st convention, held in December 1972, was again a two-parter, with identical sessions in Atlanta and Los Angeles. The increasing attendance at wholesaler conventions was beginning to stretch the capacity of the Armstrong auditorium and other Lancaster facilities, and removing the meetings to remote locations helped ease the strain.

The Floor Division took another approach to this problem in February 1973, when it held meetings for Floor Fashion Center retailers at Lancaster's Host Farm Resort. These were the equivalent of three separate conventions, held back to back. The aforementioned 51st wholesalers' convention, which had been staged just two months earlier, served as a guide for the Floor Fashion Center meetings.

For the Floor Division and its team, the convention was a familiar, even beloved, mountaintop to be scaled each December. Everyone in attendance found it a time to share information about new products, new sales promotions, new advertising campaigns, new bases of sale. It was a high-protein way of closing out the year. More important, it was a way of planning for the year ahead—with every member of the team poised at the same starting line, muscles tensing, tendons thrumming, ready to plunge forward into another seism of success.

Armstrong's flooring business: A rainbow in the rearview mirror

At its height, Armstrong's resilient flooring business formed the unbending backbone of the company's profitable growth. Not to be overlooked is what this meant to the Lancaster community. Part of this could be measured by the solid base of taxes the company provided, along with the millions of dollars flowing into the economy as represented by employees' wages and purchases made from local suppliers. But another part, not as often recognized, was the leadership provided by men and women employed by Armstrong who willingly volunteered their time, talents, and personal treasure to help public-service organizations of all kinds. Because of such volunteer efforts, just about everybody in the community benefited from the success of Armstrong flooring.

What can explain the decline in this business? The erosion began in the 1980s when consumer tastes started swinging away from vinyls. By 1995, when our story ends, its effects could be strongly felt. Although vinyl flooring still offered excellent choices, many homeowners favored hardwood or laminates or ceramic tiles. That change in tastes accounted for part of the slide. There were other contributors, also. Competition from overseas had increased. The growth of the "big box" mass merchandisers, along with the corresponding loss of many family-run flooring specialty stores, reduced Armstrong's opportunity to sell its higher-margin "best" materials, such as Solarian flooring. The company's proud stable of wholesalers, now trying to sell to the mass merchandisers along with their older accounts, were forced to give up some of their traditional functions to become, in some respects, materials handling distributors. Armstrong's management approach changed, too. It had to. As the flooring business began to level off, it changed from a strategy of managing for growth to one of maintaining a business that had reached a plateau. That called for new decisions as the company attempted to keep the flooring business as vital as possible while being buffeted by the cross-currents of change.

The thousands of men and women who were involved with the business during the period that rightly could be called "the glory years of Armstrong flooring"—the period from the end of World War II to 1995—tend to respond with regret to what has occurred in recent years. They understand what has taken place. And they're not looking to blame anybody, for they know that change happens and that sometimes no one can stop it.

The fourth of the company's Operating Principles asks Armstrong people "to serve fairly and in proper balance the interests of all groups associated with the business—customers, stockholders, employees, suppliers, community neighbors, government, and the general public." List the benefits that each of these claimant groups received from Armstrong's flooring business. It quickly becomes clear that this was an enterprise whose success rippled far, far beyond the company itself.

Maybe that's the main reason that Armstrong people find pleasure, and much pride, in remembering the glory years. They know what they helped to accomplish when the flooring business was shooting rocket after rocket into the sky, and every year looking to an even more brilliant future.

What a privilege it was to be a part of that!

Armstrong Floor Products Operations Management
1945–1995

Vice-President, Operations

Curtis N. Painter	1945–1960
James H. Binns	1961–1962
Harry A. Jensen	1962–1967
Duncan B. Tingle	1968–1972
Edgar A. Yale	1968 Vice-President, Floor Marketing
	1973 Senior Vice-President
	1979 Group Vice-President
Alfred B. Strickler, Jr.	1979–1988 Group Vice-President
Dennis M. Draeger	1988 Group Vice-President
	1993–1995 Group Vice-President,
	Worldwide Floor Products Operations

General Sales Managers

James H. Binns	1945–1961
Harry A. Jensen	1961–1962
Edgar A. Yale	1962–1968
George F. Johnston	1968–1973
Alfred B. Strickler, Jr.	1974–1979
Dennis M. Draeger	1979–1982
	1983–1988 Vice-President
James E. Humphrey	1989–1994
	1995– President,
	Floor Products Operations, Americas

General Production Managers

Clifford F. Hawker	1945–1960
Milton D. Ford	1960–1963
J. Ross McCray	1963–1967
	1968–1980 Vice-President
Edward P. Davidson	1980–1983 Vice-President
Richard A. Graff	1983–1987
Harrison C. Goff	1987–

Lancaster Floor Plant Managers

Henry J. Marshall	1945–1955
Milton D. Ford	1955–1960
J. Ross McCray	1960–1963
Edward P. Davidson	1963–1964
Leroy D. Bishop	1964–1973
Ronald K. Wilson	1973–1981
Richard A. Graff	1981–1983
Wayne W. Ackerman	1983–1990
Fred W. Joost	1990–

Leadership of Armstrong World Industries, Inc., 1945–1995

Chairmen, Presidents, and Chief Executive Officers

Chairman
Henning W. Prentis, Jr.	1950–1959
Clifford J. Backstrand	1962–1967
Maurice J. Warnock	1968–1976
James H. Binns	1978–1982
Joseph L. Jones	1983–1988
William W. Adams	1988–1994
George A. Lorch	1995–

President and Chief Executive Officer
Henning W. Prentis, Jr.	1945–1949
Clifford J. Backstrand	1950–1962
Maurice J. Warnock	1962–1968
James H. Binns	1968–1978
Harry A. Jensen	1978–1983
Joseph L. Jones	1983–1988
William W. Adams	1988–1994
George L. Lorch	1994–

Directors and Vice-Presidents of Selected Centralized Staff Departments

Research and Development
Edmund E. Claxton	1950 Director
	1957–1962 Vice-President and Director
Francis B. Menger	1962 Director
	1969–1970 Vice-President and Director
James E. Hazeltine	1970–1981 Vice-President and Director
D. Dwight Browning	1981–1986 Vice-President and Director
Joseph E. Hennessey	1986 Vice President and Director
	1995 Vice President and Director, Innovation

Product Styling and Design

Harry A. Humphreys	1945–1971 Director
Richard Flanders Smith	1972–1986 Vice-President and Director
Wendy W. Claussen	1987– Vice-President and Director
	1995 Vice-President, Corporate Design

Engineering

Clifford F. Hawker	1945–1960 Vice-President and Director of Manufacturing
George A. Reinhard	1945–1963 Director
J. Phillip Holloway	1963–1969 Director
	1969–1970 Vice-President and Director
Guy McLaughlin	1970 Director
	1972–1980 Vice-President and Director
Donald H. Betty	1981–1989 Vice-President and Director
Louis J. Varljen	1990– Vice-President and Director
	1995– Vice-President, Technical and Support Services

Advertising and Marketing Services

E. Cameron Hawley	1945–1951 Director
Max Banzhaf	1951 Director
	1963–1968 Vice-President
Craig W. Moodie	1963 Director
	1968–1972 Vice-President and Director
Donald G. Goldstrom	1972–1989 Vice-President and Director
Fredric A. Stoner	1989–1994 Vice-President and Director

Corporate Markets Sales

Richard L. Collister	1971–1974 Vice-President
Robert H. Caldwell	1974–1979 Vice-President
John B. Helmer	1980– Group Vice-President

Technical Services

Milton D. Ford	1963–1976 Vice-President and Director

Materials Management

Fredric E. Bulleit	1976 Vice-President and Director
	1983–1989 Vice-President and Director, Manufacturing Services

Employee Relations

Louis J. Bibri	1972–1982 Vice-President and Director
Jack N. Jordin	1983–1994 Vice-President and Director, Human Resources

Secretary and General Counsel

Keith Powlison	1953–1957 Secretary
Albert H. Sheaffer	1958 Secretary
	1967–1973 Vice-President and Secretary
George L. Herr	1974–1977 Vice-President and Secretary
Larry A. Pulkrabek	1977 Vice-President, Secretary, and General Counsel
	1991– Senior Vice-President and General Counsel

Controller

Keith Powlison	1945–1953 Vice-President and Controller
I. Wayne Keller	1953–1960 Controller
Frederick J. Muth	1960 Controller
	1963–1965 Vice-President and Controller
R. Leslie Ellis	1965 Controller
	1968 Vice-President and Controller;
	1976 Senior Vice-President
	1979–1984 Group Vice-President, Management Information
Ray E. Longenecker	1976–1978 Vice-President and Controller
William J. Wimer	1978–1990 Vice-President and Controller
Bruce A. Leech, Jr.	1990– Controller

Treasurer

Maurice J. Warnock	1945–1953 Treasurer
Walter E. Hoadley	1954 Treasurer; Vice-President, Treasurer
Frederick S. Donnelly	1966–1968 Treasurer
Max Banzhaf	1968–1974 Vice-President and Treasurer
Charles A. Walker, Jr.	1974–1990 Vice-President and Treasurer
William J. Wimer	1990 Senior Vice-President Finance, and Treasurer
	1994–1995 Senior Vice-President Finance

Economist

Albert G. Matamoros	1966 Chief Economist
	1968–1986 Vice-President and Chief Economist

Corporate Planning

George F. Johnston	1974–1987 Vice-President and Chief Planning Officer
Dennis J. Craig	1988 Vice-President, Corporate Planning

Business Information

D. Dwight Browning	1976–1983 Vice-President and Director, Business Information
Forbes H. Burgess	1984–1993 Vice-President and Director, Business Information

Corporate Retail Accounts Division

Stephen E. Stockwell	1995– President

APPENDIX C
List of Contributors

Thanks to those listed for their financial aid, personal interviews, and other significant contributions. Without their help this story could not have been published.

Armstrong World Industries, Inc.,
  Corporate Communications
William W. Adams
John R. Baldwin
Clarence D. Barlet
Gilbert D. Benson
Vicki Zentmyer Bergstrom
Donald H. Betty
Mr. and Mrs. James H. Binns, Jr.
Lawrence E. Bish
G. Wayne Bonsell
Joann M. Davis Brayman
D. Dwight Browning
Fredric E. Bulleit
David H. Byrne
Robert H. Caldwell
Ronald C. Carpenter
Gary A. Cross
Glen P. Dalrymple
Dennis M. Draeger
William F. Early
Charles G. Elliot
Edgar C. Fearnow
David J. Feight
Hubert J. Fitzgerald
Brian I. Gates
Donald G. Goldstrom
Richard A. Graff
Marjorie and James E. Hazeltine
John P. Hill
Burt F. Hofferth
John M. Hornberger
William E. Irwin
Eric Jensen
Harry A. Jensen
George F. Johnston

M. William Jones
Joseph L. Jones
Carolyn C. Kent
Gordon T. Levering
S. Todd Lewis
C. Eugene Moore
John H. Moore
Dr. Spencer D. Phillips
Larry A. Pulkrabek
James J. Riley
Galen D. Robbins
Galina A. Rowland
Abram Rudisill
Francis X. Schaller, Jr.
Dale R. Shenk
Joane (Mrs. Richard Flanders) Smith
Robert W. Snyder
Fred A. Spracher
Robert J. Stewart
Stephen E. Stockwell
William E. and
  Kristie Jensen Strickland
Alfred B. Strickler, Jr.
William J. VanPelt
Frank and Marie Yale Veri
Donald J. Wain
Charles A. Walker, Jr.
Biddle A. Whigham
David A. Whinfrey
C. Richard Whitson
Lester and Kathleen Yale Williams
William J. Wimer
E. Allen and Debra Yale
Wilson and Donna Yale
John H. Young
David T. Zentmyer, Jr.

George F. Johnston

George F. Johnston, a chemistry graduate of the University of Colorado, served in World War II as a Navy officer and fighter pilot.

He joined Armstrong World Industries, Inc. (then known as Armstrong Cork Company) in 1947 as a marketing representative in the Floor Division. After assignments in several district offices, including that of assistant district manager in Chicago and district manager in Cleveland, he moved to Lancaster as a marketing manager. In 1968 he was named general sales manager of the Floor Division. Five years later he was elected a vice-president of the company and was named chief planning officer. In this capacity, he played a leading role in the design and implementation of Armstrong's worldwide strategic planning process. He retired at the beginning of 1988 with 40 years of Armstrong service.

His professional affiliations include The Planning Forum, The Association for Corporate Growth, The Conference Board's Council of Planning Executives, and The Profit Impact of Marketing Strategy Institute.

In community activities, he has served as president of the Boys and Girls Club of Lancaster, as president of the Donegal Society, as president of the Hamilton Club, as regent of the Lancaster County Chapter of Pennsylvania Sons of the Revolution, and as an elder at First Presbyterian Church of Lancaster. He has served on the boards of Lancaster Cleft Palate Clinic, Homestead Village Retirement Community, and North Museum Corporation. Also, he has been active as a member of Lancaster County Historical Society, Rotary Club of Lancaster, Cliosophic Society, Lancaster Pirates, Lancaster Country Club, and the Military Officers Association of America.

He and his wife, Dawn, who live in Lancaster, have two sons and six grandchildren.

ABOUT THE AUTHOR

C. Eugene Moore, a graduate of Auburn University who earned a master's degree from Florida State University, is a former Navy officer.

He retired as Armstrong's director of public relations in 1994, having spent 37½ years in advertising and public relations work with the company.

A past chairman of the Heritage Center of Lancaster County, he remains on the board of that organization. He is a past president of the Cliosophic Society, and he currently serves as president of Sphinx lecture group. In other community work, he has been active on the boards of the Economic Development Company of Lancaster County, Lancaster Chamber of Commerce and Industry, Military Officers Association of America, Lancaster Community Concert Association, and Lancaster Opera Company. He serves on the Development Committee of South-East Lancaster Health Services and is a volunteer reader for the local radio station for the blind. He is a former member of the Public Relations Council of the National Association of Manufacturers, Washington, D.C.

Gene Moore has edited several books and is the author of two: *Inspiring Interiors from Armstrong—the 1950s*, published in 1998, and *Interior Solutions from Armstrong—the 1960s*, published in 1999. He also wrote *Forty Years' Worth of Jobs: The Story of the Economic Development Company of Lancaster County*, an illustrated history published in 2000.

He and his wife, Jan, make their home in Lancaster. They have two sons and four grandchildren.